lon

SICILY

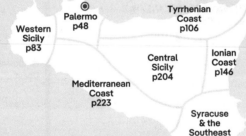

Aeolian
Islands
p125

Palermo
p48

Tyrrhenian
Coast
p106

Western
Sicily
p83

Central
Sicily
p204

Ionian
Coast
p146

Mediterranean
Coast
p223

Syracuse
& the
Southeast
p173

Nicola Williams, Sara Mostaccio

CONTENTS

Cattedrale di
Monreale (p78)

Isola Bella (p159),
Taormina

Erice (p93)

Toolkit

Storybook

From top: Cefalù (p112); *chiosco* (kiosk), Palermo (p48)

3

DANITA DELIMONT/SHUTTERSTOCK ©

Castelbuono (p117)

SICILY
THE JOURNEY BEGINS HERE

It's Sicilians' blatant ancestral love for their land and the unflagging determination with which home cooks, chefs, farmers, fishers, winemakers and other culinary creatives summon up every ounce of ingenuity they possess to nurture the *bel paese* (beautiful country) that lures me to Sicily time and again. And I always encounter something new: exotic, locally grown papayas, avocados and bananas at Palermo's open-air food markets; the experimental gin maker on Favignana who works with a botanist to cultivate the very best botanical pairings for the Aeolian Islands' natural bounty of indigenous wild herbs and flowers; the family of coffee roasters from Palermo who successfully planted coffee and harvested 30kg of native beans in 2021 for the first time in Sicilian history. A changing climate is shifting parameters, but the grassroots pedigree of Sicily's fiercely epicurean soul is unshakeable.

Nicola Williams

@tripalong

My favourite experience is hiking up hundreds of weather-beaten, volcanic-stone steps and feasting on the day's catch on Alicudi (p140), the Aeolian island where simplicity and celestial 360° sea views reign.

Nicola Williams is a journalist specialising in travel in Italy, France and Switzerland.

WHO GOES WHERE

Our second writer and expert chooses the place which, for them, defines Sicily.

ROMEOVIP_MD/SHUTTERSTOCK ©

I was born and I still live on the slopes of the volcano, Mt Etna (pictured). Whenever I can, I lace my boots up and go climbing. I love exploring hidden paths, walking on old lava flows and crossing an ever-changing landscape. At sunset, I rest on the edge of the Valle del Bove before journeying back under the moon. It is great to feel the power of the volcano under my soles and reconnect with the Earth.

Sara Mostaccio
@fritha
Sara Mostaccio is a journalist and a podcaster.

5

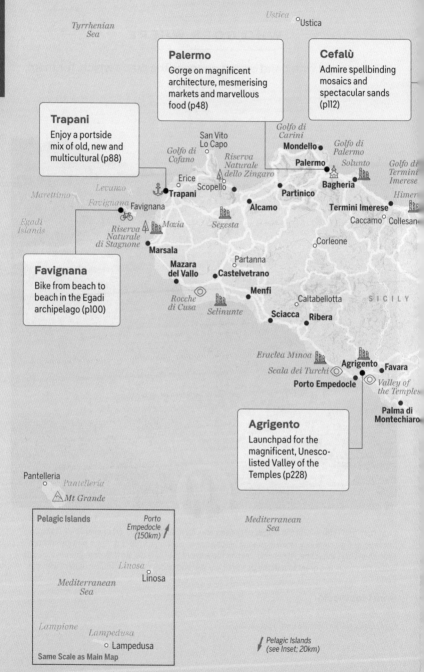

Trapani
Enjoy a portside mix of old, new and multicultural (p88)

Palermo
Gorge on magnificent architecture, mesmerising markets and marvellous food (p48)

Cefalù
Admire spellbinding mosaics and spectacular sands (p112)

Favignana
Bike from beach to beach in the Egadi archipelago (p100)

Agrigento
Launchpad for the magnificent, Unesco-listed Valley of the Temples (p228)

Tyrrhenian Sea

Ustica ○ Ustica

Golfo di Carini

San Vito Lo Capo

Golfo di Cofano

Riserva Naturale dello Zingaro

Mondello ●

Golfo di Palermo

Palermo ●

Soluto

Golfo di Termini Imerese

Erice
Scopello ●
● Trapani

Partinico ●

Bagheria ●

Himer

Marettimo

Levanzo

Favignana ● Favignana

Alcamo ●

Termini Imerese ●
Caccamo ○ Collesan

Egadi Islands

Riserva Naturale di Stagnone

Mozia

Segesta

● Corleone

Marsala ●

Mazara del Vallo ●

Castelvetrano ●

Partanna ●

Rocche di Cusa

Selinunte

Menfi ●

Caltabellotta ○

S I C I L Y

Sciacca ● Ribera ●

Eraclea Minoa

Scala dei Turchi ◎

Agrigento ● Favara ●

Porto Empedocle ●

Valley of the Temples

Palma di Montechiaro ●

Pantelleria ○ *Pantelleria*

△ Mt Grande

Mediterranean Sea

Pelagic Islands

Porto Empedocle (150km)

Linosa ○ Linosa

Mediterranean Sea

Lampione *Lampedusa*

○ Lampedusa

Same Scale as Main Map

Pelagic Islands (see Inset; 20km)

Salina

Taste the island's signature sweet Malvasia wine and sensational capers (p137).

Lipari

Sail to the Aeolian island-hopping 'capital' (p130)

Capo d'Orlando

Experience life on a lemon farm, not far from the sea (p120)

Taormina

Snag tickets for summer performances in an ancient theatre (p157)

Catania

Sicily's second-largest city in the shadow of Mt Etna (p164)

Syracuse

Uncover the greatest city of ancient Magna Graecia (p178)

Caltagirone

Meet Sicily's crafty city of ceramists (p217)

Noto

Lose yourself in a beautiful baroque hill town (p188)

Ragusa

Get giddy on brilliant baroque architecture, craftsmanship and gelato (p196)

Stromboli ○ San Vincenzo (Stromboli Town)

Aeolian Islands

Panarea ○ San Pietro

Salina Santa Marina Salina

Monte Fossa delle Felci

Lipari Town *Lipari*

○ Porto di Levante

Gran Cratere

Golfo di Milazzo

Mortelle

Ganzirri ● Villa San Giovanni

Milazzo

Messina ● Reggio di Calabria

Golfo di Patti

Barcellona

Tyndaris

Sant'Agata di Militello

Castel di Tusa

○ San Marco d'Alunzio

Parco Regionale dei Nebrodi

Savoca ○

○ **Cefalù**

Castelbuono Mistretta

Parco Naturale Regionale delle Madonie

○ Petralia Soprana

Mt Soro

Parco dell'Etna

Taormina

Giardini-Naxos

Bronte ○

Mt Etna

Giarre

Valle del Bove

Adrano

Acireale

Enna

Castello di Lombardia

Paternò

Aci Castello ○ Aci Trezza

Caltanissetta

Morgantina

Misterbianco

Catania

Villa Romana del Casale

○ Aidone

Piazza Armerina

Golfo di Catania

Ravanusa

Mazzarino

Palagonia ○

Butera

Caltagirone

Lentini

Megara Hyblaea

Augusta

Falconara

Niscemi

Necropoli di Pantalica

Castello Eurialo

Licata

Gela

Palazzolo Acreide

Floridia ○

Syracuse

Akrai

Ragusa

Avola

Ionian Sea

Modica

Noto

Eloro

Scicli

Cava d'Ispica

Riserva Naturale Oasi Faunistica di Vendicari

Pozzallo ○

Pachino ○

Isola delle Correnti

Messina ● Villa San Giovanni

Straits of Messina

Barcellona

● Reggio di Calabria

CALABRIA

Gozo

⊗ N 0 ___ 50 km
0 ___ 25 miles

7

BEACH LIFE

Be it endless golden sand for the kids to build castles on, clusters of rocks around a natural *piscina* (swimming pool) in the sea or a pebble cove for two, Sicily has a beach to suit every mood and moment. Some are pretty wild, accessible by boat or a scraggy footpath plunging down to the water. Others are easy to reach, with dedicated car parks and facilities aplenty.

Beach Season

The official summer season runs from June to September, meaning lifeguards on bigger beaches, sun loungers and parasols to rent, and a buzzing beach-bar scene.

Lido Love

Many beaches are cordoned off into public and private beaches. Entrance to a private lido or *bagno* includes a parasol-shaded sun lounger for the day.

Shoe Hack

Bring water shoes to make light work of getting across sun-scorched pebbles into the water – it can be akin to tiptoeing across burning coals in summer.

BEST BEACH EXPERIENCES

Downtown Cefalù's sweep of action-packed golden sand needs no introduction – follow locals to snorkel off rocks from **Capo Cefalù ❶** (p115)

Stretch your snorkelling legs in piercing-clear emerald waters at Cala Marinella in western Sicily's **Riserva Naturale dello Zingaro ❷** (p95)

Bike it to **Cala Rossa ❸** – as untamed as island beaches come – on Favignana's northern shore; continue to Cala Beu Marino for a food-truck lunch (p102)

Splash, snorkel and dive like a 1960s movie star in turquoise-laced beaches on **Isola Bella ❹**, a teeny island below glamour-queen Taormina (p159)

Experience the wild beauty of one of Sicily's most isolated Mediterranean beaches in the **Riserva Naturale Torre Salsa ❺** (p234)

GREEK DRAMA

Outside of Greece, nowhere else in Europe is the ancient world evoked with such drama. Not only is Sicily's unparalleled collection of ancient Greek temples and amphitheatres remarkably well preserved; scenic backdrops of wildflower-spun plains, soaring cliffs, snowcapped volcanoes and the big blue sea set off the ancient relics to spectacular effect.

Footwear

Wear closed, comfortable shoes – most sites are rough under foot, with stony paths and plenty of kilometres to walk in a day.

Summer Festivals

Tickets for summer performances in open-air theatres sell like hot cakes. Gen up on what's happening and buy tickets well in advance.

Lunch Date

Allow ample time for ambling around each site – bring plenty of water and snacks or a lunchtime picnic. On-site facilities are scant or nonexistent.

BEST ANCIENT RELIC EXPERIENCES

Cool off on the beach after being bowled over by the Greek temples with a staggering seaside backdrop at **Selinunte** ❶ (p97)

Watch drama unfold and catch the wind playing tunes amid the ruins of ancient **Segesta** ❷ in Western Sicily (p93)

You'll be forgiven for thinking you've already seen star-turn **Tempio della Concordia** ❸ – at the Valley of the Temples in Agrigento – it's the model for Unesco's logo (p230)

Bag a golden ticket for tragedy beneath the stars at the supremely well-preserved Greek amphitheatre in **Syracuse** ❹, a major power in ancient times (p181)

High-drama views of snow-capped Mt Etna and the Ionian Sea vie for the spotlight at the **Teatro Greco** ❺ in Taormina (p159)

Cappella Palatina (p56), Palazzo dei Normanni, Palermo

ILLUSTRATED HISTORY

Representing everything from biblical themes and budding bikini-clad Olympians to wild African animals, mythical monsters and deities, Sicily's unmatched collection of dazzling – and dazzlingly detailed – mosaics date to the Roman, Byzantine and Arab–Norman periods.

Cover Up

In churches bring a scarf to hide bare shoulders and thighs – or buy a shockingly inelegant €1 disposable smock to cover up at the entrance.

Pictorial Guides

Before entering said church or palazzo, buy a pictorial guide or booklet at the ticket entrance to help you identify each miniature scene depicted in mosaic.

BEST MOSAIC EXPERIENCES

See bible figures in mosaic form in Arab-Norman **Cappella Palatina ❶** in Palermo (p56)

Admire the world's finest Roman mosaics in Unesco-listed **Villa Romana del Casale ❷** (p216)

Take in shimmering gold mosaics in an Arab–Norman cathedral in **Cefalù ❸** (p113)

Travel back in time to see Christ healing a leper in the hilltop village of **Monreale ❹** (p78)

See how Romans amassed small fortunes from the island's sulphur in the mosaic-rich interiors of **Villa Romana di Durrueli ❺** near Agrigento (p234)

BAROQUE BEAUTIES

It needed an earthquake in 1693 to usher in Sicily's golden age of baroque. As flattened cities rose from the ashes, a highly flamboyant architectural style took form combining Spanish baroque with Sicilian structural and decorative elements, among them the generous use of masks and glorious riot of cheeky *putti* (cherubs).

Zoom In

Dedicated art and architecture aficionados: bring along binoculars to study intricate stuccowork and decorative details up close.

King of Cherubs

The most important artist from this period was Palermo-born Giacomo Serpotta (1656–1732), whose dazzling stuccowork fills countless Sicilian baroque churches in his home city.

QR Codes

In key churches and monuments look for information panels with a QR code – flash with your phone to access detailed guides in English.

BEST BAROQUE EXPERIENCES

Explore the tangle of nooks and lanes in **Ragusa Ibla ❶** – Duomo di San Giorgio is the grand design of superstar baroque architect Rosario Gagliardi (p197)

Linger with locals on Catania's **Piazza del Duomo ❷** – a mirage of contrasting lava and limestone buildings in the unique local baroque style (p164)

One of seven Unesco-listed baroque beauties, gold-stone **Noto ❸** is deemed the fairest of them all (p188)

Track down Giacomo Serpotta's captivating cherubs in every pose in Palermo's **I Tesori della Loggia ❹** (p74)

Marvel over a 360-degree panorama of ancient Palermo from the rooftop terraces of **Chiesa e Monastero di Santa Caterina d'Alessandria ❺** (p57)

MARKET MADNESS

Sicily's souk-like markets are pure street theatre. Tables groan under the weight of decapitated swordfish, ruby-pink prawns and trays full of clams, mussels, sea urchins and all manner of mysterious sea life. Fishmongers gut silvery fish and high-heeled customers step daintily over pools of blood-stained water. Fruit vendors hawk their wares in Sicilian dialect, and trattoria chefs sear octopus and offal over a flaming grill on the street.

Etiquette

Take your own shopping bag and don't expect to enter into any hard bargaining. Gentle haggling with a smile is acceptable.

Plan Lunch

Plan lunch around your visit. Dozens of stalls sell snacks to eat on the go, or full meals around plastic tables on the street. Watch your pockets.

Opening Hours

Some street markets operate all day, others mornings only Monday to Saturday. Whichever the case, plan a morning visit when there's the best choice of produce.

BEST MARKET EXPERIENCES

Dive into an intoxicating whirlwind of Sicilian, Asian and African smells at Palermo's oldest open-air food market **Mercato del Ballarò ❶** – dare to try *stighiola* (p55)

Treasure-hunt in vintage shacks at Palermo's flea market and poke backstage with Luciano at its **Museo del Mercato Storico delle Pulci ❷** (p65)

Tuck into freshly shucked oysters and a glass of wine at **Antico Mercato di Ortygia ❸** in Syracuse's ancient heart (p180)

Hit **La Pescheria ❹**, Sicily's premier fish market, in Catania at 7am sharp for an A to Z of Sicilian ocean fish (p166)

Hunt down a church built atop a prehistoric cave at Catania's **Fera 'o Luni ❺** open-air market on Piazza Carlo Alberto (p166)

Granita **and brioche**

GIUSEPPELOMBARDO/SHUTTERSTOCK ©, RIGHT: REDA&CO/GETTY IMAGES ©, FAR RIGHT: ANGELO GIAMPICCOLO/SHUTTERSTOCK ©

KEEP COOL

Gelato and *granita* are reason alone to visit Sicily, and sampling the rainbow of seasonal flavours is one sure way of keeping cool in summer's sizzling heat. Every town has a *gelateria* (ice-cream shop); classic island flavours include *pistacchio* (pistachio), *mandorla* (almond), *gelso* (mulberry), *anguria* (watermelon), *fico* (fig) and often *cannolo* (yes, as in the Sicilian sweet).

Bun It

Where else is it acceptable to eat an ice-cream sandwich for breakfast? *Brioche con gelato* (ice cream inside a sweet-bread roll) is a thrilling, deliciously common treat. Cones work too.

Crushed Ice

Granita (flavoured crushed ice) is typically served in a glass or plastic beaker. Order a *brioche col tuppo* (round, two-tier, sweet-bread bun) on the side to rip into chunks and dunk.

BEST ICED TREAT EXPERIENCES

Breakfast on almond *granita* and a *brioche col tuppo* with sea views on the terrace at **Da Alfredo** ❶ in Lingua, Salina (p138)

Ever tasted ricotta *granita* with candied capers? Hit **Pa.Pe.Ro** ❷ in fishing hamlet Rinella on Salina (p138)

Hunt one of Palermo's last roving **pushcarts** ❸ selling *grattatella* – ice scratchings, scraped from a block of ice (p65)

Leap off rock spires into the sea and scoff saffron-spiced amaretto gelato in quaint seaside hamlet **San Gregorio** ❹ (p121)

End a walking tour of Ragusa Ibla with wine gelato at **Gelati DiVini** ❺ (p198)

GRAPE TO GLASS

Sicily's vineyards cover nearly 120,000 hectares, making it Italy's second-largest wine-producing region. But while grapes have always been grown here, Sicilian wine is for the most part not well known outside the island. The exception is its excellent honey-sweet dessert wines, with globally celebrated Marsala leading the pack.

Tasting

In towns almost every *enoteca* (wine bar) offers *degustazione* (tasting) of one or two Sicilian wines at least. Tasting at wineries requires advance booking.

Buying

A rich, intense red from a prestigious Mt Etna winegrower or a €2 bottle of *vino da tavola* (table wine) at the market: all budgets are catered for.

Tours

Catania, Messina, Taormina and Cefalù are key spots for picking up a half- or full-day guided tour of surrounding vineyards and wineries, with tastings.

BEST VITICULTURAL EXPERIENCES

Tour the venerable 1830s cellars of a historic winemaking family at **Cantine Florio** ❶ in viticultural capital Marsala (p99)

Explore the Aeolian Island of Vulcano by scooter, climaxing with sunset wine tasting in vineyards with superlative sea views at **Soffio sulle Isole** ❷ (p137)

Pair island capers with Salina's signature sweet Malvasia wine during a guided tasting at **Azienda Agricola Carlo Hauner** ❸ (pictured far left; p138)

Sip almond wine in the 18th-century taverna where it was first bottled in 1907 in hilltop village **Castelmola** ❹ (p161)

Trundle by train through winemaking villages and past wineries in sumptuous historic villas on the volcanic slopes of Mt Etna along **Strada del Vino dell'Etna wine route** ❺ (p162)

CORAL & CLAY

From ancient grave vases, spun in clay and painted with intricate patterns to accompany the dead, to lifelike marionettes and contemporary coral jewels, Sicily's art and crafts heritage is immense. Some towns are renowned for one craft, such as Caltagirone (ceramics) in central Sicily. But island-wide, you can find artists and artisans in family workshops, faithfully celebrating and reinventing Sicily's thriving artistic tradition.

Opera dei Pupi

Pupi siciliani (Sicilian marionettes) have entertained since ancient Greek times. Watch performances in traditional puppet theatre in Palermo, Catania and Syracuse.

Artists at Work

Dozens of artists and artisans open their *bottega* (studio or workshop) to visitors – most workspaces double as a boutique where you can buy their work.

Hands-on Crafting

Many artisans run intimate, small-group workshops allowing you to try your hand at their craft – ceramics, pottery and painting are the most widespread.

VLADIMIR KOROSTYSHEVSKIY/SHUTTERSTOCK © FAR LEFT: PAOLO GALLO/SHUTTERSTOCK © LEFT: DOV MAKABAW/ALAMY STOCK PHOTO ©

BEST ARTS & CRAFTS EXPERIENCES

Learn about traditional puppet theatre at a puppeteer's workshop and catch a show in **Palermo ❶** (p75)

Enjoy a private tour of rare majolica tiles and overnight in a tile collector's home at Palermo's extraordinary **Stanze al Genio ❷** (p69)

In **Caltagirone ❸** craft clay in a hands-on ceramic workshop and see the town's iconic ceramic-inlaid staircase lit with thousands of twinkling oil lamps (p217)

Shop for contemporary jewellery set with local, naturally sustainable coral by goldsmith and jeweller Sabrina Orafa in **Sciacca ❹** (p236)

Watch a pair of world-famous cart artisans paint bold, colourful and intricate motifs on a Fiat, traditional cart or other object in their workshop in **Ragusa Ibla ❺** (p197)

NOA_80/SHUTTERSTOCK ©

Chiosco (kiosk), Catania

URBAN LIFE

Palermo and Catania – Sicily's largest cities – are a mesmerising mashup of suburban dishevelment and soul-stirring beauty. To get under the skin of these urban creatures where almost 1.5 million Sicilians live and work, join locals for a morning mooch around an open-air food market, grilled intestines on sticks and a *passeggiata* (afternoon stroll) through town.

Street Art

Keep your eyes peeled for works – often Mafia- or eco-themed – by Nicolò Amato, Tutto e Niente and other Sicilian street artists.

Aperitivi

The late-afternoon *aperitivo* (aperitif) is sacrosanct. Hit a cafe on any central people-watching piazza or head up high to sunset-watch atop a rooftop.

BEST URBAN EXPERIENCES

Honour unsung heroes who've died in Sicily's anti-Mafia fight on a DIY street-art tour in Palermo's **Il Capo ❶** (p65)

Grab a spleen sandwich from Palermo's **'king of street food' ❷** to scoff on the waterfront (p70)

Shop for *dolci* (cakes and sweets) cooked up in *pasticcerie* hidden inside monasteries in Palermo and **Agrigento ❸** (p228)

Stop by a 19th-century *chiosco* (kiosk) and knock back a refreshing *seltz limone e sale* in **Catania ❹** (p164)

Scale Catania's rooftops for majestic views of central square **Piazza del Duomo ❺**, the sea and Mt Etna (p167)

ANDRAS_CSONTCS/SHUTTERSTOCK ©

Gole dell'Alcantara (p162)

WILD SICILY

Abandoned hilltop castles staring moodily out to sea, ancient quarries re-spun as botanical gardens, lost beaches only accessible by boat: Sicily's wild side promises peace, solitude and natural beauty in spades. Whether you're a mountain, river or seafaring type, the island has an unspoilt retreat with your name on it.

Gear

Despite the searing heat, a pair of comfortable closed shoes is key. Binoculars for spotting birds and other fauna are also handy.

Getting Around

You'll need your own wheels or the services of a boatman to reach Sicily's wildest spots. Hook up with a local guide to hike remote trails.

BEST WILD EXPERIENCES

Climb to the top of **Alicudi ❶**, the Aeolian's least developed island, where mules are the only transport (p140)

See where hermits once lived in the **Valle degli Eremiti ❷** and scale Monte Poverello for a 'two-sea' panorama (p156)

Take an ice-cold wild swim in the vertiginous lava gorges of **Gole dell'Alcantara ❸** (p162)

Revel in solitude and spot sea turtles in the windswept sands of the **Riserva Naturale Torre Salsa ❹** (p234)

Dive off **Lipari ❺** to study the habitats of octopuses, eels, groupers and other critters up close (p132)

21

SLOW TRAVEL

No island is more bound up with the fruits of its volcanic soil than Sicily, a down-to-earth destination where the best travel is grassroots stuff. From road trips and train journeys in quest of a fine Mt Etna wine or a soul-soaring panorama even grander than the last, the most memorable journeys here are slow and in tune with the natural landscape. Join the lemon or olive harvest, be welcomed onto a family farm, and discover the side of Sicily where time almost stands still.

Join the Harvest

Harvesting is an opportunity to get your hands dirty with locals – and learn. Collecting manna in Madonie ash forests with Mario (madonieexplorers.com) is a highlight.

Ark of Taste

Look for endangered food products in Slow Food's Ark of Taste – the Etna silver goat, Favignana tuna roe and Iblei Mountains thyme honey are among the 100-odd listed.

Agriturismi

Overnight in an *agriturismo* (farmstay) – anything from a lemon farm or winery to a restored *palmento* where grapes from Etna's slopes were once pressed.

Salt pans, Trapani

BEST SLOW EXPERIENCES

Take part in the olive or lemon harvest and taste oil at organic farm **Azienda Agricola Paparoni Agricontura ❶**, near Capo d'Orlando (p121)

Join a guided day trek from **Palermo ❷** to a goat farm and artisan dairy in the hills – watch ricotta being made (p80)

Become a salt worker for the day in salt pans south of **Trapani ❸** – watch them blaze pink at sunset (p93)

Follow ancient Aeolian pathways into the hills, along centurion mule tracks fringed with prickly pears and dry-stone walls – be guided by a botanist or biologist from Nesos in **Lipari ❹** (p134)

Road trip into the **Madonie mountains ❺**, ending with a traditional dinner feast at Casale Drinzi above Collesano (p117)

REGIONS & CITIES

Find the places that tick all your boxes.

Western Sicily

ANCIENT RUINS & SLOW ISLANDS

Sensational seafood (lobster soup alert!), sweet Marsala wine and a unique local cuisine woo taste buds in the epicurean west. Ancient Greek temples and theatres at Segesta and Selinunte blast time travellers to the island's rich classical past. Boats transport island-hoppers from Trapani to the serene Egadi archipelago.

p83

Palermo

MASTERPIECE ARCHITECTURE & EXTRAORDINARY FOOD

Arab domes, shimmering Byzantine mosaics, Norman palace walls – Sicily's largest metropolis sizzles with architectural gems. Pair this gargantuan artistic heritage with an intoxicating whirlwind of urban street life, historic markets, a vibrant cultural scene and a string of top-drawer day trips.

p48

Palermo
p48

Western
Sicily
p83

Mediterranean
Coast
p223

Mediterranean Coast

SEA & TEMPLES

Greek genius in the Valley of the Temples or contemporary funk at Farm Cultural Park: the artistic marvels span centuries along Sicily's southern shores. West of main town Agrigento, it's a walk on the wild side on golden sand beaches, dazzling white chalk cliffs and tracts of unspoilt countryside.

p223

Central Sicily

SILENT LANDSCAPE & TRADITION

Slow right down to really get under the skin of Sicily's wild and empty interior – a timeless landscape of sunburnt peaks, greystone villages and forgotten valleys. Greek ruins and Roman mosaics, noble *palazzi* and Caltagirone's staircase to heaven and endless pastoral tradition reward those who venture this far.

p204

Tyrrhenian Coast

BEACHES, FOOD & MOUNTAIN CAPERS

This northern wedge bottles a taste of Sicily's two extremes. Beach-hop in high season along the crowded coast with seemingly half of Italy – don't miss Cefalù's endless sweep of sandy gold spiaggia and enchanting old town. Then head inland to find peace and pristine nature in the remote Madonie and Nebrodi mountains

p106

Aeolian Islands

SLOW ESCAPES & OUTDOOR ADVENTURE

Hike up volcanic slopes at sunset, watch Stromboli spit and fume, paddle around a smoking crater or into an iridescent sea cave: these seven Unesco-listed islands are paradise on earth. Each one has its own character, meaning cobalt-blue waters and clandestine coves to match every mood and moment.

p125

Aeolian Islands
p125

Tyrrhenian Coast
p106

Central Sicily
p204

Ionian Coast
p146

Ionian Coast

BETWEEN MYTH & HISTORY

Wedged between the menacing hulk of mighty Mt Etna and the storied Ionian Sea, Sicily's far east is a hypnotic beast. It's here you'll find the skinny Strait of Messina, volcanic vineyards yielding exceptional vino, the world's most spectacularly located ancient Greek theatre and Catania – a buzzy, Unesco-listed city cut from lava stone.

p146

Syracuse &
the Southeast
p173

Syracuse & the Southeast

HISTORY & NATURE

The past and present collide in a magnificent drama of Graeco-Roman ruins and baroque hill towns, sweeping topaz beaches and cutthroat canyons. Syracuse on the coast and the string of historic beauties – Noto, Modica, Ragusa and Scicli – in the undulating Val di Noto are priceless. Then there's the chocolate...

p173

WHEN **TO GO**

Join the crowds in July and August, or visit during the shoulder seasons to enjoy mellow days and handsome scapes spun from extraordinary light and colour.

There is so much more to Sicily these days than flopping on the sand and dipping in gin-clear turquoise water. Traditional water-based activities like snorkelling, diving and boating are as hot as ever during the sun-scorched high season. But as there is growing interest in slow, meditative exploration of rural landscapes and traditions, it's the cooler shoulder seasons that are increasingly popular.

When assessing the warmth and what you need to pack, consider the altitude. Holidaying on the slopes of Europe's highest volcano is dramatically different to hanging around at sea level on the Aeolian and Egadi Islands.

Want a Bargain?

Low season, between November and March, might see offshore islands and coastal resorts largely shut down. But this is the time when accommodation rates drop by 30% or more.

⊘ I LIVE HERE

AUTUMNAL ENERGY

Favignana Islander Stefania Prodida is an art teacher and bilingual tour guide, specialising in botany and gardens.

'The place I go to get away from the routine is Marettimo in autumn: the walks at dawn towards the summit of Pizzo Falcone (750m), the clear air, the blue sky, the smell of wet grass, plants bathed in intense colour, the feeling of being refreshed and purified. Nature is generous to those who know how to love it.'

LEFT: MARCO OSSINO/SHUTTERSTOCK ©
RIGHT: IMANTAS PAKALNIS/SHUTTERSTOCK ©

SNOWFALL

Mt Etna and the highest peaks of the Madonie and Nebrodi Mountains are typically snow-capped from December to late March. January is the best month to hit the slopes in ski resorts Piano Provenzana and Nicolosi (p171) and Piano Battaglia (p119).

Hiker near Mt Etna (p169)

Weather through the year

JANUARY	FEBRUARY	MARCH	APRIL	MAY	JUNE
Ave. daytime max: **16°C**	Ave. daytime max: **16°C**	Ave. daytime max: **18.6°C**	Ave. daytime max: **21.9°C**	Ave. daytime max: **26.8°C**	Ave. daytime max: **31.6°C**
Days of rainfall: **9.1**	Days of rainfall: **9.4**	Days of rainfall: **8.6**	Days of rainfall: **8.8**	Days of rainfall: **4.1**	Days of rainfall: **1.9**

SIROCCO

It's not difficult to recognise the Sirocco wind: think a horribly hot, 'hairdryer' wind that blows in from the south in August and has been known to reach near-on hurricane speeds. Dust from the North African deserts sometimes reddens Sicilian skies and temperatures soar.

The Big Music & Arts Festivals

World-class actors perform at Syracuse's 5th-century-BCE amphitheatre during the **Festival del Teatro Greco** (p181). ☀ **May to July**

Catania's four-night world music festival **Marranzano** (p166) brings acts from all over the globe into historic Monastero dei Benedettini. ☀ **June**

Taormina Arte raises the curtain on opera, dance, theatre and live-music performances at Taormina's Teatro Greco. ☀ **June to September**

On the eco-conscious Aeolian Islands, **Festa di Teatro Ecologico** ushers in 10 days of electricity-free theatre, dance and music on an open-air stage on Stromboli. ☀ **July**

Catch live jazz beneath the stars in the spectacular ruins of a 16th-century church during Palermo's **Sicilia Jazz Festival**. ☀ **September**

Dozens of venues open their doors to celebrate their cultural heritage during **Le Vie dei Tesori**, an eight-week, island-wide 'Open House'. ☀ **September and October**

Carnivals & Patron Saints

During the week before Ash Wednesday, many towns stage **Carnevale**. The most flamboyant are in Sciacca (wwwsciaccarnevale.it; p236) and Acireale (www.carnevaleacireale.com; p169). ☀ **February**

One million Catanians follow a silver reliquary of Sant'Agata through the streets during Catania's **Festa di Sant'Agata**, accompanied by fireworks. ☀ **February**

Traditional *maestranze* (guilds) in Trapani parade life-sized wooden statues of

the Virgin Mary and other Biblical figures through the streets for four days during **La Processione dei Misteri** (p90). ☀ **April**

Drums, confetti and fireworks set a hypnotic scene as a statue of Modica's patron saint is raced through the streets during the **Festa di San Giorgio**. ☀ **April**

Palermo's biggest annual festival, **Festino di Santa Rosalia** (p80), celebrates its patron saint with a multi-day party, grand parade and celebratory fireworks. ☀ **July**

Parco Naturale Regionale dell Madonie (p119)

THREE SEAS

Depending on where you stay in Sicily, you dip into one of three seas: the Ionian, the Tyrrhenian or the Mediterranean. The average water temperature hovers around 27°C in summer, and 15°C in winter.

JULY	AUGUST	SEPTEMBER	OCTOBER	NOVEMBER	DECEMBER
Ave. daytime max: **34.9°C**	Ave. daytime max: **35°C**	Ave. daytime max: **30.7°C**	Ave. daytime max: **26.1°C**	Ave. daytime max: **21.1°C**	Ave. daytime max: **17.1°C**
Days of rainfall: **1.2**	Days of rainfall: **2.4**	Days of rainfall: **5.5**	Days of rainfall: **8.4**	Days of rainfall: **10.6**	Days of rainfall: **12.2**

MEET THE SICILIANS

It is not easy to define Sicilians univocally but one thing is certain: they are the most hospitable people you will ever meet. We learned it from the Greeks. SARA MOSTACCIO introduces her people.

THE COMISO-BORN AUTHOR Gesualdo Bufalino wrote that 'the concept of an island usually corresponds to a solid clump of races and customs, while here everything is odd, mixed up, changing, as in the most hybrid continent. It's true that there are many Sicilies, we won't ever be able to count them all.' The position of Sicily as a stepping stone in the centre of the Mediterranean Basin has lent it strategic importance throughout history, resulting in an endless procession of conquerors. Being colonised for centuries, Sicilians have absorbed myriad traits. That's why the Sicilian soul is such a mix, full of contradictions. According to the writer, Sicilians 'suffer from an excess of identity'. This complexity, due to centuries-old interwoven bloodlines, is still visible as a constant tension between a sense of seclusion, and the intimacy of an island perceived as a nest, versus the openness to the world. Sicilians can be very diffident, warmly welcoming, deeply pessimistic, even fatalistic, but also resourceful and always ready to look into the future. Sometimes they feel oppressed by a sense of inferiority but they also cultivate a strong sense of being different. It won't be surprising to know that they generally define themselves as Sicilians rather than Italians.

THE DIASPORA

Sicily's population is approximately 5 million while an additional 10 million people of Sicilian descent live around the world – mostly in the United States, Argentina, Australia and other EU countries. The island is home to growing communities of immigrants from the Balkans, Africa, India and China.

Today it is not easy to make blanket assertions about who Sicilians are, not only because of this multi-layered personality but also because of the marked difference between cities and rural areas. Palermo and Catania boast a vibrant youth culture and a liberal lifestyle, while in rural areas vestiges of traditional life remain, especially those linked to family loyalty, fear of losing honour, and the obsession with putting forward the *bella figura*, a good impression. This asphyxiating atmosphere, no less than economic needs, has induced many Sicilians to leave the island in search of better opportunities and a more open mindset elsewhere. On the other hand, increasing migratory flows have continued to bring new life and fresh energies, confirming that Sicily is still a land of passage. Here many different roots give life to a unique people whose most recurring feature is hospitality. From the Greeks we learned the value of hospitality. Sicilians are a caring, friendly people, and they always do their best to make everyone feel at ease. If you happen to be invited to a Sicilian home, you will never leave hungry, as food is our way of connecting with people, even when language barriers might seem difficult to overcome. Be prepared to hear the word *mangia!* (eat!) often.

Pictured clockwise from top left: Sicilian folk performer; Sicilians, Enna; beachgoer, Taormina; man carrying aubergines

I'M SICILIAN & I DECIDED TO STAY

I was born in Catania and still live in Sicily. I went away for quite a while, but I always decided to come back and, ultimately, to stay. Despite all its contradictions, Sicily is home. I feel the duty to take care of it by trying to change what doesn't work and keep everything that is precious. Part of my family had to emigrate – to Switzerland, the USA and Australia – between the 1930s and 1950s. This openness to the world, although dictated by economic needs, has always had a powerful influence on me. Sicily itself, conquered many times over the centuries and now a destination for migration, has always been open to the world. My deep-seated roots intertwine with remote peoples who have left traces as they passed through – even in my DNA as I was born with blue eyes, fair skin and dark hair and from an early age I was called the Norman.

LEFT, SUN_SHINE/SHUTTERSTOCK © RIGHT, CBS PHOTO ARCHIVE/GETTY IMAGES ©

Piazza Duomo (p158), Taormina

GET PREPARED
FOR SICILY

Useful things to load in your bag, your ears and your brain

Clothes

Appearances Matter Sicilians take the concept of *la bella figura* (literally 'making a good impression') seriously. In towns and cities, suitable clothing for men is trousers and shirts or polo shirts, and for women, skirts, dresses and trousers. Summer ushers in shorts and T-shirts.

Scarves Bring a sarong or scarf to cover up in churches. Bare chests on the street are a strict no-go.

Footwear Flip-flops and sandals are beach-perfect, but pack shoes with decent grip for towns and hilltop villages where time-worn pavements and cobbles are slippery. Bring closed shoes – trainers or hiking shoes – for exploring archaeological sites, the Aeolian Islands and nature parks in the mountainous interior.

Manners

Never intrude on a church service. Be quiet and respectful when visiting religious sites; cover shoulders, torsos and thighs.

Don't discuss the Mafia – it can be a touchy subject.

When dining in an Italian home, bring sweets *(dolci)* or wine. Dress well.

Cannoli are meant to be eaten with your fingers, not a knife and fork! Ditto for street food.

Hats In summer you won't make it through the day without a decent sunhat. In winter, the sun remains strong – don't leave your hat at home.

📖 READ

Beautiful Antonio
(Vitaliano Brancati;
1949) Sicilian machismo:
the tale of a young man
from Catania returning
home to wed.

The Invention of Sicily
(Jamie Mackay; 2021) A
riveting romp through
the island's rich history,
myths, culture and
people.

**Sicily: A Literary Guide
for Travellers** (Andrew
& Suzanne Edwards;
2014) Sicily's cultural
landscape through the
eyes of writers.

**Pomp & Sustenance:
25 Centuries of Sicilian
Food** (Mary Taylor
Simeti; 1998) Recipes
and stories of Sicily's
dishes and customs.

Words

'Buongiorno' (bwon-*jor*-no),
meaning 'good day', and
'buona sera' (bwon-a *se*-ra),
used from late afternoon
onwards to say 'good
evening', is the standard
greeting for strangers.

Use **'lei'** (formal 'you') in
polite company and **'tu'**
(informal 'you') with friends
and children.

'Come stai?' (kom-e stai),
accompanied by a kiss on
both cheeks, is the way to
greet friends and ask 'how
are you?' Reply with **'Bene.
E lei/tu?'** (*be*-ne e lay/too)
meaning 'Fine. And you?'

'Per favore' (per fa-*vo*-re)
is the standard way to say
'please'. It is also what
you use in restaurants to
summon the waiter. **'Grazie'**
(*gra*-tsye) is 'thank you'.

If you don't understand
something someone has
said to you in Italian, you
can say **'Non capisco'**
(non ka-*pee*-sko) or 'I don't
understand'.

Say **'mi scusi'** (mee *skoo*-
zee) or 'excuse me' to get
someone's attention.

Say **'permesso'** (per-
mess-o) when you want to
pass someone in a crowd.

In restaurants and trattorie,
when deciding what dish to
order, don't hesitate to ask
what the regional or town
speciality is. Say **'Qual'è
la specialità di questa
regione/città?'** (kwa-*le* la
spe-cha-lee-*ta* dee kwes-ta
re-*jo*-ne/chee-*ta*). You can
also ask the waiter **'Cosa
mi consiglia?'** (*ko*-za mee
kon-*see*-lya) meaning 'What
do you recommend?'

'Salute!' (sa-*loo*-te) literally
means 'health'. You say it
after someone sneezes or
as a toast before drinking.
Don't confuse it with **'Saluti'**
(sa-*loo*-tee) which means
'Greetings!' or 'Hi'.

📺 WATCH

The Godfather (Francis Ford
Coppola; 1972–90) Masterpiece
trilogy starring Marlon Brando
and Al Pacino as powerful leaders
of an Italian-American crime
family in the 1940s and '50s.

Stromboli (Roberto Rossellini;
1950) The explosive love affair
between a Lithuanian refugee and
a fisherman on a volcanic island.

Nuovo Cinema Paradiso
(Giuseppe Tornatore; 1988)
Oscar-winning film celebrating
Sicilian cinema and life in a village
after WWII.

**Framed! A Sicilian Murder
Mystery** (Salvatore Ficarra &
Valentino Picone; 2022) Netflix
comic crime drama set in Sicily.

🎧 LISTEN

FLEURs
(Franco Battiato; 1999)
Considered the best
album of the Sicilian
singer (1945–2021)
nicknamed *'il maestro'*.

D'acqua e di rosi
(*Love Songs of Sicily;*
Mario Incudine;
2017) The voice of
contemporary Sicilian
folk music.

Punto e a Capo (Lello
Analfino; 2022) Debut
solo album from Lello
Analfino, lead singer
of Sicily's wildly
successful rock band
Tinturia.

**The Platinum
Collection** (Carmen
Consoli; 2017) The
best 'best of' album of
Catania-born Consoli,
Sicily's best known
singer-songwriter.

SERGII KOVAL/SHUTTERSTOCK ©

Caponata

THE FOOD SCENE

It's not all temples and churches. Such is the scope of Sicilian cuisine that it's perfectly feasible to simply eat your way around the island.

In a nutshell: Sicily boasts one of the sassiest, oldest and least-known cuisines in Italy, standing out for its uniqueness and quality in an epicurean nation pretty much fuelled by food.

Regional variations are such that within Sicily, each town, village, even mountain has its own specialities and traditional dishes mirroring the lay of the land, season and ancestral heritage. Help harvest lemons in Capo d'Orlando or artisan salt in Trapani and unearth unique, privileged insight into local culinary life displayed in no museum.

Over the centuries successive waves of invaders, poverty and deprivation have all shaped and spiced the island's rich pantry with foreign flavours and smart tricks. Facing a changing climate, Sicilian farmers and winemakers continue to innovate. As they experiment with new ways to grow old crops – and indeed seek new crops to replace old crops – the current food scene remains a moveable feast. Dig in and savour, preferably around a table with friends in a cheek-to-jowl-packed trattoria, family-run *agriturismo* (farm) or on a seafront terrace within a wave's splash of the big blue.

Ancient Roots

Sicily's diverse pantry has its roots in the island's fertile volcanic soil and waters – Mediterranean fish and shellfish form one of the lasting foundations of Sicilian cuisine. An abundance of fruit and vegetables has also been evident since ancient Greek times.

Best Sicilian Cakes & Sweets	CANNOLO	FRUTTA MARTORANA	PASTA DI MANDORLA	TORTINA PARADISO
	Crisp tube of fried pastry dough, filled with creamy ricotta.	Marzipan exquisitely shaped to resemble fruits.	One-bite almond cake, perfect with an espresso.	Almond sponge, soaked in rum, apricot jam and sugar syrup.

Homer famously wrote about wild fennel and caper bushes growing on the hills and said of the island, 'Here luxuriant trees are always in their prime, pomegranates and pears, and apples glowing red, succulent figs and olives swelling sleek and dark'.

With the arrival of the Arabs, Sicilian cuisine really took shape. The Saracens brought the ever-present aubergine (eggplant), as well as citrus fruits, and they are believed to have introduced pasta to the island. They also spiced things up with saffron and sultanas, and contrasted the dishes' delicate flavours with the crunch of almonds and pistachios. Seafood couscous became a menu staple and sugar cane was hauled onto shore. Don't leave your sweet tooth at home!

Home Staples

Bread is an ancient staple. Made from durum wheat, Sicilian bread is coarse and golden, fashioned into myriad ritualistic and regional shapes, from braids to rings to flowers, and sometimes finished off with sesame seeds. Baked bread is treated with the greatest respect and in the past only the head of the family had the privilege of slicing the loaf.

A bread-dough base is the secret behind *sfincione* (the Sicilian version of pizza made

with tomatoes, onions and sometimes anchovies), *impanata* (bread-dough snacks stuffed with meat, vegetables or cheese) and *scaccie* (pancake-like discs of bread dough spread with a filling and rolled up). No Sicilian larder is complete without a tub of breadcrumbs – a hand-me-down from the days when peasants substituted meat with *melanzane* (aubergines) and grated cheese with *mollica* (breadcrumbs) to create age-old classics such as *pasta con le*

WEAD/SHUTTERSTOCK ©

CELEBRATING FOOD

Sagra della Ricotta (p221) Time your trip to Vizzini, 30km east of Caltagirone, for late April when villagers celebrate ricotta.

Sagra delle Minni di Virgini (p238) May celebrates Sicily's cake infamously shaped like a 'virgin's breast', created by a nun in Sambuca di Sicilia in 1725.

StraGusto (p88) This street-food fest in July fills Trapani's old fish-market square with three days of tastings, dining and live cooking.

Couscous Fest (p95) San Vito Lo Capo celebrates Trapani's beloved local dish for six days in September.

Funghi Fest (p119) Inland from the Tyrrhenian Coast, hit epicurean Castelbuono for October's mushroom festival.

Scale del Gusto (p198) October ushers in Ragusa Ibla's fabulous food festival, with tastings, master classes, live cooking and endless eating.

ROSARIOSCALIA/SHUTTERSTOCK ©

Mpanatigghi

Minni di Virgini

CASSATA SICILIANA	MPANATIGGHI	MINNA DI VIRGINI	CASSATELLA DI MONTEVAGO
Ricotta, sugar, candied fruit and chocolate, flavoured with vanilla and maraschino liqueur, encased in sponge cake.	Sweet biscuits filled with chocolate, spices and minced beef (really).	Small, round, white-iced cake with a cherry on the top.	Fried pastry filled with ricotta, honey and lemon zest; a speciality of the southeast.

VINCENZO SCARANTINO/SHUTTERSTOCK ©

HOW TO EAT CANNOLI

Unspoken rules surround Sicily's most iconic sweet treat, *cannoli* (singular: *cannolo*).

A truly good *cannolo* is filled on the spot with fresh ricotta. Avoid pre-filled shells; left to sit for too long, the shell gets soggy, killing the whole crunchy bliss of the experience.

Eating is strictly fingers only. Even in top-end restaurants, it's perfectly acceptable to grasp the *cannolo* between thumb and forefinger and bite in. Alternate ends when eating.

The best cannoli are 100% homemade. The *cialda* or *scorza* (crispy pastry shell) is never a perfect cylinder and the velvety cream filling is *lavorata a mano* (worked by hand) to blend fresh sheep ricotta with sugar.

November to May is the best time for *cannoli* when the milk used to make the fresh ricotta comes from ewes grazing on fresh green grass. During Sicily's scorching summer, sheep are fed dry foliage and ricotta is often made with a mix of sheep and cow milk.

aroma (smell the artichoke, citrus and almond groves surrounding those olive trees). Vinegar can be balsamic, apple cider, white wine – even pomegranate (sublime!). On Salina and other Aeolian Islands, tangy capers are picked up from a neighbouring farm, street-side or in a recycled glass jam jar at the local grocery store.

Vegetarians & Vegans

Vegetarianism is not specifically catered to in Sicily but the abundance of excellent local produce means that many antipasti, pastas and *contorni* (side dishes) only feature veg. You won't go wrong with *caponata*, the classic Sicilian appetiser of aubergine, tomatoes, olives and capers – at its best in the Aeolian Islands. *Pane cuzato* (open sandwiches), piled high with a variety of toppings, are meals in themselves. Salads are common and tasty, though you'll need to watch out for the odd anchovy or slice of ham.

Vegans will be in for a tough time, with many dishes featuring some sort of animal product (butter, eggs or animal stock). When buying *cannoli* check what oil the shell was deep-fried in – traditionally it's pork lard, though many pastry chefs use vegetable oil these days.

sarde (pasta with sardines, pine nuts, raisins, wild fennel and breadcrumbs) and *involtini* (meat or fish slices wrapped around a sometimes-spicy breadcrumb stuffing, then pan-fried or grilled).

Then there's the sacrosanct bottle of olive oil – essential for transforming stale bread into *pane cuzato*. Most households buy local oil, pressed from a variety of fruity olives bursting with Sicilian sunshine and

GANDOLFO CANNATELLA/SHUTTERSTOCK ©

Stigghiole

MUCCUNETTO	TORTA DI RICOTTA	FEDDA DEL CANCELLIERE	MINNA DI SANT'AGATA
Single-bite, gooey, almond cake crafted by traditional pastry cooks in Mazara del Vallo.	Ricotta cake.	Marzipan clam shell filled with apricot jam and almond milk.	An iced cake for Catania's patron saint: candied fruit, dark chocolate and ricotta in crumbly shortcrust pastry.

Sicilian Specialities

Couscous & Pasta

Couscous alla trapanese Trapani's North African-inspired fish couscous, seasoned with saffron, garlic, tomatoes and parsley.

Pasta alla norma Catania's signature pasta dish, made with aubergines, ricotta, basil and tomatoes.

Pasta con le sarde Palermo marries pasta with sardines, pine nuts, raisins and wild fennel.

Busiate alla trapanese Hand-twirled, spaghetti-like pasta with Trapani's pesto of tomatoes, basil, garlic and almonds.

Pasta che paddunedda A traditional broth of noodle-like pasta and small veal meatballs.

Favourite Fish

Frittura mista Battered, deep-fried mix of shrimp, squid and/or fish.

Carpaccio di spada Swordfish carpaccio.

Tonno rosso alla griglia Grilled tuna steak.

Tonno scottato al pistacchio Seared tuna encrusted in pistachio nuts.

Agghiotta di pesce spada Swordfish with pine nuts, sultanas, capers, olives and tomatoes: a Messina special

Swordfish carpaccio

Pesce spada alla ghiotta Swordfish fillets with tomatoes, capers and olives.

Snacks & Street Food

Pane e panelle Chickpea fritters, fried aubergine and potato croquettes with a touch of mint, served on a sesame roll.

Stigghiola Seasoned and barbecued skewers of lamb or kid intestines, cooked on grills in street food markets.

Pani câ mèusa A bread roll filled with calf's spleen and lung, caciocavallo cheese, a drizzle of hot lard and squeeze of lime juice.

Arancini Rice balls stuffed with a variety of meat, cheese or nut fillings (often pistachio), coated with breadcrumbs and fried.

MEALS OF A LIFETIME

Gagini, Palermo (p76) Enjoy the modern Sicilian cuisine of Italian–Brazilian chef Mauricio Zillo at Palermo's only Michelin-starred restaurant.

Locanda Don Serafino, Ragusa Ibla (p197) Michelin-starred dining in a series of rocky caves.

Il Cappero, Vulcano (p137) A 10-course menu celebrating island produce thrills at this food temple with sea view. In the kitchen: Michelin-starred, Palermo-born Giuseppe Biuso.

Trattoria Il Veliero, Marettimo (p105) Phone this waterfront trattoria at least 24 hours in advance to order its masterpiece lobster soup and *frascatole* (handmade couscous).

Cortile Arabo, Marzamemi (p197) Sensational dining and an unmatched sea view in a fishing village 30 minutes from Noto.

THE YEAR IN FOOD

SPRING

Asparagus, artichokes, fennel, fava beans and wild strawberries flood market stalls. Wheat fields are pea-green and Easter specialities fill bakery windows. Tuna and swordfish swim into season.

SUMMER

Aubergines, peppers, berries, seafood and capers. Beat the heat with *granita* (crushed ice with fruit) or gelato on brioche. Mulberry, pomegranate, pistachio and watermelon are hot August flavours.

AUTUMN

Food festivals galore, grape and olive harvests, and time to visit the mountains for chestnuts, hazelnuts, mushrooms and wild game. Farmers pick almonds, pistachios, and yellow and red Leonforte peaches.

WINTER

The orange harvest begins and ricotta is made from the milk of sheep grazing on lush green pastures. Christmas ushers in *buccellati* – sweet dough rings stuffed with fruit and almonds. Eat sea urchins in January.

FRANK LAMBERT/SHUTTERSTOCK ©

Hiking on Vulcano (p137)

THE OUTDOORS

With its bluebird climate and Garden of Eden mix of landscapes, Sicily is an enticing outdoor playground – whatever your chosen sport or activity, on land or sea.

Sicily's varied landscape makes a dramatic first impression – and demands action. There really are fewer more stunning backdrops in which to run wild than the island's natural juxtaposition of sea, volcano and mountain scenery. Hikers can wind along precipitous coastlines, scale volcanoes (Europe's highest to boot, at 3372m) and traipse through flower-strewn mountain meadows. Birders benefit from the plethora of species on the Africa–Europe migration route and divers and swimmers enjoy some of the Mediterranean's most pristine waters. Whatever your personal predilections, Sicily offers enough activities to build an entire holiday around.

Hiking

A coastline spilling across three seas and mountains that capture every traveller's full attention with their explosive volcanic heritage make Sicily superb hiking terrain. Marked trails lead to ancient Greek temples and once-splendid Roman villas in archaeological parks, along time-trodden mule tracks to shepherds' huts where ricotta is crafted over an open wood fire, up smoking volcanoes and down hillsides stitched from centurion dry-stone walls and prickly pears. Spring (April to May), June and autumn (September to October) offer the best conditions – high summer is busy and

More Outdoor Thrills

COASTEERING & CANYONING
Explore island shores with Eugenio Viviani on Vulcano (p136). Canyon in the Gole dell'Alcantara (p162).

KITE SURFING
Ride the wind on lagoon Laguna dello Stagnone (p94) near Trapani in western Sicily. On the Med, windy Torre di Gaffe (p239) is another kite hub.

SAILING & KAYAKING
Explore the coastlines, beaches, sea stacks and grottoes of the Aeolian Islands (p125).

FAMILY ADVENTURES

Take a short island hike up to the **ruins of a Bronze Age village** (p138) on Filicudi.

Float in a **natural swimming pool** (p79) carved from rocks on Ustica.

Walk with a naturalist guide and **learn how to make ricotta cheese** (p80) on a goat farm.

Speed in a motorboat around Levanzo island to uncover **prehistoric cave art** (p104).

Tombstone off rocky outcrops (p121) from hidden beaches in San Gregorio near Capo d'Orlando.

Spend the day on a **black-sand beach** (p142) on Stromboli.

Trek with a donkey on Mt Etna or in the Madonie mountains.

Explore the coast around Syracuse (p180) by bicycle – traditional or e-bike. Or **beach-hop by bike** (p101) on the Aeolian Island of Favignana.

---

too hot. Whatever the season, bring ample water and a sunhat.

Sicily's active volcanoes have strict access rules and are either off-limits completely or require a guide to access higher slopes (p000). On Stromboli you need a guide beyond 290m (up to 400m) and on Mt Etna, from 2450m (up to the authorised crater area at 2920m). The volcano on the island of Vulcano is no longer accessible.

Even when it's hot at lower altitudes, it's windy higher up and temperatures can fall below freezing on Etna (3372m). Bring proper walking boots/shoes, a wind jacket, warm headgear, gloves, sunhat and sunglasses. If you don't have your own, trekking specialists at Rifugio Sapienza (at 1920m, next to the lower station of the Funivia dell'Etna cable car; www.rifugiosapienza.com) on Etna and Totem Trekking (www.totemtrekkingstromboli.com) in Stromboli rent all the gear. For Mt Etna maps, trails and guides, see www.unescoparcoetna.it and download the Parco dell'Etna app.

Trails on the Aeolian Islands and in the Madonie and Nebrodi mountains can be poorly marked. Pick up locally produced maps before setting out, and if in any doubt, book up a local guide: Nesos (www.nesos.org) for all the Aeolians; Sicilian Experience (www.sicilianexperience.com) and Madonie Explorers (https://madonieexplorers.com) in Madonie; Vai Col Trekking Sicilia (www.vaicoltrekkingsicilia.com) in Nebrodi.

Beaches & Swimming

With almost 1500km of coastline and 15 offshore islands (including Ustica, Pantelleria and the Aeolian, Pelagic and Egadi Islands), Sicily sports a beach for every taste. Clear, deep blue and emerald-green waters lapping the shoreline are clean and warm in summer and autumn – for optimum swimming conditions, bathe between June and early October. Beaches range from pebbly to sandy, and from crowded bathing lidos where you can rent sun loungers and parasols to hidden coves and long expanses of sand.

Diving & Snorkelling

May to October, diving and snorkelling opportunities abound in Sicily, most notably in the waters surrounding its offshore islands. Ustica and the Aeolian Islands are the region's leading dive destinations. On Lipari, key diving school La Gorgonia (www.lagorgoniadiving.it) can kit you out and arrange dives. Offshore from the Mediterranean coast, Lampedusa is another hot spot.

SKIING & SNOWSHOEING
There's nothing quite like skiing Sicily's two ski mountains, Mt Etna (p171) and Monte Mufara.

STAND-UP PADDLEBOARDING
Glide along shorelines bejewelled with caves, cliffs and fantastical rock formations around Capo d'Orlando (p120).

BIRDWATCHING
Witness the annual passage of flamingos, herons and other birds through the marshlands of Vendicari (p194) on the Ionian Coast.

HORSE RIDING
Trek on horseback along ancient mule tracks through protected nature reserves on Etna, Madonie and Nebrodi mountains.

ACTION AREAS

Where to find Sicily's best outdoor activities.

Ustica

Tyrrhenian Sea

San Vito Lo Capo

Golfo di Cofano

Golfo di Carini

Mondello

Golfo di Palermo

Palermo

Bagheria

Golfo di Termini Imerese

Erice

Scopello

Partinico

Castellammare del Golfo

Termini Imerese

Levanzo

Trapani

Alcamo

Caccamo

Collesan

Marettimo

Favignana

Favignana

Bosco della Ficuzza

Egadi Islands

Marsala

Corleone

Partanna

Mazara del Vallo

Castelvetrano

Menfi

Caltabellotta

SICILY

Sciacca

Ribera

Beaches

1. Spiaggia di Cefalù (p115)
2. Spiaggia di San Vito (p95)
3. Spiaggia di Scala dei Turchi (p234)
4. Spiaggia San Gregorio (p121)
5. Spiaggia di Torre Salsa (p234)
6. Spiaggia dei Conigli (p240)
7. Spiaggia Valle Muria (p132)

Mediterranean Sea

Agrigento

Favara

Porto Empedocle

Palma di Montechiaro

National Parks

1. Parco Regionale dei Nebrodi (p123)
2. Parco Naturale Regionale delle Madonie (p119)
3. Parco dell'Etna
4. Riserva Naturale dello Zingaro (p95)
5. Riserva Naturale Torre Salsa (p234)
6. Riserva Naturale di Vendicari (p193)
7. Riserva di Cavagrande del Cassibile (p193)
8. Riserva Naturale Saline di Trapani e Paceco (p93)
9. Riserva Naturale di Stagnone
10. Riserva Naturale Fiumedinisi (p155)

Pantelleria

Pantelleria

Pelagic Islands

Porto Empedocle (150km)

Linosa

Linosa

Mediterranean Sea

Lampione

Lampedusa

Lampedusa

Same Scale as Main Map

Pelagic Islands (see Inset; 20km)

Strómboli
San Vincenzo
(Stromboli Town)

Aeolian
Islands

Basiluzzo

Panarea
San Pietro

Salina
Santa Marina Salina

Alicudi

Filicudi

Lipari

Lipari Town

Porto di Levante

Vulcano

Golfo di
Gioia

Golfo di
Milazzo

Mortelle

Messina

Milazzo
Ganzirri

Villa San Giovanni

Capo
d'Orlando

Golfo
di Patti

Barcellona

Reggio di Calabria

Sant'Agata
di Militello

San Marco
d'Alunzio

Riserva
Naturale
Fiumedinisi

Straits of
Messina

Cefalù

Castel
di Tusa

Savoca

CALABRIA

Castelbuono

Mistretta

Parco
Regionale
dei Nebrodi

Taormina

Parco
Naturale
Regionale
delle Madonie

Giardini-Naxos

Petralia Soprana

Bronte

Parco
dell'Etna

Valle
del Bove

Giarre

Adrano

Acireale

Enna

Paternò

Aci
Castello

Aci
Trezza

Riviera dei Ciclopi

Caltanissetta

Misterbianco

Catania

Piazza
Armerina

Aidone

Golfo di
Catania

Ionian
Coast

Mazzarino

Palagonia

Ravanusa

Lentini

Augusta

Butera

Caltagirone

Falconara

Niscemi

Licata

Gela

Palazzolo
Acreide

Floridia

Syracuse

Golfo
di Gela

Vittòria

Riserva di
Cavagrande
del Cassibile

Ragusa

Modica

Noto

Avola

Golfo
di Noto

Ionian
Sea

Scicli

Pozzallo

Pachino

Isola
Capo
Passero

Isola
delle
Correnti

Gozo

Snorkelling/Diving

1 Ustica (p79)
2 Lipari (p132)
3 Filicudi (p138)
4 Riserva Naturale dello
Zingaro (p95)
5 Isola Bella (p159)
6 Lampedusa (p240)
7 Riserva Naturale di
Vendicari (p194)

Walking/Hiking

1 Sciara del Fuoco Viewpoint,
Stromboli (p142)
2 Mt Etna (p169)
3 Dorsale dei Nebrodi (p123)
4 Monte Fossa delle Felci (p138)
5 Monte Montagnola, Alicudi (p140)
6 Punta del Corvo, Panarea (p145)
7 Pizzo Carbonara (p119)

N
0   50 km
0   25 miles

Cattedrale di Monreale (p78)

ITINERARIES

Highlights of Sicily

Allow: 10 days   **Distance:** 755km

This circular grand tour takes you from the Byzantine mosaics, Arabesque domes and frescoed cupolas of urban Palermo to ancient Greek temples by the sea, beautiful baroque hill towns and magnificent Mt Etna. Feasting exceedingly well on traditional and modern Sicilian cuisine is unavoidable.

❶ PALERMO ⏱ 2 DAYS

Start in **Palermo** (p48), exploring its monumental cathedral, royal palace and churches glittering with Byzantine mosaics. Mooch vibrant markets, art-plastered backstreets and lanes specked with artisan boutiques.

🚗 *2-hour drive*

🚐 **Detour:** Catch a bus to hilltop **Monreale** (p78) for shimmering mosaics and sea views in its Unesco-listed Norman cathedral. ⏱ 5 hours

❷ AGRIGENTO ⏱ 1 DAY

From **Agrigento** (p228) spend the day uncovering Sicily's most enthralling archaeological site at **Valley of the Temples** (p230), then return to town for an old-town meander (don't miss Monastero di Santo Spirito with its hidden bakery) and dinner.

🚗 *2½- to 3-hour drive*

🚐 **Detour:** Leaving Palermo, you could explore remarkably preserved Greek temples at **Segesta** (p93) and **Selinunte** (p97). ⏱ 1 day

❸ SYRACUSE ⏱ 2 DAYS

Split your time in **Syracuse** (p178) between the ancient island-city of Ortygia, with oysters at the market for lunch, and the Parco Archeologico's vast ruins. Potter along the coast towards **Noto** (p188) for a sunset swim.

🚗 *1-hour drive*

🚐 **Detour:** Cherry-pick a showpiece baroque town in Val di Noto; **Scicli** (p202) is the most relaxed place for an overnight stay. ⏱ 5 hours

ELESI/SHUTTERSTOCK ©, GRAHAM MCANDREW/SHUTTERSTOCK ©, AURALAURA/SHUTTERSTOCK ©

JEROME LABOUYRIE/SHUTTERSTOCK ©

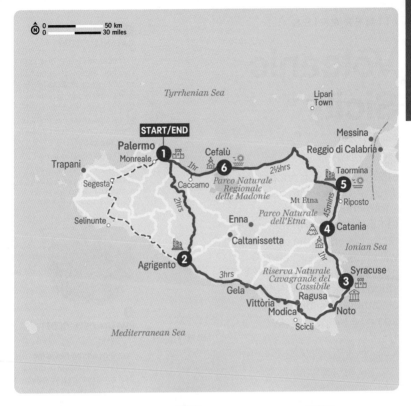

0 — 50 km
0 — 30 miles

Tyrrhenian Sea

Lipari Town

START/END

Messina

Palermo ❶

Cefalù ❻

Reggio di Calabria

Monreale

Trapani

1hr

Taormina ❺

Segesta

Caccamo

2½hrs

Riposto

Parco Naturale Regionale delle Madonie

2hrs

Mt Etna

45mins

Selinunte

Parco Naturale dell'Etna

Enna

Catania ❹

Caltanissetta

Ionian Sea

1hr

Agrigento ❷

3hrs

Riserva Naturale Cavagrande del Cassibile

Syracuse ❸

Gela

Ragusa

Noto

Vittòria

Modica

Scicli

Mediterranean Sea

❹ CATANIA ⏱ 3 DAYS

Continue up the coast to **Catania** (p164), Sicily's second-largest city. Its Unesco-listed old town and baroque piazzas, stucco-stitched churches, Roman ruins and raucous fish market make light work of a couple of days. Dining is also sensational. Navigate the menacing slopes of **Mt Etna** (p169) with a mashup of cable car, 4WD and on foot.

🚗 *45-minute drive*

❺ TAORMINA ⏱ 1 DAY

Take your foot off the pedal in super-chic resort town **Taormina** (p157). Chill atop cliffs with breathtaking Mt Etna views, meander old-world alleys, sea dip and catch a moonlit performance in the town's spectacular Greek theatre.

🚗 *2½- hour drive*

〰️ *Detour:* Break from driving with a narrow-gauge train tour of Etna's prestigious vineyards; hop aboard in **Riposto** (p162). ⏱ 1 day

❻ CEFALÙ ⏱ 1 DAY

Loop back to Palermo along the beach-laced **Tyrrhenian Coast** (p106). Spend the day in **Cefalù** (p112) where Sicily's finest stretch of powder-soft sand and Unesco-prized 12th-century cathedral vie for your attention.

🚗 *1-hour drive*

〰️ *Detour: En route to Palermo dose up on green mountain splendour and hilltop castles in the Madonie peaks;* **Caccamo** (p118) *is an excellent starting point.* ⏱ 3 hours

ITINERARIES

Volcanic Sicily

Allow: 1 week
Distance: 185km

Sicily's active volcanoes – Mt Etna, Stromboli and Vulcano – form the dramatic backdrop to this tour of northeastern Sicily. Lovers of the outdoors will enjoy the walks and activities inspired by the smouldering peaks, but there are ample ops for serene admiring from afar too.

Mt Etna (p169)

ALBERTO MASNOVO/SHUTTERSTOCK ©

❶ CATANIA ⏱1 DAY

From **Catania** (p164), built from lava from the volcanic eruption of 1669, hike up **Mt Etna** (p169). Admire this brooding giant – Italy's highest mountain south of the Alps – from the rooftop of Catania's **Chiesa della Badia di Sant'Agata** (p167).

🚆 35-minute to 1-hour train ride

🔺 *Detour: If you have wheels, dip or canyon in the icy waters of **Gole dell'Alcantara** (p162), lava gorges formed over millennia.* ⏱5 hours

❷ RIVIERA DEI CICLOPI ⏱1 DAY

Dizzying cliffs and towering black rocks rising out of the sea bear witness to past volcanic activity along the coast. Take it in from seaside resort **Taormina** (p157). Its Teatro Greco, suspended between sea and sky with Mt Etna looming beyond, is the world's most dramatically situated Greek theatre.

🚌 4-hour bus and boat trip

❸ LIPARI ⏱1 DAY

Arriving by hydrofoil from **Milazzo** (p123), explore the largest Aeolian island **Lipari** (p130). Learn about the archipelago's fiery history, geology and volcanology at the top-notch Museo Archeologico Regionale Eoliano inside castle walls, and shop for artisan jewellery set with jet-black obsidian (glass formed by solidifying magma) and crafted in gold smelted in lava rock.

🚆 20-minute crossing

LANDSCAPE NATURE PHOTO/SHUTTERSTOCK ©

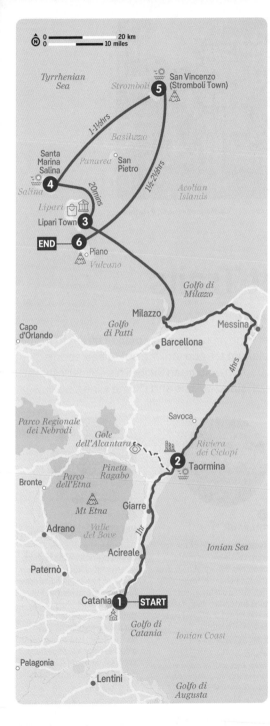

④ SALINA ⏱ 1 DAY

Hop to the most verdant of the islands, **Salina** (p137), whose twin extinct volcanoes are among the Aeolians' highest peaks. Bus it to Lingua to taste Salina's sweet Malvasia wine and beach-flop with some of Sicily's best *granita*. End on the island's western shore with a killer sunset in fishing hamlet Pollara and gourmet dinner at Hotel Signum.

🚢 *1- to 1½-hour crossing*

⑤ STROMBOLI ⏱ 2 DAYS

Walking up the black slopes of Stromboli's active **volcano** (p141) to watch its nightly eruptions light up the sky is a once-in-a-lifetime must. Reserve your guided sunset hike to 400m in advance. Spend the day exploring the island's black-sand beaches. Second day, hike around Ginostra and savour the island's alfresco drinking, dining and movie scenes after dark.

🚢 *1½- to 2½-hour crossing*

⑥ VULCANO ⏱ 1 DAY

Stromboli's little sister, likewise presided over by an active volcano, is a spot worth lingering. From the sulphurous fumes that hit you on arrival to the smoking crater visible from almost every point, **Vulcano** (p136) is a fascinating window on daily life with a volcano. Consider a guided tour by stand-up paddleboard.

JUAN GARCIA HINOJOSA/SHUTTERSTOCK ©

Via Maqueda (p64), Palermo

ITINERARIES

Gourmet Trails

Allow: 5 days **Distance:** 435km

From a lard-dripping offal sandwich on a noisy market street to a white-tablecloth dinner on an elegant terrace looking out to sea, foodie experiences know no bounds in epicurean Sicily. This culinary sampler covers the full spectrum of island cuisine and its fine wines.

❶ MARSALA ⏱ 1 DAY

Graceful **Marsala** (p99) is a charming viticultural town. Tour cellars and taste the famous wine at Cantine Florio, meet winegrowers at Palazzo Fici, dine on stunning food-wine pairings at Ciacco Putia Gourmet.

🚗 *40-minute drive*

🚗 *Detour: Drive the Via del Sal (Salt Road; p93) between Marsala and Trapani, lingering at Saline Ettore e Infersa to learn about salt production on a saltpan tour.* ⏱ *5 hours*

❷ TRAPANI ⏱ 1 DAY

Trapani's position on the sea route to Tunisia has made couscous the signature dish of this tempting port town (p88). Explore its old town, learn about tuna and coral fishing, feast on couscous at a Slow Food–endorsed trattoria.

🚗 *1½-hour drive*

🚗 *Detour: Whizz up to hilltop village Erice (p93) for coffee and cakes in a secret garden at Pasticceria di Maria Grammatico.* ⏱ *5 hours*

❸ PALERMO ⏱ 1 DAY

Diving into the souk-esque torrent of produce and aromas at the open-air food markets of epicurian heavyweight **Palermo** (p48) is gourmet heaven. Flit from heirloom pushcart and trattoria to African lounge bar and community-driven garden. Learn how to cook with a duchess, eat marzipan fruits, scoff a spleen-and-lung bun, drink *aperitivo* on a rooftop…

🚗 *1½-hour drive*

④ PETRALIA SOPRANA
⏱ HALF A DAY

Head east, skirting the Madonie and Nebrodi mountains, to the pretty hill town of **Petralia Soprana** (p117). Sample local black pork, ricotta, pecorino, mushrooms, hazelnuts and other fruits of the earth in traditional trattorias like Da Salvatore.

🚗 *2-hour drive*

🔀 *Detour:* Go mad over forest mushrooms and wild boar in **Castelbuono** (p117). ⏱ *5 hours*

⑤ CATANIA ⏱ 1 DAY

Eat your way around Sicily's **second-largest city** (p164), kicking off with its rowdy, chaotic fish market La Pescheria. Break over a refreshing *seltz limone e sale* (fresh lemon juice and sparkling water) with locals at a traditional *chiosco* (street kiosk), snack on artisan *arancini* and lunch on Catania's signature pasta dish, *pasta alla Norma,* in an urban trattoria.

🚊 *40-minute train ride*

⑥ BRONTE ⏱ HALF A DAY

Enjoy a scenic train ride, past acres of nut groves and vineyards on the western flanks of Mt Etna, to **Bronte** (p171). Feast on Sicilian 'green gold' in the small town, famous throughout Italy for its pistachios, grown on the lava soil and harvested by hand in late August to October every two years. Lunch at Protosteria.

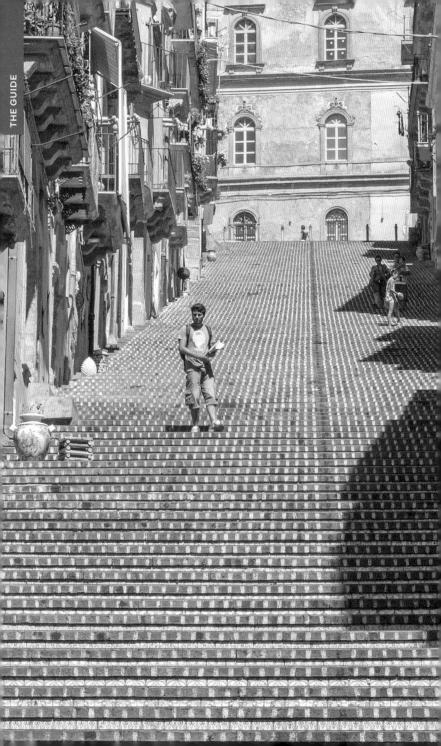

SICILY

THE GUIDE

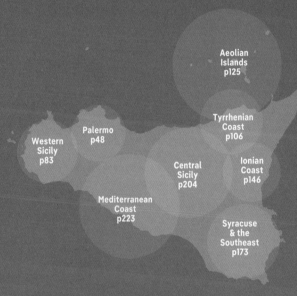

Aeolian
Islands
p125

Tyrrhenian
Coast
p106

Palermo
p48

Western
Sicily
p83

Ionian
Coast
p146

Central
Sicily
p204

Mediterranean
Coast
p223

Syracuse
& the
Southeast
p173

Chapters in this section are organised by
hubs and their surrounding areas. We see
the hub as your base in the destination,
where you'll find unique experiences,
local insights, insider tips and expert
recommendations. It's also your gateway to
the surrounding area, where you'll see what
and how much you can do from there.

Scalinata di Santa Maria del Monte (p218), Caltagirone

PALERMO

ARCHITECTURE & FOOD

Sicily's largest city is a cryptic creature, a place where nefarious neglect and soul-stirring beauty link arms and rattle your soul.

Flamboyant, feisty and disarmingly aristocratic, Palermo is a seething mass of contradictions. Pock-marked buildings, broken pavements and decrepit infrastructure reveal deep political and economic cracks, yet all are easy to forgive when you enter a church full of luminously beautiful Byzantine mosaics, wander a street of elegant baroque *palazzi* (palaces) or stumble upon live jazz after dark in the moonlit ruins of a medieval monastery.

Not far from the waterfront, on the Gothic facade of a medieval hospice for the poor, there's a curious hole in the wall. Unsurprisingly for this city of wild, incongruous contrasts, the hole is in marble. Commemorating two anti-Bourbon patriots who escaped the church in 1860 after women on the street staged a fight to distract soldiers outside, the Buca della Salvezza ('Hole of Salvation') safeguards one of a zillion extraordinary stories of rebellion, bravery, squalor and solidarity embedded in Palermo's bewitching labyrinth of ancient, sun-scorched streets and squares.

Centuries of dizzying highs and crushing lows have created a complex metropolis. Nearly 3000 years old, Palermo was born as a huddle of Phoenician stores on a peaceful bay surrounded by the fertile Conca d'Oro. Conquered by the Arabs in 831 CE, the Greek port flourished and when the Normans invaded in 1072, Roger I (1031–1101) made it the seat of his enlightened 'kingdom of the sun', encouraging resident Arabs, Byzantines, Greeks and Italians to remain. Palermo has remained at the crossroads of civilisations ever since, delivering a delicious, heavily spiced mix of Byzantine mosaics, Arabesque domes and frescoed cupolas.

Contemporary Palermo is a place where Piero wraps a huge block of ice in the same faded old cloth each morning for another day at the market. It is where reformed juveniles bake sweet biscuits to sell in artisan kitchens and historic workshops that once crafted Europe's finest art nouveau furniture are reborn as a hipster cultural centre. Talented street artists take up arms against the Mafia and locals chat in Albanian and Arabic in this captivating melting pot of history and cultures. Be inquisitive. Allow yourself the time to peek into that citrus-filled cloister, cherub-spun chapel or trash-strewn back alley, and you really will be astonished by what you find.

JONATHON STOKES/LONELY PLANET ©

THE MAIN AREAS

ALBERGHERIA & BALLARÒ	IL CAPO	LA KALSA	VUCCIRIA	BEYOND THE CITY CENTRE
Sightseeing and shopping p54	The city centre p61	Trendy and alternative p67	Markets and nightlife p73	Urban escapes p77

Via Parta di Castro, Ballarò (p54). Left: Cafe outside Teatro Massimo (p63)

0.25 km

0

0.1 miles

NEW CITY

Teatro dei Pupi di
Mimmo Cuticchio

VUCCIRIA
p73

Teatro Massimo

Mercato del Capo

IL CAPO
p61

Via Maqueda

Fontana
Pretoria

Chiesa e Monastero
di Santa Caterina
d'Alessandria

Cattedrale di Palermo

Corso Vittorio Emanuele

ALBERGHERIA & BALLARÒ
p58

Mercato di Ballarò

Palazzo dei Normanni

FROM THE AIRPORT

Getting into town is swift and efficient.
Whether you opt for the train or the bus,
the journey time is about 50 minutes from
Palermo's Aeroporto Falcone Borsellino in
Punta Raisi, 35km northwest, to Palermo
Centrale train station and adjoining Via
Tommaso Fazello bus station.

WALK

Hands down, the best way to explore
central Palermo is on foot. Wear sturdy,
comfortable shoes or sandals – flimsy
flip-flops don't fly – to combat uneven
pavements, dusty streets and slippery
stone paving. Expect to get 'lost' in the old
city's bewitching maze.

Find Your Way

Larger-than-life Palermo is large but walkable – lapping up this charismatic city's chaotic vibe on foot is an experience in itself. Two main streets in the new town, Via Maqueda and Via Vittorio Emanuele (also called Corso Vittorio Emanuele), meet at the Quattro Canti (Four Corners) to neatly slice the *centro storico* (historic centre) into four intoxicatingly vibrant quarters.

Via della Cala

Foro Italico Umberto I

Galleria Regionale della Sicilia

Villa a Mare

Galleria d'Arte Moderna

LA KALSA
p67

Villa Giulia

Via Roma

Orto Botanico di Palermo

Via Abramo Lincoln

Piazza Giulio Cesare

Palermo Centrale

ELECTRIC SCOOTER & BIKE

Zip around on an electric scooter (operators include Tier, BiT, Link, Helbiz and Bird) or a Ridemovi e-bike. Use your smartphone to download the app, locate free-floating wheels and pay. Scooters and bikes are usually lined up on Piazza Giuseppe Verdi, Piazza del Parlamento and other major squares.

BUS & TAXI

Watch for pickpockets on AMAT bus 101 linking the port with Via Roma and buses to/from out-of-town Monreale and Mondello. In town, city sightseeing buses allow you to hop on/off at sights. Or hop in a three-wheel Piaggio Ape taxi, lined up by the cathedral, Palazzo dei Normanni, Piazza Giuseppe Verdi and Quattro Canti.

Plan Your Days

Grab an espresso and *cornetto* (pastry) in a cafe before diving into the labyrinthine historic centre: find breathtaking churches and *palazzi* galleries, artisan workshops, street markets and edible temptations at every turn.

Piazza Bellini (p59)

JONATHON STOKES/LONELY PLANET ©

DAY 1

Morning

● Explore Palermo's crown jewel, Cappella Palatina, inside **Palazzo dei Normanni** (p56). Weave your way through backstreet Albergheria to **Mercato di Ballaró** (p55) for a street gawp and a lunch of grilled intestines.

Afternoon

● Visit **Chiesa del Gesù** (p55) on your way to **Piazza Bellini** (p59), with its flush of churches: **La Martorana**, **San Cataldo** and **Chiesa e Monastero di Santa Caterina d'Alessandria** (p57) with rooftop view of the architectural ensemble. Join locals for a *passeggiata* on **Via Maqueda** (p64). Shop on **Corso Vittorio Emanuele**.

Evening

● Enjoy *aperitivo* with **Fontana Pretoria** (p58) at rooftop bar **Le Terrazze del Sole**. Dine at **Le Angeliche** (p65).

YOU'LL ALSO WANT TO...

Dig into the city's famous street food, discover its traditional crafts scene, chill on the beach and enjoy alfresco concerts.

SLEEP IN A MUSEUM

Overnight B&B-style in the private *palazzo* home of an art collector and enjoy a private tour of rare majolica tiles at **Stanze al Genio**.

HIT THE BEACH

On summer weekends follow Palermo's street-smart set to the golden sands of beach resort **Mondello**.

MEET THE MAFIA

Learn history and tune into the anti-Mafia movement at the **No Mafia Memorial** exhibition and **Wall of Legality** street mural.

VIRAG NOBILE/SHUTTERSTOCK ©, HOLGER LEUE/GETTY IMAGES ©, STEFANO MONTESI-CORBIS/GETTY IMAGES ©

DAY 2

Morning
● Visit the Arab-Norman **Cattedrale** (p62) and neighbouring **Diocesan Museum** (p62) in the archbishop's palace. Come back down to earth with street art in **Il Capo** (p65).

Afternoon
● Go backstage at **Teatro Massimo** (p63). Visit a puppeteer's workshop and tour the puppet museum in **Palazzo Branciforte** (p75). Time travel at **Museo Archeologico Regionale Antonio Salinas** (p76); relax in its peaceful courtyard gardens.

Evening
● Catch Giacomo Serpotta's stuccowork at **Oratorio di San Lorenzo** (p74). Lap up the after-dark vibe around Piazza San Francesco d'Assisi: buy artisan souvenirs on Via Alessandro Paternostro and sip cocktails at **Goccio** (p71); dine at Slow Food–endorsed **Osteria Ballarò** (p72).

DAY 3

Morning
● Catch a bus to **Monreale** (p78) for its Unesco-listed cathedral. Back in Palermo, meet well-dressed dead at **Catacombe dei Cappuccini** (p79) or skip the skeletons and head straight to **La Kalsa** (p67) for lunch with sea view at **Le Cattive** (p72).

Afternoon
● Swoon over Sicilian art at **Galleria Regionale della Sicilia** (p68) and modern gems at **GAM** (p68). Browse artisan workshops and artsy boutiques on Piazza Aragona. End the afternoon amid citrus groves, centurion ficus and tea in leafy **Orto Botanico di Palermo** (p72).

Evening
● Dip into Vucciria's pulsating night scene. Go for drinks in the market at **Ciwara** (p74) and dinner on Via dei Cassari; **Gagini** (p76) is gourmet nirvana.

EAT MARZIPAN FRUITS	CATCH LIVE JAZZ	SCOFF OFFAL	ISLAND CAPERS
A pear or pomegranate, perhaps, sculpted in marzipan at historic **Pasticceria Costa** is a foodie rite of passage.	Starlit concerts at roofless church **Chiesa di Santa Maria dello Spasimo** in La Kalsa are an unforgettable, under-the-radar date.	Track down *pane cà mueusa* (spleen-and-lung buns) and other street-food icons at street stalls and carts in **city markets**.	Sea dip, hike and feast on organic, farm-grown produce – lentils, pomegranates and capers – on the idyllic island of **Ustica**.

ALBERGHERIA
& BALLARÒ

SIGHTSEEING & SHOPPING

A melting pot of treasured, Unesco-listed historic monuments and unfettered street life, this incongruous twinset of old-city neighbourhoods intrigues. From mosaic-gilt chapels to ruined medieval cloisters and shabby backstreets, it is an area of wild contrasts.

Once the home of Norman kings and a romantic stop on 18th-century Grand Tour itineraries, Albergheria has been a poor and ramshackle quarter since the end of WWII. Nevertheless, it is a vibrant snapshot of Palermo today. Its sizeable immigrant population is revitalising the streets and injecting energy into the local arts and crafts scene, kitchens, cultural and social projects. The city's oldest street market, Mercato del Ballarò, plunges visitors into an intoxicating whirlwind of Sicilian, Asian and African smells and sounds that have scarcely changed since Arab traders struck deals here in the 9th century.

TOP TIP

In summer watch for concerts and cultural events at top sights like Palazzo dei Normanni, and openings of bell towers and monuments inaccessible the rest of the year. The sound-and-light shows and themed 'Sicilian kitchen' tastings illuminating Chiesa e Monastero di Santa Caterina d'Alessandria are spectacular.

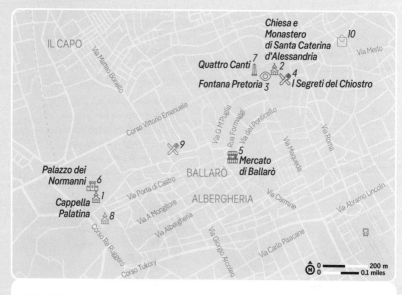

HIGHLIGHTS
1 Cappella Palatina
2 Chiesa e Monastero di Santa Caterina d'Alessandria

3 Fontana Pretoria
4 I Segreti del Chiostro
5 Mercato di Ballarò
6 Palazzo dei Normanni
7 Quattro Canti

SIGHTS
8 Chiesa di San Giovanni degli Eremiti
EATING
9 Giardino Bistro Al Fresco

SHOPPING
10 Ideestortepaper

Mercato di Ballarò

A SENSORY MARKET MEANDER

Lose all sense of time and direction in Palermo's oldest street market – a hypnotic jumble of outdoor stalls and open shopfronts piled high with fruit and veg, fish, olives and spices, caged birds, plastic buckets, knock-off padded bras and more.

Follow the stream of locals shuffling beneath the tunnel of parasols, tarps and corrugated-iron sunshades along Via Ballarò. On the corner of Via Alberghia a **black whale** by Messina-born street artist Nicolò Amato swims across a graffitied wall; the environment activist signs his marine-themed frescoes as NessuNettuno. Further along Via Ballarò, pause to admire **Chiesa del Carmine Maggiore**'s eye-catching cupola with stucco atlantes and polychrome maiolica in the traditional colours of the Carmelite Order. The best dome views are actually from the church's 19th-century bell tower – if you can, snag a spot on a weekend visit or an occasional atmospheric night opening in August. Not far away, **Chiesa del Gesù**'s 17th-century baroque extravagance and Pietro Novelli frescos are another breathtakingly beautiful antidote to Ballarò's backstreet market squalor.

Mooch south to the intersection of Via Giovanni Grasso and Via Giovanni Naso where market stalls and vintage pushcarts hawking hand-shaved *granita* or oily chunks of *sfincione* (focaccia with tomato sauce, anchovies, oregano and caciocavallo cheese) peter out. Join the queue at **Bancarella Del Polpottavio** for a plastic plate of grilled octopus barbecued while you wait or try-if-you-dare *stigghiola* (grilled intestines).

GRILLED INTESTINES

At quick glance it looks like an ordinary sausage. It's not. Introduced to the city by the Greeks some 2000 years ago, Palermo's beloved *stigghiola* sees veal, lamb or goat intestines wrapped around a spring onion or leek, seasoned with parsley, and barbecued to a crisp on a charcoal- or wood-fired grill. El Bocadillo, on the corner of Via Ballarò and Via Alberghia, is one of several fast-food joints at Mercato di Ballarò to grill *stigghiola* alfresco. The street snack is always served chopped into chunks and salted. Squeeze over the accompanying wedge of lime and tuck in.

Mercato di Ballarò

DEYMOSHR/SHUTTERSTOCK ©

Palazzo dei Normanni

GLITTERING MOSAICS IN A ROYAL PALACE

Norman Sicily's compelling cultural complexity is beautifully evoked at Palermo's star attraction: **Cappella Palatina**, squirrelled away like a rare jewel inside Palazzo dei Normanni (also called Palazzo Reale). The landmark monument, built by conquering Arabs on the highest point of the city in the 9th century, morphed from defensive fortress to pleasure palace with the arrival of the Normans in Palermo in the 11th century. Since 1947 it has been the seat of the Sicilian Regional Assembly.

The lavish royal apartments can be visited Friday to Monday: admire the Sala d'Ercole (Hall of Hercules) where the Regional Assembly convenes the other days of the week; the king's bedroom; and the Sala dei Venti (Hall of Winds) with Byzantine mosaics and 18th-century wooden ceiling.

But it is the shimmering-gold chapel, designed by Roger II in 1130 in the palace loggia, that takes your breath away. The Norman king brought in the finest Byzantine Greek craftsmen to inlay the interior with gemstones and marble. The detail, expression and movement captured by the figurative mosaics are extraordinary. Revel in the life of Christ, the Saints, Prophets and Evangelists in the presbytery; Cristo Pantocratore (Christ Almighty) and angels in the apse and dome; and the Old Testament in the central nave.

FATIMID ART

In the chapel's trio of naves, don't forget to look up. A lively menagerie of camels, lions, griffins, scribes, musicians, wrestlers, nude belly dancers and various other profane court entertainers of the day practically pops off the vaulted ceilings. Carved in wood and painted by Muslim artists, the ceiling is a rare example of 12th-century Fatimid art in the Mediterranean basin and unique for a Christian church. Inscriptions in Kufic script surround the blaze of Islamic star-shaped polygons and between the ceiling and walls, ornately wood-carved muqarnas drip down like decorative honeycomb.

Cappella Palatina

GONZALO AZUMENDI/GETTY IMAGES ©

Monastero di Santa Caterina d'Alessandria

Chiesa e Monastero di Santa Caterina d'Alessandria

BAROQUE ART AND BIRD'S EYE VIEWS

A 360° panorama of ancient Palermo jostles for the limelight with baroque masterpieces at this early 14th-century hospice-turned-convent. Its rooftop terraces alone – best visited late afternoon – demand unlimited swooning.

Count two hours to explore the richly decorated interiors. The single-nave church, built between 1580 and 1596, hat tips the Italian Renaissance with its frescoed dome depicting the *Triumph of the Holy Dominicans* (1751) by Vito D'Anna and intricate filigree ornamentation in gold leaf and marble inlays. On the sumptuous main altar, a tabernacle encrusted in amethyst and lapis lazuli gemstones dazzles. Baroque artist Filippo Randazzo executed the vault fresco depicting the *Triumph of Saint Catherine* (1744), and notable 17th-century paintings by Vincenzo Marchese and Giacomo Lo Verdo – students of baroque master Pietro Novelli – adorn the side chapels. End your visit in the gloriously peaceful majolica cloister, ringed with unusual balconied cells overlooking a fountain by late baroque Palermo sculptor Ignazio Marabitti (1719–97).

I Segreti del Chiostro

HOLY SWEETS & CAKES

Buy a sweet bite – the *torte di ricotta* (ricotta cakes), *cassatina antica* and monster-sized *cannoli* filled to order are all sinfully good – from Santa Catarina's antique *pasticceria* to munch beneath an orange tree in its perfumed cloister garden. Hidden on the 1st floor of the monastery complex, I Segreti del Chiostro ('The Cloister's Secrets') only uses recipes shared between generations of nuns in honour of Sicily's centuries-old tradition of convent pastry-making. Ooh and aah over beautifully arranged plates of *biscotti di mandorle* (almond biscuits), *fedde del Cancelliere* (marzipan clam shells filled with apricot jam and almond milk) and naughty-but-nice *minne di vergine* ('Virgin breasts' or white cakes with a candied cherry on the top).

Minni di vergini

Fontana Pretoria

Quattro Canti

BACKSTAGE AT THE
SUN THEATRE

Quattro Canti – as the
elegant intersection of
Via Vittorio Emanuele and
Via Maqueda is commonly
known – does more than
only mark the epicentre
of Palermo's sizeable old
city. The iconic square
(officially Piazza Vigliena)
is also nicknamed Il Teatro
del Sole (Theatre of the
Sun) because of the light
show that unfolds each
day on its perfect circle of
curvilinear facades.
Return to the people-busy
crossroads at different
times of day to see the
sun lighting up a different
facade – unlit facades
disappear up to the
China-blue vault of the
sky in a clever display of
perspective. Religious
believers preaching
speakers-corner style,
waiting taxis blaring
music on portable
loudspeakers and horse-
drawn carriages only add
to the show.

Fontana Pretoria

SUNSET DRINKS AT THE FOUNTAIN OF SHAME

So scandalised were Sicilian churchgoers by the flagrant nudity of cheek-baring nymphs, tritons and frolicking river gods sculpted in marble on Piazza Pretoria's monumental fountain that they dubbed it Fontana della Vergogna (Fountain of Shame). Actually designed by Florentine sculptor Francesco Camilliani between 1554 and 1555 for the Tuscan villa of Don Pedro di Toledo, it was bought by Palermo in 1573 in a bid to outshine Messina's newly crafted Fontana di Orione. The play of light on the nudes posing in the fountain's tiered basins is theatrical any time of day – and never the same twice. Return several times to admire the whimsical scene in different lights. Come sunset, enjoy it from above over alfresco drinks at Le Terrazze del Sole, the rooftop bar of Palermo's historic Grand Albergo Sole (now Hotel B&B Palermo Quattro Canti) at No 291 on Via Vittorio Emanuele.

Quattro Canti

ELESI/SHUTTERSTOCK ©

Piazza Bellini

ARAB-NORMAN UNESCO TREASURES

Pack a scarf or sarong for covering up bare shoulders to ensure you don't miss out on the city's most unique treasures: East-meets-West, Arab-Norman churches and *palazzi* whose beguiling blend of unmatched Byzantine, Islamic and Latin beauty sent mesmerised scholars, intellectuals and Grand Tour romantics into raptures in the 18th and 19th centuries.

Between 1130 and 1194 the Normans collaborated with Byzantine and Arab architects and artisans to transform Greek temples into basilicas and build innovative new structures reflecting a unique mix of architectural and artistic influences, including mosaics. Palermo's Capella Palatina, Cattedrale di Monreale and the Duomo in Cefalù (p113) – all granted World Heritage status by Unesco in 2015 along with six other Arab-Norman monuments in Palermo – are the glittering stars of this period.

MORE IN ALBERGHERIA & BALLARÒ

Piazza Bellini

PEOPLE-WATCHING WITH STRIKING CHURCH VIEW

Watch the world go by from a bench – beware of greedy, dive-bombing pigeons – on this harmonious neighbourhood square, hemmed in by three dramatically different churches, including Chiesa e Monastero di Santa Catarina d'Alessandria (p57).

The luminously beautiful, 12th-century **Chiesa di Santa Maria dell'Ammiraglio** was endowed by King Roger's Syrian emir and was originally planned as a mosque. **Chiesa Capitolare di San Cataldo** blends Arab and Norman architectural styles with its striking dusky-pink domes, squat square form, blind arcading and delicate tracery. If you nip inside, the austere interior – with inlaid floor and lovely stone and brickwork – won't disappoint.

Linger late afternoon on the square when the sinking sun shows off Piazza Bellini's disparate collection of architectural styles in Insta-happy hues of soft pink, peach and gold.

WHERE TO STAY IN ALBERGHERIA & BALLARÒ

B&B Hotels – Hotel Palermo Quattro Canti
Unmatched location and rooftop view make this three-star hotel excellent value. €–€€

De Bellini Apartments
Stylish, architect-designed apartments in a 17th-century palazzo on the 'hood's finest square. €€€

Il Giardino di Ballarò
Earthy colours, cooking classes, garden and sun terrace with jacuzzi cocoon at this boutique B&B. €€

Artisan jeweller and environmentalist **Nanà Aristova** recommends her favourite spots for artisan crafts and eco-conscious creations.

Ideestortepaper
This amazing place resembles a *bottega* (workshop), but it's actually a publishing house specialising in hand drawings in watercolour pastels (Via Alessandro Paternostro 85).

La Profumoteca
This family-owned business handcrafts fragrances – all refillable and recyclable. Master perfumers only use traditional techniques to produce every perfume (Via Ruggiero Settimo 74E).

Sicilia Inspired
Find drawings in Etna lava pigments and luminous agave-plant sculptures in this space hosting artists representing Sicily. (Via Vittorio Emanuele 292).

Slow Design
SHOP FOR HANDCRAFTED SOUVENIRS

Look beyond the sea of street vendors selling cheap fridge magnets and other mass-produced souvenirs on Corso Vittorio Emanuele to uncover artist studios. It's a five-minute walk from the royal palace to the *laboratorio d'arte* (art lab) of **Angela Tripi** where you'll be stunned twice: once by the talented ceramist's teeny terracotta *presepi* (traditional crib figurines) and again by the 15th-century palazzo courtyard at No 452 in which her gallery resides.

Walk another five minutes along Via Vittorio Emanuele to meet Siberia-born, Palermo-adopted jeweller **Naná Aristova** at No 314. Sicilian volcanoes and towns inspire her contemporary jewellery, handcrafted using traditional techniques. Don't miss the onyx-beaded bracelets knitted from brass wire.

You'll always find something to please at **Spazio a Tempo**, a slow-design boutique at No 297. Decorative elements from traditional majolica, historical monuments and urban flora leap off the paper craft, homewares, puppets and jewellery of graphic designer Manuela Baldanza and photographer Cristina Ferrara.

Chiesa di San Giovanni degli Eremiti
A GARDEN RETREAT WHERE TIME STANDS STILL

When the incessant tourist bustle of downtown Palermo tires, escape to a stone bench in the enchanting walled garden of Chiesa di San Giovanni degli Eremiti. The 12th-century church is named after Sicilian hermit-monk and miraculous wolf tamer St William of Montervergine and there's no doubt about it: modern-day hermits will fall hopelessly in love with this shady retreat (bring a book!) spun from olive, fig, pomegranate and citrus trees, citrus groves, and bewitching cloister ruins.

MORE ARTSY SHOPPING

Near Piazza San Francesco d'Assisi in La Kalsa, enchanting artist workshops dot narrow Via Alessandro Paternostro; fantastic street art too. Or walk towards the sea to pocket a city monument in terracotta from **La Cittàcotte di Vizzari** (p71).

WHERE TO EAT IN ALBERGHERIA & BALLARÒ

Moltivolti
Couscous, *caponata* or baba ganoush: this co-working cafe is a delicious melting pot of culture and cuisine. €

Santamarina Bistrot
Live jazz and wine tastings enliven this locally loved Albergheria bistro, with terrace on a hidden square. €–€€

Locanda del Gusto
Modern Sicilian cuisine in an elegant palazzo courtyard off Via Vittorio Emanuele. €€€

IL CAPO

THE CITY CENTRE

Directly north of Albergheria, Il Capo is an ~~and blind alleys in the *centro storico* (histor~~ century Arab rule, this was a raucous der~~rates and *schiavoni* (slave traders) haggled out~~ ing; the popular street market, Mercato del Capo, rema~~its colourful past. Pass street hawkers flogging 2L plastic bo~~cheap wine or walk along backstreets festooned with sun-bleache~~drapes and you quickly feel the resilient pulse of this neighbourhood.

On the other end of the spectrum, Palermo's treasured Norman cathedral dazzles on Il Capo's southwestern fringe. Its northeastern limits are grandly guarded by bronze lions flanking steps up to 19th-century opera house Teatro Massimo. On the vast square in front, Art Nouveau kiosks sell tobacco and cold drinks as they've done since 1894, and horse-drawn carriages wait for tourists to take them for a ride. Take your cue from locals and opt instead for one of the rainbow of e-scooters and e-bikes lined up here.

Cattedrale di

ROYAL TOMBS, TRE~

THE GUIDE

PALERMO

A sensual feast~
majolica cupo~
larger-than~
chitectura~
intarsia~
Islamic~
fruit~
Ital~
sh~

fro~
terrace.~
churches and~
double as venues
for music concerts,
theatrical tours and fun
children's workshops
during the summer-long
RestART Show arts
festival.

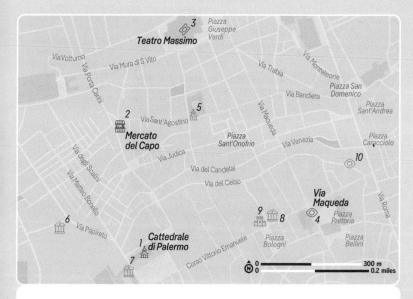

Palermo

of geometric patterns, ziggurat crenellations, las and blind arches, Palermo's cathedral is a ife example of Sicily's unique Arab-Norman ar- style. Above its magnificent entrance, admire the decoration depicting the tree of life in a complex -style geometric composition of 12 roundels featuring humans and animals. It's thought to date back to 1296. interior, while impressive in scale, is essentially a marble ell whose most interesting features are the royal Norman ombs (containing the remains of two of Sicily's greatest rulers, Roger II and Frederick II of Hohenstaufen) and the treasury (see Constance of Aragon's gem-encrusted 13th-century crown, made by local craftspeople in fine gold filigree, and silver reliquaries safeguarding a tooth and ashes of Santa Rosalia). Save the best for last: the cinematic spiral up 110 steep stone steps to the cathedral's roof terraces, with panoramic city views.

On the southern porch, a column inscribed with a passage from the Koran is all that remains of the 9th-century mosque on which construction of the cathedral began in 1184. Over time the building has been much altered, sometimes with great success (as in Antonio Gambara's 15th-century three-arched portico that became a masterpiece of Catalan Gothic architecture), and sometimes with less fortunate results (Ferdinando Fuga's clumsy dome, added between 1781 and 1801).

ARCHBISHOPS' PALACE

Skip the cathedral's habitual, high-season ticket queue (for the royal tombs and terrace) by first diving into the archbishops' palace next door. Admission to the **Museo Diocesano** (Diocesan Museum) here covers the cathedral sights too. Don't miss *Veduta della Cattedrale di Palermo* (View of Palermo Cathedral) – a rare depiction of the exterior of the medieval cathedral before its 18th-century alterations, which included the addition of the dome – by Sicily's most significant painter of the early 17th century, Monrealese Pietro Novelli (1608–47).

Cattedrale di Palermo

DAVID IONUT/SHUTTERSTOCK ©

Mercato del Capo

Backstage at Teatro Massimo

ITALY'S LARGEST THEATRE

If you miss the opera season (September to June), revel in the opulence of Ernesto Basile's art-nouveau masterpiece (1875–97) – Europe's third-largest opera house – on a guided backstage tour instead. Nip onto Via Maqueda to admire Teatro Massimo's majestic, pale-green cupola from afar before ducking backstage. Stand on the steps where the iconic Mafia shooting scene from Francis Ford Coppola's *Godfather* trilogy was shot. Swoon over the six-tiered auditorium, lit by lamps in pink Murano glass, from the 27-seater royal box. Sing an aria of your own in the extraordinary Echo Room, and gorge on city views from the panorama roof terrace. End with lunch, drinks or dinner in the theatre's contemporary, garden-clad restaurant Giardino del Massimo.

Mercato del Capo

THE OPEN-AIR FOOD MARKET WHERE LOCALS SHOP

Palermo's premier fruit-and-veg market feels as souk-esque as it did when Arab traders, pirates and slave merchants peddled goods in its labyrinthine streets in the 9th century. Watch pockets and bags as you push your way through the crowds from Porta Carini – one of Palermo's original city gates, re-built in 1782 – along Via Porta Carini and Via Beati Paoli.

Stalls piled high with fist-sized lemons, plastic beakers of fresh coconut, wild strawberries and more pack Via Porta Carini to bursting. **Sit & Mancia** (No 63) is one of several spots to sip local Birra dei Vespri craft beer and lunch on *pastelle* (deep-fried slices of seasonal veg), pistachio-stuffed sardines or marinated swordfish at a plastic table between stalls.

Break from the market din at medieval **Chiesa di Sant'Agostino**. A textile market on Via Sant'Agostino drapes the church's plain 13th-century facade in a curtain of colourful fabrics and laces. But once inside, celestial stuccos by 17th-century master Giacomo Serpotta and a tranquil cloister garden soothe.

Teatro Massimo

Via Maqueda Passeggiata

STROLL & STREET FOOD ON THE CATWALK OF PALERMO

No pastime exposes Palermitani's passion for eating quite like a traditional *passeggiata* (afternoon stroll) along pedestrian strip Via Maqueda. Adopt locals' leisurely pace to absorb the hypnotic whirlwind of shops, screeching street hawkers and pushcarts selling cheap jewellery, faux majolica-print caps, sundresses, Mickey Mouse balloons, beakers of Aperol Spritz...

Mooching south from theatre-clad Piazza Giuseppe Verdi, the terrace at new-gen pizzeria **Biga** (No 282) is always packed. Sink your teeth into a pizza slice loaded with seasonal zero-km ingredients on dough naturally leavened for 48 hours. The Porchetta delle Madonie (with artisanal Madonie pork, smoked scamorza cheese and sweet Giarratana onions), paired with craft beer, is a Slow Food favourite.

Further south, snack on *arancini* (fried rice balls) with different meaty, veg and vegan fillings at **Ke Palle** (No 270). Or hit neighbouring **Cannoli & Co** for ricotta-filled *cannoli,* a velvety *cassata* (rich sponge cake, with green icing and candied fruit) and artisan *granite*. Burn some calories with a duck east down Salita Castellana to Salita Sant'Antonio. Scribble a poem or thought on a piece of paper and add it to the collection of verse pegged on a string running the length of the quiet, neglected backstreet. Return to Via Maqueda for drinks and/or dinner on the street at vintage-styled **Bisso Bistrot** (No 172), inside an old bookshop.

Via Maqueda

FRUTTA MARTORANA

Don't miss **Pasticceria Costa** at No 174. So realistic is the historic pastry shop's *frutta martorana* (marzipan fruit) – figs, oranges, lemons, pomegranates, pears – displayed beneath glass domes, it is almost sacrilege to eat them. Moulded from almond-rich marzipan, the fruit-shaped confections were cooked up by nuns at 12th-century La Martorana to impress the king during a royal visit to their monastery. Buy a baby-blue box of fruits to take home – traditionally Sicilians feast on *frutta martorana* to celebrate Ognissanti (All Souls' Day) in November, but these days, they're devoured year-round.

YULIA GRIGORYEVA/SHUTTERSTOCK ©

Mercato delle Pulci

MORE IN IL CAPO

Mercato delle Pulci

TREASURE HUNTING AT ANTIQUE & FLEA MARKETS

Palermo's oldest flea market is squirrelled away behind the cathedral on Piazza Domenico Peranni. With a sharp eye and patience, you can uncover some real treasures: antiquarian books and dolls, gramophones and vinyls, vintage glassware, Catholic kitsch, jewellery, etc. The jewel in the crown is Museo del **Mercato Storico delle Pulci** and if you're lucky, passionate collector Luciano Ienna will guide you around his collection of curiosities spanning the 18th century to 1970s. He and his family built the one-room museum – the oldest of 20-odd shacks at the permanent flea market – from *palazzi* bombed here during WWII. In the 15th century the area was a damp wetland, rife with papyrus reeds and malaria.

Grattatella Carts

THE OLD-FASHIONED ART OF KEEPING COOL

Track down Palermo's roving pushcarts selling old-fashioned *grattatella* – ice scratchings, scraped by hand from a

WHERE TO STAY & EAT IN IL CAPO

Massimo Plaza Hotel
Wake up to iconic views of Teatro Massimo at this traditional hotel with wrought-iron balconies. €€

Palazzo Pantaleo
On Capo's northern fringe, this attractive B&B has six rooms in a 19th-century *palazzo;* free parking. €

Le Angeliche
Sicilian culinary tradition is honoured at this Slow Food trattoria, footsteps from the market. €€

BEST COCKTAILS & MUSIC

Mak Mixology
Mixology cocktails
are paired with
modern cuisine at this
fashionable bar in a
1930s shopping gallery
off Via Maqueda.

Malox
Don't miss the house
cocktail at this cult
bar: a Malox Negroni
mixes Bulldog gin
with Cinzano 1757 and
zesty Bèrto Bitter.

SciùRum
Cocktails are the star
turn at this elegant
lounge bar-restaurant
with designer fittings.

**Terzo Tempo
Cocktail Lab**
Superb signature
cocktails (try Sicilian
Shepherds!) or
personalise with your
pick of boutique gins,
rums and whiskies.

block of ice wrapped in a cloth and served in a plastic beaker with one of a dozen-odd different fresh fruit syrups. Lemon is the classic, but **Grattatella da Tonino** serves mint, banana, tropical rose, orgeat, coca cola and a rainbow of other modern flavours from his brightly painted cart often parked around the intersection of Via Maqueda and Via Vittorio Emanuele on Quattro Canti.

Piero Caccamo works the cart of his late father-in-law Vincenzo Tirenna, a Palermo legend nicknamed *'il re della grattatella'* ('the king of grattatella') who crafted the city's iconic summertime thirstquencher for 40-odd years from his **Grattatella all'antica no Zu' Vicè** cart in front of Teatro Massimo. You can usually find Piero these days juicing fresh pomegranates and scratching ice to order at Mercatò del Capo, opposite Via Porta Carini 20.

No Mafia Memorial

LEARN PALERMO'S MAFIA STORY

You will never truly understand what makes this city until you've made the brutal journey through its horrifying Mafia past. Words and pictures speak for themselves at the No Mafia Memorial, a compelling multimedia space evoking Mafia and anti-Mafia history and activities in a palazzo on main street Corso Vittorio Emanucle. Allow yourself at least two hours to digest the B&W photographs, newspaper clippings and highly emotive memorials – bring tissues – to those who've died in Mafia hands. Modern-day murders and massacres aside, the exhibition provides a fascinating insight into Mafiosi roots: feudal lords in the 15th century hired *bravos* (bandits) to steal farmers' livestock and by the 16th century, gangsters were working the city's markets for *pizzo* (extortion money).

Palazzo Riso

CONTEMPORARY ART & SUMMER CONCERTS

SICILIAN DESIGN

Patrizia Italiano (ceramics) and
Briuccia Sicilian Style (designer
boxer shorts) are among the Sicilian
designers sold in Palazzo Riso's
fantastic boutique. For
more Sicilian-designer
shopping, see p60.

Catch an alternative interpretation of Sicily's gargantuan artistic heritage at the city's bastion of modern and contemporary art. Impeccably restored, neoclassical Palazzo Riso (1784) on Corso Vittorio Emanuele is the striking backdrop for the sassy permanent installations – think 19 'floating' wardrobes by Greek artist Jannis Kounellis – and thought-provoking temporary exhibitions at the Museo Regional d'Arte Moderna e Contemporanea della Sicilia (Regional Museum of Contemporary Art of Sicily). Bewitching music concerts, Sicily Film Festival movie screenings – even occasional wine tastings – fill the *palazzo* with music and gaiety and assure a summertime dolce vita.

WHERE TO EAT IN IL CAPO

L'Acerba
On-point *osteria dinamica*
serving creative Sicilian, Sunday
brunch, cocktails and live music
on an idyllic square. €€

NonnAngé
Snag the window swing seat
and tuck into breakfast or
brunch at this contemporary
coffee shop. €

La Galleria
An excellent choice of wine
accompanies Sicilian dishes at
this rustic *osteria* behind the
cathedral. €€

LA KALSA

TRENDY & ALTERNATIVE

A juxtaposition of time-warped elegance and contemporary street culture, this historic neighbourhood stretching east from the *centro storico* to the sea is Palermo in a nutshell. Plagued by poverty, La Kalsa has long been one of the city's most notorious areas. Urban regeneration has blessed some of its abandoned *palazzi* and derelict streets with petite bohemian bars, fashionable eateries and powerful art. Splendid residences where Sicilian nobles once hobnobbed are enjoying a renaissance as top modern-art galleries: Galleria Regionale della Sicilia, Galleria d'Arte Moderna, Palazzo Butera.

The destruction caused by WWII bombings is still highly visible in La Kalsa, where musicians take to the stage in ruined churches and street artists 'shout' protest messages from half-wrecked rooftops. It's no coincidence that the city's most polished murals – including Rosk e Loste's portrait of slain anti-Mafia magistrates Giovanni Falcone and Paolo Borsellino overlooking fishing boats at pleasure port La Cala – are in impoverished, irresistible La Kalsa.

TOP TIP

It's a five-minute walk from Palermo Centrale train and bus stations to main square Piazza Magione on La Kalsa's southern fringe. En route, grab some of the city's finest gelato at Gelateria Ciccio Adelfio. Go local with *cannolo,* mulberry or pistachio gelato sandwiched in a sweet brioche bun.

Galleria Regionale della Sicilia

SICILIAN MASTERPIECES IN A MAGNIFICENT PALAZZO

Spend a few hours exploring Palermo's top art museum inside Palazzo Abatellis. The mansion was built for the city's harbour master, Francesco Abatellis, and his wife Eleonora Soler in 1490 – spot their family coats of arms (his a snout, hers a sun) near the front-porch capitals.

You'll struggle to tear your eyes off the macabre star turn, *Trionfo della morte* (Triumph of Death) – a monumental fresco (artist unknown) reminding us of the bubonic plague that threatened Mediterranean port cities like Palermo throughout the Middle Ages. Equally compelling is Sicily's 'Mona Lisa', aka the enigmatic *L'Annunciata* (Virgin Annunciate) by the island's best-known artist Antonello da Messina (1430–79).

Galleria d'Arte Moderna

Galleria d'Arte Moderna

A MODERN-ART AMBLE

Get under the neighbourhood's artsy skin with a half-day stroll around the mellow, art-laden squares and backstreets around top-drawer Galleria d'Arte Moderna (GAM). Take your time exploring the modern art gallery's permanent collection, spanning the late 1800s to 20th century, in an atmospheric 15th-century *palazzo* which later became a Franciscan cloistered convent. Meet Sicily's 'Sun Thief', aka Palermo painter Francesco Lojacono (1838–1915); his pioneering portrayal of light in his luminous Palermo land- and seascapes transformed Sicilian art.

Later amble to neighbouring **Piazza Aragona**, dubbed 'Artisans' Square' after its edgy mix of artists' workshops, boutiques and public art. Meet local artists and shop for funky furnishings and homewares crafted from discarded sails and other upcycled materials at **Junkle** (No 13), jewellery and ceramics at **InsimuLab** (No 19–20), and leather crafts at **Ciatu** (No 3). End with coffee at buzzy neighbourhood cafe **NewArt108** or head to I Corrieri on nearby Piazza Cattolica where more artist collectives and grungy garage studios await.

Palazzo Abatellis

Stanze al Genio

A NIGHT IN A MAJOLICA HOUSE-MUSEUM

Multicultural Sicily has been a melting pot of different populations and cultures since birth, and few traditional crafts illustrate the island's rich diversity as colourfully as majolica – eye-catching red-clay earthenware, fired at high temperatures to create decorative motifs in bold, brilliant colours on a glossy-white background.

Art collector Pio Mellina has collected majolica tiles hand-painted by Sicilian and Neapolitan ceramists for decades and staying overnight in his home, Stanze al Genio ('Rooms at the Genius') – on the high-ceilinged piano nobile of a 16th-century *palazzo* on Via Giuseppe Garibaldi – is a unique opportunity to fall asleep beneath a geometric frieze of six-pointed blue stars and breakfast between flowering vine shoots, arabesque garlands and birds of paradise. Count two hours to check in: private house tours offered to guests of the 2300 tiles spanning the 16th to early 20th centuries mean you appreciate the decorative tiles in your B&B room from a whole new perspective.

Stanze al Genio

Piazza Magione to Piazza della Kalsa

STREET ART, PARK LIFE & FOOD TRUCKS

Stroll around strangely compelling **Piazza Magione** to uncover a microcosm of contemporary Palermo. A manicured garden under the 'golden age' Fatimid dynasty, the unkempt lawns are now the stage for community projects. While the faithful find peace in a cloister garden at **Chiesa della Magione**, lost souls loiter around the street-art-tagged ruins of an 18th-century girls' convent school, bombed during WWII. Pick out fading works by Zolta and Sten & Lex over a coffee from food truck **Da Ginetto**.

Large-scale murals brighten shabby apartment blocks on nearby **Via della Spasimo**: Rosk e Loste's woman of African descent celebrates cultural diversity. Towards Piazza della Kalsa, admire Ema Jons' mural colouring another half-destroyed building before lunch on Palermo's best *pane e panelle* (sesame bread with chickpea fritters) at kerbside **Friggitoria Chiluzzo**.

VIRAG NOBILE/SHUTTERSTOCK ©

69

Pani câ mèusa

Piazza San Francesco d'Assisi

ALFRESCO DINING ON A PICTURE-PERFECT PIAZZA

Romantics seeking the quintessential Sicilian piazza: look no further than this bijou square anchored in a labyrinth of stone-paved lanes (uncover gorgeous artisan boutiques festooned with fun street art on neighbouring **Via Alessandro Paternostro**). The Romanesque facade of **Chiesa di San Francesco d'Assisi** frames the square's eastern side and the lively, parasol-shaded terrace of **Antica Focacceria San Francesco** fills the rest. This retro bakery has been cooking up *focaccia con la milza* (spleen focaccia), *arancini* (deep-fried rice balls), *pane panelle e cazzilli* (chickpea fritters and potato croquettes in a bun) and regular trattoria dishes since 1834, and is packed from dawn to dark. *Buon appetito!*

Pani Câ Mèusa

KING OF PALERMO STREET FOOD

The queue stretching down the street says it all: Palermitan street food doesn't get finer or cheaper than the monster panini hawked from **Francu U Vastiddaru**, near Piazza Marina. If you're serious about street food, Palermo's signature *pani câ mèusa* (Sicilian) or *pane con la milza* (Italian) – a soft bread bun stuffed with boiled and lard-fried beef spleen, lung and trachea – is the only respectable choice. Ask for it *maritata* ('married' rather than *schietta* or 'single') if you fancy ricotta or caciocavallo cheese with the strong-tasting offal.

Order *panelle* (chickpea fritters) or *crocchè* (potato croquettes) sides, and walk around the corner to **Giardino Garibaldi** to scoff the lot amid the handsome shade and aerial roots of Palermo's oldest ficus tree. Or walk five minutes north to the fishing port of **La Cala**, with benches overlooking bobbing boats. If you're a dedicated foodie, repeat the *pani câ mèusa* experience at **Pane Câ Meusa – Porta Carbone**. In the offal biz since 1943, its spleen bun is considered among the city's best.

Antica Focacceria San Francesco

DRMOROND/SHUTTERSTOCK ©

Palazzo Mirto

WHY I LOVE LA KALSA

Nicola Williams
@socialhandle

It's the incongruous onslaught of industrious endeavour and wanton abandon that hits you on almost every street in La Kalsa yet makes the 'hood so ludicrously seductive. Trash-strewn backstreets lead to painstakingly restored *palazzi*, fronted with handsome sea-facing terraces or vintage pergolas draped in the magnificent, coconut-perfumed trumpet blooms of creeping solandra plants. The sea is never far away. Palazzo Butera (p72), hidden behind a curious promenade designed for widows to walk in peace, is one of my favourite spots to bask in this irreverent mashup of old, new, chaos and calm. The modern gallery offers no descriptive panels or labels with individual artworks – it's all about using your intuition to appreciate the harmonious ensemble.

MORE IN LA KALSA

Palazzo Mirto
INSIDE PEEK AT A LOST WORLD

Time-travel for a couple of hours into the lost world of Sicilian nobility at this 17th-century *palazzo,* home to the Filangeri family for four centuries. Precious silks, velvet and Cordovan leather, embroidery, frescoes and stuccos, hand-painted majolica tiles, mosaics and marbles carpet the walls, ceilings and floors in rooms on two floors. Don't miss the black-lacquered Salottino Cinese (Chinese Salon) with conceited ceiling painting of aristocrats viewing the room from above, or the ingenious swivelling Apollo statue in the Salottino di Diana – it leads to a secret passageway.

La Cittàcotte di Vizzari
RESIZING THE CITY'S ARCHITECTURAL ICONS

For a unique handcrafted souvenir, visit this historic workshop on Corso Vittorio Emanuele where the city's iconic churches and palaces come to life in enchanting doll's house form. Watch Palermo architect Vincenzo Vizzari at work as he

WHERE TO GO FOR LATE-NIGHT DRINKS IN LA KALSA

Farmacia Alcolica
Chink cocktails with urban hipsters in a funky interior crafted from flea-market finds.

Goccio – L'art de miscelare
Homemade syrups, craft spirits and a gourmet *aperitivi* platter make this industrial-styled bar a fashionable spot.

Cantavespri Art Café
Mellow cocktails on a terrace facing Teatro Santa Cecilia morph into late-night food, tunes and occasional dancing.

painstakingly moulds soft orange clay into elegant terracotta miniatures – perfectly to scale with the original and reflecting the city's centuries-old artisan tradition.

Mura delle Cattive

JOG IN THE FOOTSTEPS OF WIDOWS

If you're an urban runner searching for a scenic spot to jog along with locals at weekends, hit **Foro Italica** – the grassy seafront area linking fishing port **La Cala** with city park **Villa Giulia**. In the 19th century an elegant, elevated walkway was built atop the old city walls here for widows in mourning to promenade away from the Foro Italica hoi polloi: incorporate this sea-facing terrace, called Mura delle Cattive (Wall of the Prisoners) after these 'prisoners of grief', in your morning run. Linger afterwards over coffee or lunch at **Le Cattive** and consider an art stop at experimental gallery **Palazzo Butera**. Should you fancy a day cooking with a duchess, sign up for a one-day course with Duchess Nicoletta Polo Lanza Tomasi (www.butera28.it) in her seafront palace here.

Chiesa di Santa Maria dello Spasimo

LIVE JAZZ BENEATH THE STARS

With the exception of Palermo's out-of-town, 2200-seat Teatro di Verdura, this ruined 16th-century church is the city's most spectacular open-air stage. Cross its fountain-pierced interior courtyard off Via dello Spasimo and duck under the porch into the romantic church nave – a breathlessly beautiful, roofless space with medieval stone walls and trees soaring up to an open sky.

Poke around ruined side chapels with flapping pigeons by day, and admire striking contemporary-art installations. Come dark, it's all about sensational live jazz by the resident Sicilian Jazz Orchestra and Brass Group Music School; their concert season runs July to September. In late June, it's a venue for Palermo's Sicilia Jazz Festival.

Orto Botanico di Palermo

BIRD-WATCHING AND BOTANICAL DISCOVERY

Solace for the weary urban soul, these prestigious botanical gardens tell the story of Palermo's diverse landscape. Enter via the 18th-century wrought-iron gate and mooch silk-floss-tree-shaded alleys punctuated with weathered busts on pedestals, terracotta-potted cacti and footpaths scented with citrus fruits and fig blossom. See Palermo's diverse roots mirrored in the garden's mix of Mediterranean, tropical and subtropical flora, and learn about endangered Sicilian species. If you're a birder, pick up the DIY bird-watching trail.

BEST STYLISH DINES

Osteria Ballarò
It's strictly Sicilian produce all the way at this stylish, Slow Food–approved *osteria* in former *palazzo* stables. Exceptional wine list.

Quattro Mani
Sicilian home cooking, fuelled in the kitchen by local, predominantly organic produce.

Ciccio ... in pentola
Creative fish and seafood dishes paired with excellent service make this elegant *ristorante* a local foodie favourite.

Le Cattive
Sophisticated dining by Sicily's Tasca d'Almerita winery, with sea-facing tables on the Mura delle Cattive.

MORE MÈUSARI

Track down one of the last of Palermo's *mèusari* – street vendors selling *pani câ mèusa* from a hand-pushed cart – at **Mercato della Vucciria** (p74).

WHERE TO STAY IN LA KALSA

B&B Dimora Sinibaldi
Lavish breakfast and 360° panorama from its rooftop are highlights of this beautifully located *palazzo* B&B. €€

Grand Hotel Piazza Borsa
Four-star grandeur in Palermo's former stock exchange – a magnificent *palazzo* of course. €€€

Butera 28
Self-catering apartments in the 18th-century home of *The Leopard* author Giuseppe Tomasi di Lampedusa. €€

VUCCIRIA

MARKETS & NIGHTLIFE

Also called Loggia after the *logge* (loggia) used for public meetings that once graced ramshackle Piazza Garraffello, Vucciria is synonymous with its market today. But don't expect the masterpiece of colourful stalls overflowing with gluttonous aubergines and fennel, peppers, butchered meat and cheese at Mercato della Vucciria that Sicilian painter Renato Guttuso portrayed in his famous painting, La Vucciria (1974). Dramatically smaller today, the poorly stocked market on market square Piazza Caracciolo is a pale reflection of its vibrant past.

Notice street names when strolling about this endearingly shabby part of the old city, butting La Kalsa to the north and tumbling east into the sea at bijou fishing port La Cala. Vucciria was the stomping ground of seafaring merchants from Pisa, Amalfi, the Orient in Arab times, and later, 14th-century craft guilds: dyers worked on Via dei Tintori, silversmiths on Via degli Argentieri, doll makers on Via dei Bambinai.

At one time the heart of poverty-stricken Palermo and a den of crime and filth, Vucciria illustrated the medieval chasm that existed between rich and poor in Sicily until the 1950s. By no means gentrified, the winds of change are blowing. Entrepreneurs and visionaries Franco Virga and Stefania Milano are single-handedly transforming tiny Via dei Cassari, steps from the port, into an epicentre of modern dining. Time nor dirt can detract from the dazzling stuccowork by Baroque genius Gercamo Serpotta in Vucciria's treasure chest of churches – an exquisite, timeless seduction.

TOP TIP

Walking is the best way to experience the atmosphere, architecture and all-round buzz of this traditional quarter – most dark, narrow streets around market square Piazza Caracciolo are pedestrian. For a bird's eye panorama of the entire neighbourhood, indulge in a coffee or drink at Il Bar, the rooftop cafe-bar of department store La Rinascente on Via Roma.

HIGHLIGHTS

1 Mercato della Vucciria
2 Oratorio di San Domenico
3 Oratorio di Santa Cita
4 Teatro dei Pupi di Mimmo Cuticchio

SIGHTS

5 Museo Archeologico Regionale Antonio Salinas
6 Palazzo Branciforte
7 Piazza San Domenico

ACTIVITIES, COURSES & TOURS

8 Laboratorio Teatrale

Vuccìria

I Tesori della Loggia

A STUDY IN SICILIAN STUCCO

Palermo-born sculptor Giacomo Serpotta (1656–1732) – Sicily's greatest late baroque and rococo artist – transformed Italian stuccowork into high art. Admire his lifelike figures and narrative scenes in several 17th-century churches, collectively called I Tesori della Loggia. Cheeky *putti* (cherubs) modelled on local street urchins prop up stucco drapes framing Serpotto's elaborate Battle of Lepanto scene in Oratorio di Santa Cita. Nearby at Oratorio del Rosario di San Domenico, children twirl arabesques and garlands beneath niches adorned with Charity, Purity, Strength and other sensual figures representing the Virtues. Serpotta's name meant 'lizard' and he often included these signature reptiles in his work – spot one!

Mercato della Vuccìria

STREET MARKET MAYHEM

Feel the city's historical ties with the Arab world and proximity to North Africa pulsating in the mayhem of this noisy, graffiti- and litter-strewn market. Spilling across **Piazza Caracciolo** in Vuccìria's ancient heart, this open-air food market is Palermo's most dishevelled and underwhelming. But its bloody history – 13th-century meat market and slaughterhouse – and iconic characters lend it 'charm'. Follow your nose (literally) to the tiny square where **Rocky Basile** doles out some of the finest *pani câ mèusa* in town; come dusk, the wizened and weather-beaten *mèusari* wheels his mobile pushcart to the pavement in front of Corso Vittorio Emanuele 216.

If *polpo bollito* (boiled octopus) or *frittura di pesce* (deep-fried fish) better rocks your boat, grab a plate to take away or devour at a plastic table from Maddalena and Angela at **Al Tentacolo**. Or opt for African cuisine, cocktails and rip-roaringly fun music gigs that get everyone dancing in the square to the multicultural beat of Senegalese artist Doudou Adib at African restaurant and lounge bar **Ciwara**.

Cherub by Giacomo Serpotta, Oratorio di San Lorenzo

Teatro dei Pupi

EXPLORE THE CITY'S TRADITIONAL PUPPET THEATRE

If you meander east from Palermo's opera house into the web of lanes behind the landmark monument on Piazza Giuseppe Verdi, you'll stumble upon the hidden **Teatro dei Pupi di Mimmo Cuticchio** on Via Bara all'Olivella. Push open the door of the enchanting, pocket-sized theatre to uncover the spellbinding world of Sicilian puppetry. *Puparo* (puppetmaster) Giacomo Cuticchio inherited the 1970s theatre from his father, and his shows (at 6.30pm on weekends, September to June) skilfully combine pianola music with script to plunge audiences into a folkloric world of chivalry, romance, courtly love, heroic battles and tragedy.

Before attending a performance, it's well worth nipping into the **Laboratorio Teatreale**, across the street at No 48, where Giacomo crafts and fashions bloodthirsty Saracen warriors, sorcerers, monsters, knights, princesses and other puppets. To learn more about his Palermitan marionettes – carved from beech, olive or lemon-tree wood, and attached to iron rods – head to Palazzo Branciforte, a two-minute walk. From 1848 until 1979, there was a pawn house in the 16th-century palazzo and the original wood shelving – arranged in four tiers beneath a 14m-high ceiling – now displays the Cuticchio family's vintage puppet collection. Guided tours talk you through the different scenes and characters: Bradamante, the only female soldier, is easy to spot as she's the only puppet with glass eyes and real human hair.

A Cuticchio family puppet theatre

SPATULETAIL/SHUTTERSTOCK ©

SPANISH ORIGINS

The Spanish arrived on the island with *pupi* (marionettes) in the 18th century and Sicilians, enthralled with the re-enacted tales of Charlemagne and his heroic knights Orlando and Rinaldo, quickly embraced the art form. Effectively soap operas of the day, puppet shows expounded the deepest, otherwise-unspoken sentiments of life – unrequited love, treachery, thirst for justice, anger and frustration of the oppressed. Puppeteers were judged on the dramatic effect they could create – lots of stamping feet, thundering and a gripping running commentary – and the speed and skilled ease with which they manipulated more complex battle scenes.

**I LIVE HERE:
WALKING WITH
THE LEOPARD**

Michele Anselmi
from literary walks association Sicilia Letteraria recommends evocative spots in the city where Sicilian novelist Giuseppe Tomasi di Lampedusa set *Il Gattopardo* (The Leopard).

Via Lampedusa
Our walking tour links the two houses of the writer, beginning with the house where he was born in 1896.

Piazza San Domenico
The search for Ponteleone Palace, where Lampedusa set the ball episode, ends on this square in front of the Vucciria market. What makes this spot special is that the *palazzo* doesn't exist, but the guide narrates details to evoke it.

Via Butera
The death of the prince is remembered as the guide reads a moving passage from the novel, in front of the last Lampedusa house overlooking the sea.

Museo Archeologico Regionale Antonio Salinas

ANCIENT TREASURES IN A CLOISTER GARDEN RETREAT

Bookworms rejoice: the cloister garden at this Renaissance monastery turned Sicily's oldest public museum is heaven on earth. Plant yourself on an old stone bench beneath banana trees and contemplate the courtyard collection of Phoenician sarcophagi from the 5th century BCE (or simply read your book in meditative silence).

All three courtyards at Palermo's archaeological museum are stunning: water turtles frolic in a fountain in the first; and ancient and modern worlds collide in the centrepiece glass-ceilinged courtyard displaying a life-size reconstruction of a pediment from Temple C at Selinunte (p97). Allow ample time for the original decorative friezes from Selinunte – the detail, such as Actaeon being torn apart by dogs as punishment for seeing Artemis naked, is utterly thrilling.

Gagini

FINE DINING IN A RENAISSANCE ART STUDIO

Palermo sumac, Nubia garlic, Mediterranean crab and lobster, yellow Monreale plums, Ispica sesame and pungent *cucina* (caper flowers) from the Aeolian island of Salina: experience gourmet heaven with local foodies at the contemporary kitchen of Italian-Brazilian chef Mauricio Zillo – Palermo's only Michelin-starred address. Reserve well in advance to bag a table in the 16th-century mansion – the Renaissance workshop of Palermitan sculptor Antonello Gagini (1478–1536) and contemporary gallery for local artists whose canvases hang on exposed gold-stone walls. Skip lunch to max out on the eight-course tasting menu.

WHERE TO DINE WELL IN VUCCIRIA

Aja Mola
Outstanding seafood on a boxed-hedge terrace, with glimpses of bobbing boats beyond. €€–€€€

Buatta
Feast on sweetbreads or ricotta ravioli with offal at this contemporary, Slow Food–loved *cucina popolana*. €€

Trattoria Ferro di Cavallo
Going strong since 1944, this unflaggingly faithful, old-school trattoria won't disappoint. €

BEYOND THE CITY CENTRE

EASY URBAN ESCAPES

Urban Palermo's natural charisma is indisputable, but when the need for respite kicks in, the city delivers with soul-soothing half-day and day trips. The location of Palermo assures restful green landscapes, sandy beaches east along the coast and islands where time has stood still – all within a bus trip, walk, electric scoot or boat ride from the centre. Already north of Teatro Massimo on Piazza Giuseppe Verdi, away from the dark and tightly entwined *centro storico,* neoclassical and Liberty buildings evoke Sicily's last golden age in architecture and lend the new part of the city an exuberant, belle époque vibe. Sumptuous villas here safeguard Sicilian fine art and one of Europe's finest examples of 18th-century chinoiserie. A side trip to hillside Monreale and its World Heritage–listed Cattedrale di Monreale is non-negotiable.

TOP TIP

Dozens of organised tours whisk tourists off for the day to Mondello, Monreale and beyond (hotels have details), but it's cheaper and easy to DIY with public transport. Additionally, hop-on-hop-off buses operated by City Sightseeing (www.city-sightseeing.it/en/palermo) take in blockbuster destinations Monreale and Mondello.

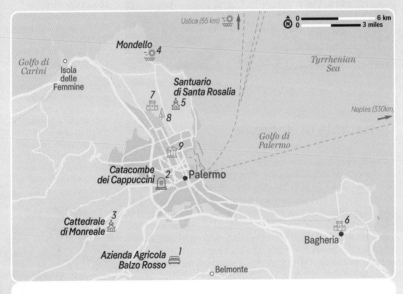

HIGHLIGHTS	3 Cattedrale di	SIGHTS
1 Azienda Agricola	Monreale	6 Bagheria
Balzo Rosso	4 Mondello	7 Palazzina Cinese
2 Catacombe dei	5 Santuario di Santa	8 Parco della Favorita
Cappuccini	Rosalia	9 Pinacoteca Villa Zito

Cattedrale di Monreale

Cattedrale di Monreale

SICILY'S TEMPLE OF GOLD

Travel back in time to the architectural pomp of the Italian Middle Ages in a hilltop village. Walking up from the bus stop at the foot of Monreale (AMAT line 389 from Palermo's Piazza Indipendenza), it's hard to believe a humble spot can contain Sicily's finest example of Norman architecture, built by William II to upstage grandfather Roger II's efforts in Cefalù and Palermo.

In the cathedral's golden mosaic interior, scout out Noah's ark atop the waves, Rebecca watering camels, Christ healing a leper infected with leopard-sized spots, the murder of Abel, and Adam and Eve. Medieval mosaicists hailed from Sicily and Venice, but the stylised influence of the Byzantines pervades their work, completed in 1184. Buy the €1 brochure mapping out all 42 biblical scenes in the cathedral bookshop. In the romantic cloister, look for William II offering the cathedral to the Madonna. End with the cathedral terrace with celestial aerial views of the cloister garden, cathedral's majolica rooftops and city of Palermo lounging on the horizon by the sea.

Catacombe dei Cappuccini

THE SLEEPING BEAUTY OF PALERMO

Back in Palermo, hop off the bus on Piazza Indipendenza and walk 1.2km west along Via Cappuccini to these catacombs – not for the young or faint-hearted. Hidden in tufa tunnels beneath 16th-century Chiesa dei Cappuccini, the cemetery houses skeletons and mummified bodies of 2000 Palermitans from the 17th to 19th centuries. Monks arranged the dead according to earthly power, gender, religion and professional status. Sections are set aside for children, families, even virgins. Palermo's 'sleeping beauty' – a golden-locked, two-year-old girl preserved by the city's finest embalmer of the time – was the last to be buried here in 1920.

Catacombe dei Cappucchini

Ustica
ISLAND HIKES, SEA DIPS & LENTILS

Pick a blue-sky day to sail to this tiny volcanic island, a 90-minute hydrofoil ride from Palermo's ferry port. Natural habitat to the Sicilian bee, this green escape languishes within a marine reserve created by local fishers to protect their fishing waters and marine life. Keep your eyes peeled for dolphins and sea turtles as you approach the rocky shoreline, bejewelled with grottoes. May to October, this is scuba-diving and snorkelling paradise.

From Ustica's teeny port, dive into island life with a coastal hike along **Sentiero del Mezzogiorno** to the lighthouse, 6km west on Punta Cavazzi. Rocky footpaths undulate past hibiscus flowers, prickly pears and dry-stone walls built with red volcanic rock. Occasional staircases stagger down to the sea for dips off rocks and signs guide you to **Grotta 'Za Azzurra** and other hidden caves. Inland, hardy islanders have farmed olives, almonds, pomegranates, capers and sweet Zibibbo Muscat grapes for centuries, but it is their *lenticchie di Ustica* (lentils) – Italy's finest– that is the prized crop, a Slow Food presidium.

Arriving at the lighthouse, cool off in **Piscina Naturale**, a swimming pool formed by scraggy rocks. Or follow the footpath five minutes more to beach bar **Il Faro Ustica**, with food, drink, canoes to rent (€15/hr) and sunloungers (€16 to €20/day) on a concrete waterfront terrace. Lunch at yacht club restaurant **La Rosa d'Eventi**, the hottest ticket on the island for sunset drinks, live music and dance parties.

DISCOVERING ITALY'S TASTIEST LENTILS

Taste Ustica's famous brown lentils – small, deliciously firm and strong-tasting – as *polpettine di lenticchie* (lentil meatballs) in the village at **Trattoria Da Umberto**. Or head 1.8km west to **Agriturismo Hibiscus**, an organic lentil farm with self-catering accommodation and a small museum exploring the island's agricultural and seafaring traditions. Learn how lentil plants are sown with horse-drawn ploughs in December, harvested and dried in June, then crushed and 'sieved' by hand to sort the lentil from the 'straw' during the traditional *pistata delle lenticchie*.

Port, Ustica

L NOYAN YILMAZ/SHUTTERSTOCK ©

Slow Trekking & Cheese

MAKE RICOTTA ON A GOAT FARM

South of Palermo, the milk from goats and sheep grazing on mountains between Belmonte Mezzagno and Altofonte is handcrafted into cheese at artisan dairies. Hook up with naturalist guide Marco Giordano (www.facebook.com/MarcoGiordanoGuida Naturalistica) to explore Palermo's ancient pastoral surrounds on a day hike, and learn how to milk goats or make fresh ricotta at Azienda Agricola Balzo Rosso. Marta Spera inherited the smallholding with a flock of sheep from her grandfather a decade ago and only makes her organic cheeses with raw, unpasteurised milk.

Mondello

Santuario di Santa Rosalia

Mondello Beach Life

PALERMO'S SUMMER PLAYGROUND

It's not difficult to find where everyone is on a summer weekend. Don your shades and hop aboard AMAT bus 806 on Piazza Sturzo or charter a motorboat from La Cala to decamp with what feels like the rest of the city to their favourite beach resort. Once a muddy, malaria-ridden port, the golden sands of Mondello have been fashionable since the 19th century when the rich and wealthy built opulent summer villas here. Gorge on old-school glamour on the huge Liberty-style pier and grandiose bathing establishment from 1913, now the top-notch restaurant Alle Terrazze with on-trend *crudo* (raw) bar and unmatched sunset sea views.

Celebrating Santa Rosalia

MOUNTAIN NIGHT HIKE TO A SAINTLY SANCTUARY

U Fistinu or Festino di Santa Rosalia, Palermo's biggest festival celebrating its patron saint who saved 17th-century Palermo from the plague, needs no introduction: crowds fill Alberghheria and La Kalsa on 14 July when Saint Rosalia's relics are paraded on a triumphal chariot from Palazzo dei Normanni to the waterfront, where fireworks and merriment ensue. But to see the cave where noble-born Rosalia (1130–66) lived – her bones were found here in 1624 – join Palermitans for L'Acchianata. This slow and celebratory, 4km-long walk by torchlight up Monte Pelligrino to Santuario di Santa Rosalia takes place during the night of 3 September. Celebrations continue the next day as more pilgrims arrive at the chapel, built into the rocky mountainside in 1629.

Palazzina Cinese

18TH-CENTURY ROMANTICISM IN A CHINESE PAVILION

When the urge for a quieter life strikes, follow the example of King Ferdinand IV (1751–1825) and his wife Maria Carolina and nip off for the afternoon to this regal Chinese Pavilion. Bus 107 to Piazza Giovanni Paolo II, then bus 615 or 645 to the stop 'Duca degli Abruzzi – Palazzina Cinese' is the quickest route from downtown Palermo. The flamboyant, pagoda-inspired pavilion is a stunning evocation of 18th-century Europe's love of Oriental exotica and the Chinese, Egyptian, Islamic and Pompeiian motifs adorning its endless rooms are really quite mesmerising. Factor in time to explore surrounding Parco della Favorita, a sprawling park created by Ferdinand IV in 1799 as a royal hunting ground and breeding ground for pheasants, hares and partridges.

Pinacoteca Villa Zito

ADMIRE SICILY THROUGH ARTISTS' EYES

If you don't have time to visit other parts of Sicily, this distinguished art gallery is the place to see Europe's largest active volcano erupt or Favignana fishers catching and killing tuna in the comfort of a sumptuous 18th-century villa, 2km north of Piazza Giuseppe Verdi. Its sharply curated collection of mainly Sicilian-themed art spans the 17th to 20th centuries, with works by leading Sicilian painters. Don't miss works by Ettore De Maria Bergler (the foremost Italian painter of the Liberty era) and Sicilian futurist Pippo Rizzo (1897–1964). Land- and seascapes by Palermo 'sun thief' Francesco Lojacono (1838–1915), and 20th-century heavyweights Ugo Attardi, Fausto Pirandello, Filippo De Pisis, Carlo Carrà and Renato Guttuso. End with drinks in the villa's stylish garden.

I LIVE HERE: REDISCOVERING BAGHERIA

Suzanne Edwards, co-author of *Sicily: A Literary Guide for Travellers*, shares one of her favourite day trips from Palermo.

'Long in decline, Bagheria, 30 minutes from Palermo, has undergone something of a rebirth. The town was a summer retreat for Palermitan aristocracy and several of their *palazzi* can be visited. The most fascinating is Villa Palagonia (1715). The circular building is beautiful in itself, but the garden wall displays the most surprising aspect: fantastical statuary, from periwigged aristocrats to hunch-backed gnomes, commissioned by former owner Francesco Ferdinando Gravina. Rumours about his motivation included that the statues satirised his wife's many lovers, and the locals refused to look at them – especially pregnant women – believing they were cursed.'

WHERE TO GET GREAT GELATO

Gelateria della Piazzetta
Crunchy almond, liquorice and cinnamon are standout flavours at this Monreale hangout, with tables on a teeny piazza. €

Caffè Traina
Hike up the steps from the port to the village to uncover the Ustica favourite for gelato since 1931. €

Latte Pa
Does it get any better than brioche on Mondello's beach oozing mulberry, pistachio or watermelon gelato? €

Temple E (p97), Selinunte. Right: *Grotta* (cave), Cala Bue Marino (p101), Favignana

WESTERN SICILY

ANCIENT RUINS & SLOW ISLANDS

Sicily's windswept western coast has beckoned invaders for millennia. Its fish-rich waters, hilltop vineyards and coastal saltpans have long inspired envy and desire.

The Phoenicians, Greeks, Romans and Normans have all coveted this part of the island and, in turn, influenced its deliciously varied landscape and culture. Even the English left their mark, with 18th-century entrepreneurs lured here and made rich by one of the world's most famous sweet wines, Marsala.

Hugging the harbour where Peter of Aragon landed in 1282 to begin the Spanish occupation of Sicily, the sickle-shaped spit of land occupied by Trapani once sat at the heart of a powerful trading network that stretched from Carthage to Venice. The region's main town traditionally thrived on coral and tuna fishing, and artisanal sea salt continues to be harvested from shimmering pink *saline* (saltpans) south along the coast. Traditional tuna fishing with drift nets, once a lucrative source of income, is now prohibited by the EU, and catches are subject to strict quotas.

Trapani's busy port today buzzes primarily with ferries sailing overnight to the mysterious volcanic rock island of Pantelleria, not far from Tunisia, and zippy hydrofoils whisking holidaymakers to dreamy pebble beaches and secret coves in the Egadi archipelago. Protected by the Egadi Marine Protected Area – the largest marine reserve in Europe – these islands are the place to savour slow food, pristine nature and an evocative dash of history. They only became part of the Italian state in 1937.

THE MAIN AREAS

TRAPANI	SELINUNTE	FAVIGNANA
Architecture, beaches, street life in a port town. **p88**	An ancient Greek city with captivating ruins to explore. **p96**	A pretty island and a jumping-off point for the Egadi archipelago. **p100**

Capo Grosso

Egadi Islands

Levanzo

Levanzo

Rosso Corallo

Erice

Valderic

Mt Eryx

Chiesa Anime Sante del Purgatorio

Trapani

Nubia

Paceco

Ex-Stabilimento Florio delle Tonnare di Favignana e Formica

Favignana

Saline di Trapani

Favignana

Castello di Santa Caterina
Cala Rossa

Cala Bue Marino

Vincenzo Florio Airport

Giardino dell'Impossibile

San Pantaleo

Stagnone Islands

Favignana, p100

The largest island in the Egadi archipelago is an attractive launchpad for boats to smaller, surrounding islands.

Trapani, p88

It's all about old-town architecture, beaches and street life in this small port town. Saltpans, and a coastal nature reserve lie beyond.

Marsala

Capo Boeo

Mediterranean Sea

Mazara del Vallo

Find Your Way

You'll fit plenty of walking into your stay in western Sicily. There are no cities and even the region's largest town, Trapani, is easily walkable – buses cover longer distances in and out of town. An efficient boat system makes light work of accessing the Egadi Islands, although winter services are heavily reduced.

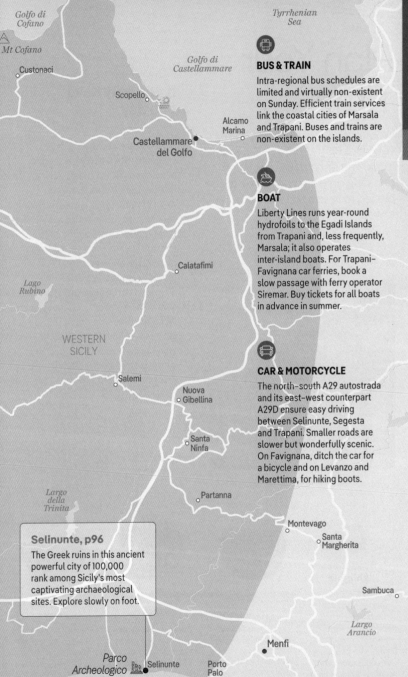

BUS & TRAIN

Intra-regional bus schedules are limited and virtually non-existent on Sunday. Efficient train services link the coastal cities of Marsala and Trapani. Buses and trains are non-existent on the islands.

BOAT

Liberty Lines runs year-round hydrofoils to the Egadi Islands from Trapani and, less frequently, Marsala; it also operates inter-island boats. For Trapani–Favignana car ferries, book a slow passage with ferry operator Siremar. Buy tickets for all boats in advance in summer.

CAR & MOTORCYCLE

The north–south A29 autostrada and its east–west counterpart A29D ensure easy driving between Selinunte, Segesta and Trapani. Smaller roads are slower but wonderfully scenic. On Favignana, ditch the car for a bicycle and on Levanzo and Marettima, for hiking boots.

Selinunte, p96

The Greek ruins in this ancient powerful city of 100,000 rank among Sicily's most captivating archaeological sites. Explore slowly on foot.

Golfo di Cofano

Tyrrhenian Sea

Mt Cofano

Golfo di Castellammare

Custonaci

Scopello

Alcamo Marina

Castellammare del Golfo

Lago Rubino

Calatafimi

WESTERN SICILY

Salemi

Nuova Gibellina

Santa Ninfa

Largo della Trinita

Partanna

Montevago

Santa Margherita

Sambuca

Largo Arancio

Menfi

Parco Archeologico di Selinunte

Selinunte

Porto Palo

0   10 km
0   6 miles

Plan Your Time

Western Sicily is a place to take your foot right off the pedal and relax. The only tricky part is deciding on which beach or sun-blazed rock to lay down your towel.

OLENA TATARINTSEVA/SHUTTERSTOCK ©

Riserva Naturale dello Zingaro (p95)

If you only have one day

● Devote the day to an invigorating hike along the rugged coastline of Sicily's oldest nature reserve, the **Riserva Naturale dello Zingaro** (p95). Museums, beaches and picnic tables along the way offer ample opportunities to catch your breath, soak up some rays or take a dip in crystal-clear turquoise waters. Post-hike, drive 30 minutes to **Segesta** (p93) to admire the majestic Greek temples in the soft, late-afternoon light. Continue an hour to the coast to enjoy an evening with seafood and sunset on the beach at **Da Vittorio** (p96) in Porto Palo.

Seasonal highlights

Summer in this western part of Sicily can be extremely hot. Fortunately, water is never far away. Spring, with its bouquet of wildflowers, and Autumn – harvest time! – are the best seasons for gentle hiking.

MARCH
Springtime flowers bloom. Fields around Segesta blaze yellow with wild fennel. Chefs flavour traditional *pasta con le sarde* with it.

APRIL
The week before Easter is marked by Trapani's quite extraordinary Misteri processions; reserve accommodation well in advance.

MAY
The salt harvest begins (and continues until August). The first sun-spun fruits are picked from sunken orchards on Favignana.

ALTRENDO IMAGES/SHUTTERSTOCK ©, DANITA DELIMONT/SHUTTERSTOCK ©, STEFANO_VALERI/SHUTTERSTOCK ©

Three days to travel around

● Explore **Trapani** (p88). Spend the morning ambling around the old town and admiring its elegant baroque architecture. Shop for coral and lunch at **La Bettolaccia** (p90) or **Tentazioni di Gusto** (p90). Ride the funicular up to hilltop **Erice** (p93) in the afternoon, not missing cakes at Maria Grammatico, then hit the beach. Reserve a table at **Caupona Taverna di Sicilia** (p90) for a traditional couscous dinner. Next day, drive south to **Saline di Trapani** (p93) and later to sweet wine town **Marsala** (p99). Pair ancient ruins in **Selinunte** (p97) and **Segesta** (p93) on day three.

If you have more time

● Pair the above three days with a trip to the Egadi Islands. Spend a couple of days exploring **Favignana** (p100). Don't miss a hike up to its hilltop fort, a morning learning about the region's tuna heritage and a bike ride to the **Giardino dell'Impossibile** (p102) – consider overnighting in the quarry gardens. Then move onto **Marettimo** (p105) for wild walks and a meal of a lifetime – lobster soup – at Trattoria Il Veliero (reserve!). On **Levanzo** (p104), a boat trip to **Grotta del Genovese** (p104) uncovers the island's prehistoric past.

JUNE	JULY	AUGUST	SEPTEMBER
Kitesurfing season (until September) kicks off on Punta Tipa in Trapani and Lo Stagnone near Marsala.	Time to hit the beach. This is also the best month to see saltpans between Trapani and Marsala shimmer brilliant pink.	Busy beaches sizzle. Islanders feast on figs and the fresh pods of carob trees. Segesta's theatre festival opens.	Marsala celebrates its grape harvest. Beach clubs and restaurants shut for winter by month's end. The first pomegranates ripen.

TRAPANI

Trapani   Palermo

A melting pot of old and new, this small port town seduces with ancient churches, goldstone *palazzi* (mansions) and traditional dining spun from local produce and fair trade. In the historic centre, pedestrian main street Via Garibaldi is a mellow place to stroll, both for locals enjoying a *passeggiata* (afternoon walk) and travellers awaiting their next boat.

Food is of the utmost importance to this ancient fishing town where trattorias cook up couscous, *busiate alla trapanese* (spaghetti-like pasta with pesto made from tomatoes, basil, garlic and almonds) and dishes with capers from Pantelleria island. On main beach Spiaggia di San Giuliano, a 30-minute walk from Piazza Vittoria Emanuele, sun-worshippers clink cocktails in beach clubs and stand in line for corn on the cob chargrilled to order, salted and wrapped in a leaf from an old-school pushcart on the golden sand. Across the street, at the town cemetery, the Murale di Licuado wall mural by Uruguayan street artists Camilo Nuñez and Florencia Durán is an artistic shout-out to Trapani's rich multicultural heritage.

TOP TIP

Watch for summertime festivals and cultural happenings: organ concerts at the cathedral; free guided tours of Palazzo Riccio di Morana on Via Garibaldi; Trapani's street-food festival Stragusto (www.stragusto.it) in July, filling Piazza Mercato del Pesce with three days of outrageously delicious tastings and live cooking shows.

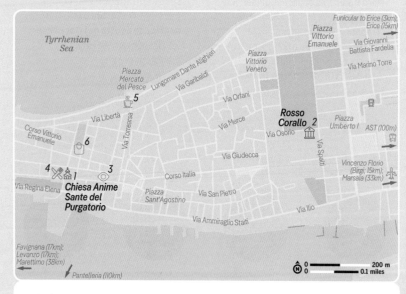

HIGHLIGHTS
1 Chiesa Anime Sante del Purgatorio
2 Rosso Corallo

SIGHTS
3 Piazza Lucatelli

EATING
4 La Bettolaccia

DRINKING & NIGHTLIFE
5 BrigBar

SHOPPING
6 Bottega del Corallo

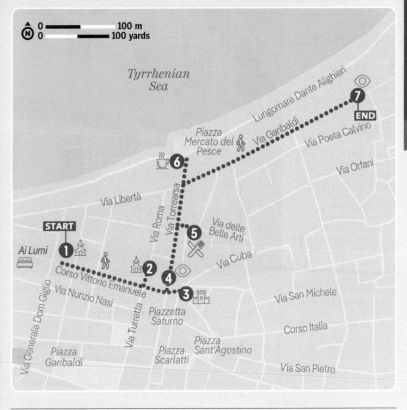

WALTZ THROUGH 17TH- & 18TH-CENTURY BAROQUE

While Trapani's golden-hued historic centre is Moorish, the city takes most of its character from its 17th- and 18th-century baroque architecture from the Spanish period. Begin in front of **1 Cattedrale di San Lorenzo**, built in 1421 but modified over the years to arrive at its 18th-century baroque look by architect Giovanni Biagio Amico.

Waltz east along pedestrianised main strip Corso Vittorio Emanuele. At No 12, monumental **2 Chiesa dei Gesuiti** (1614) illustrates the transition from mannerism to baroque. Admire its richly decorated interior, with ornate marble inlays evocative of Palermo's dazzling baroque churches. At the eastern end of the street, 3 **Palazzo Senatorio** (1672) seduces with peach-stone facade and elegant statues in niches.

Walk north along **4 Via Torrearsa** and turn right onto Via Carosio for old-school coffee, *biscotti di fichi* (fig biscuits) and Trapani's best *cannoli* at **5 Antica Pasticceria Colicchia** (1885), in 18th-century Palazzo dei Signori Carosio. Continue north for an iced latte or cold brew at BrigBar, with terrace overlooking Trapani's historic open-air fish market on **6 Piazza Mercato del Pesce**. The 19th-century ensemble of arched porticoes by Venetian architect Giambattista Talotti, cradling a fountain of Venus emerging from the sea, is pure romance. End with a handsome stroll east along **7 Via Garibaldi**, bejewelled with baroque *palazzi*. To sleep and dream baroque, check into Ai Lumi (p90) inside 18th-century Palazzo Berardo Ferro on Corso Vittorio Emanuele.

COUSCOUS ALLA TRAPANESE

Trapani's unique position on the sea route to Tunisia has made couscous a local speciality. Table reservations are essential at side-street **La Bettolaccia**, with a sharp white interior, and family-run **Caupona Taverna di Sicilia**, with summer terrace eyeballing the sculpted facade of **Chiesa Anime Sante dei Purgatorio**. Both are unwaveringly authentic, Slow Food favourites for traditional *couscous alla trapanese* – couscous accompanied by a broth of seafood, garlic, chilli, tomatoes, saffron, parsley and wine, which you ladle over according to taste. Share as a *primo* or order as a meal in itself.

Easter parade, Trapani

La Processione dei Misteri

MEET THE CITY'S CELEBRATED MISTERI

It goes without saying. If you're in town at Easter, witnessing Trapani's traditional four-day celebration of the Passion of Christ is non-negotiable. Even if you're not religious, feeling the delirious fervour of the crowd – matched only by that of the Semana Santa parades in Seville, Spain – as the town's celebrated *misteri* (life-sized wooden statues of Mary, Jesus and other biblical figures), accompanied by a Trapanese band, process through town is unforgettable.

If you're not in town over Easter, devote a morning to studying the *misteri* in **Chiesa Anime Sante del Purgatorio** (www.processionemisteritp.it). Carved in cypress or cork wood, painted by hand and clothed, the statuary groupings represent 20 scenes from the Passion and Death of Christ. Most are originals from the 17th century; some were heavily repaired or replaced after WWII.

On the Tuesday before Easter Sunday, Trapani inhabitants – represented by 20 traditional *maestranze* (guilds) – parade the life-sized Virgin Mary through town. Nightly

MORE BAROQUE

Consider visiting the churches showcasing Giacomo Serpotta's stuccowork in Palermo's **I Tesori della Loggia** collection (p74) and cathedrals in **Modica** (p201), **Noto** (p189) and **Ragusa** (p197).

WHERE TO STAY & EAT IN TRAPANI

Residenza La Gancia
Elegant rooms and a rooftop terrace for breakfast and sunset cocktails with Favignana craft gin. €€

Ai Lumi
Little beats this B&B with kitchenette-clad apartments in an 18th-century palazzo; enter via a courtyard full of plants. €

Tentazioni di Gusto
Lobsters wriggle in a tank and seafood dishes ooze creativity at this elegant address, with tables filling a tiny lane.

processions of the other *misteri,* accompanied by musicians playing dirges to the slow steady beat of a drum, make their way to a chapel on **Piazza Lucatelli** before returning to Chiesa Anime Sante del Purgatorio. Celebrations peak around 2pm on Good Friday when the 20 guilds emerge from the church. Bearers carry the statues at shoulder height on flower-adorned floats and walk with a forward-side step to heighten the drama. The all-night procession weaves through the old town, returning to the church Saturday afternoon.

Trapani Coral

MEET ARTISANS & MODERN MASTERS

Delve into Trapani's rich coral tradition at **Rosso Corallo**, the family workshop of Platimiro Fiorenza (b. 1944). Son of a coral-goldsmith and Unesco Living Human Treasure, Trapani's most distinguished coral master famously sculpted a Madonna di Trapani in coral, gold and precious stones for the Pope (displayed in Rome's Vatican Museums) and created a red-leather handbag covered in coral and silver for Italian fashion house Fendi to celebrate its iconic 'baguette' bag. Workshop visits at Via Osorio 36 tango through local coral-working history and demonstrate Platimiro's *retroincastro* (reverse-embedding) technique, introduced by Trapani craftsman in the 17th century.

For more affordable coral necklaces, earrings or a simple droplet of red coral straight from a coral fisher's net, browse Bottega del Corallo, the workshop-boutique of coral jeweller Marzia Cipriano Novata at Corso Vittorio Emanuele 47.

Coral carving dates to 1416 when local fishermen uncovered coral reefs offshore from Trapani and later San Vito Lo Capo. Dazzling chalices, relic boxes and *presepe* (nativity scenes) at the **Museo Nazionale Pepoli** illustrate the prized artisanship of Trapani *corallari* between the 16th and 18th centuries. The decorative-arts museum, hidden like a precious gem in the cloister of a 14th-century monastery, showcases the collection of local count Agostino Pepoli (1848–1910). He devoted his life to salvaging Trapani's local arts and crafts, notably coral carvings, all the rage in Europe until the 18th century when Trapani's coral banks were decimated.

THE BEAUTY OF SCIACCA

Trapani coral - the blood of Medusa's severed head, according to myth - is soft red in colour. Rare orange coral is harvested from the Mediterranean, a few nautical miles from **Sciacca** (p236).

BEST FOR COFFEE, COCKTAILS & WINE

BrigBar
Serious coffee and food all day using local produce and goods (coffee, beer) transported sustainably to Trapani by sailing ship.

Moai
DJs spin lounge tunes and hipsters bag dress-circle stools by the wall to enjoy sunset cocktails; unmatched sea/sunset views.

Bar Il Salotto
Pomegranate juice squeezed to order and street terrace with sofa seating cocoons at The Drawing Room.

Tenuta Adragna
On bar-packed Corso Vittorio Emanuele, choose this rustic vineria with pavement cushions and excellent wine from its out-of-town vineyards.

Bardia Nuova
June to September ushers in this chic rooftop lounge bar - a near-perfect spot for aperitivo and drinks after dark.

GETTING AROUND

AST buses link Trapani–Birgi Vincenzo Florio with Trapani port; taxis to either Trapani or Marsala charge a fixed €30 rate. Once in town, ATM city buses are useful to the beaches and the lower funicular station for Erice.

San Vito
Lo Capo

Riserva Natura
dello Zingaro

Bonagia
Trapani   Scopello
Erice

Via del Sal   Segesta

Mozia

Beyond Trapani

Whether you're atop a medieval hilltop village,
amid Greek theatre ruins or saltpans, views here
are out of this world.

The obvious day trips from Trapani aren't necessarily by boat.
While the summer crowd piles onto ferries and hydrofoils at
Trapani port, bound for Favignana (p100) and other Egadi
Islands, there's plenty of 'mainland' entertainment. Inland,
the remarkable preservation of ancient ruins and the majesty of their sublime rural setting at Segesta combine to form
one of Sicily's enduring highlights.

Along the coast, two pristine wetlands beguile: Riserva Naturale Saline di Trapani e Paceco north near Trapani, and Riserva Naturale di Stagnone to the south, embracing the island
of San Pantaleo and archaeological site of Mozia. Wherever
you go, look for hand-filled tins of artisanal Tre Torri tuna –
conserved using local olive oil and salt from Trapani's prized
pans – to enjoy back home.

TOP TIP

Plan your trip to Trapani's
saltpans in advance; the
most interesting activities
at Saline Ettore e Infersa
require advance booking.

Saline **(shallow salt pools; p94) and windmils**

ESSEVU/SHUTTERSTOCK ©

Segesta

MAGIC AMID ANCIENT RUINS

It's not hard to create your own magic in Segesta, 32km west of Trapani. Simply staring in wonder at its centrepiece **Doric temple** in fields of wildflowers and grasses, or watching drama unfold on a hot summer night beneath stars in a 3rd-century BCE **Greek theatre**, is nothing short of celestial. Set on the edge of a deep canyon amid desolate mountains, these 5th-century BCE ruins are among the world's most evocative ancient sites.

The remarkably well-preserved temple, a five-minute walk uphill from the ticket office, has retained all of its 36 columns – on windy days they become an organ, producing mysterious notes. The theatre, a 1.25km walk or shuttle-bus ride from the office, crowns the summit of Monte Bàrbaro and affords sweeping views north to the stunning Golfo di Castellammare. Allow at least a half-day to fully take in the ruins' remarkable state of preservation and the majesty of their bucolic, rural setting.

Medieval Erice

RUINS, VIEWS AND SENSATIONAL CAKES

It's difficult to pinpoint one highlight of a day trip to Erice, a medieval hilltop village watching over Trapani from its mountain perch atop the legendary peak of Eryx. The funicular ride up is a treat in itself – choose a bluebird day – as a spectacular panorama extending from San Vito Lo Capo to Trapani's saltpans unfolds. Inside the walled 12th-century village, get lost in a mesmerising tangle of polished, slippery, stone-paved lanes – wear shoes with decent grip. Spend an hour exploring the grassy, evocative ruins of 12th- to 13th-century **Castello di Venere**, built by the Normans over the Temple of Venus, and break over coffee and cakes in the secret garden of legendary **Pasticceria di Maria Grammatico**.

The Salt Road

HELP HARVEST ITALY'S FINEST SALT

Along the coast between Trapani and Marsala lies an evocative landscape of *saline* (shallow salt pools) and

ANCI
CIVII

Long
arriv
Seg
principal city of the
Elymians, an ancient
civilisation claiming
descent from the
Trojans that settled
in Sicily in the Bronze
Age. The Elymians
were in constant
conflict with Greek
Selinunte, whose
destruction (in 409
BCE) they pursued
with bloodthirsty
determination.
More than 100 years
later the Greek
tyrant Agathocles
slaughtered over
10,000 Elymians and
repopulated Segesta
with Greeks.

GREEK THEATRE

Watching a performance in Segesta's Greek theatre during August's Segesta Teatro Festival is goosebump stuff. Elsewhere, Taormina's Teatro Greco stages theatre and classic concerts with a Mt Etna backdrop during July's Taormina Arte festival and Greek tragedies unfold in Syracuse at the summer-long **Festival del Teatro Greco** (p181).

🍴 WHERE TO LUNCH IN ERICE

Gusto Il Panino Gourmet	**Ristorante Monte San Giuliano**	**Liparoti**
Gourmet *panini*, salads and Bruno Ribadi craft beer brewed an hour along the coast.	A stone archway leads to a vine-shaded garden promising an idyllic lunch; cuisine is average.	Skip *dolci* for outstanding *granita:* try almond, pistachio and lemon peel or salted caramel and peanut.

LANDSCAPE NATURE PHOTO/SHUTTERSTOCK ©

Riserva Naturale dello Zingaro

I LIVE HERE: NEGRONI APERITIVI & SALTY SUNSETS

One-time Italian Barista of the Year and all-time bon vivant **Giulio Panciatici** moved from Turin to Trapani to shake up the local coffee scene at new-wave coffee shop BrigBar. He shares his favourite addresses in and out of town.

'After a hard day's work I always go to Bar Piccadilly on Via Torrearsa for a negroni. I'm a romantic and you can't leave Trapani without seeing the sunset in the *saline* (saltpans). The sky turns deep pink over the white saltpans. There is a little restaurant by the Laguna Lo Stagnone where you can eat and watch the sun sink. It's exceptional.'

decommissioned *mulini* (windmills). As you drive along the Via del Sal or Salt Road in summer from Trapani – SP21 on maps – spot salt workers harvesting Italy's finest salt from rosy-pink saltpans glinting in the sun. Only a cottage industry remains today, providing discerning tables with prized *fior di sal* (rock salt), *cristalli di sal* (salt crystals) and *sale marino dei Trapani IGP* (table salt).

Learn about salt production and take part in a guided saltpan walk or salt tasting at Saline Ettore e Infersa (www.seisaline.it), a salt museum in a 16th-century windmill, 25km south of Trapani. May to August, try being a salt worker for a half-day, harvesting salt (boots provided); or sail 20 minutes in a traditional lagoon boat across Stagnone di Marsala to the uninhabited islet of Isola Lunga. Back at the mill, tuck into an alfresco lunch, sunset drinks or dinner overlooking saltpans at Mamma Caura.

 WHERE TO STAY & EAT BEYOND TRAPANI

Agriturismo Vultaggio
Safari tents, B&B rooms and a zero-kilometre farm restaurant make this retreat, 15km south of Trapani, hard to resist. €

Baglio La Luna
Escape to this hillside farmhouse B&B with hypnotic sea views, 2km north of the Zingaro reserve. €€

La Tonnara di Scopello
Dream tuna at Scopello's historic tuna fishery; self-catering apartments and hotel rooms on the water's edge. €€

Mozia

A FERRY RIDE TO ANCIENT PHOENICIA

Hop aboard the teeny half-hourly ferry from **Imbarcadero Salina Infersa**, 25km south of Trapani, to ancient Mozia on the tiny island of San Pantaleo. Established in the 8th century BCE and coveted for its strategic position, this was one of the Mediterranean's most important Phoenician settlements. The entire island was bought by the ornithologist and amateur archaeologist Joseph Whitaker (1850–1936) whose unique collection of Phoenician artefacts fills **Museo Whitaker**. Pick up trail maps here to explore the island strewn with ruins from ancient Phoenicia.

Riserva Naturale dello Zingaro

A HIKER'S SEASIDE PARADISE

Stride out along a 7km walking trail bejewelled with blockbuster sea views in this wild, off-the-beaten-track coastal nature reserve. Keep your eyes peeled for the rare Bonelli's eagle, majestic buzzard, kestrel and 40 other bird species. Wild carob, bright yellow euphorbia and a mountain of other Mediterranean flora dust the hillsides, and narrow paths cut down to hidden rocky coves with pebble beaches and tranquil swimming. The hot spot for snorkelling is **Cala Marinella**, a bijou cove midway along the coastal path with piercing emerald-green waters and mountains of rocks from which to access the water; there is no beach as such. Buy admission tickets and pick up a free trail map at the park's southern entrance, 2km north of Scopello, or northern entrance in San Vito Lo Capo.

The Tuna Route

EXPLORING LOCAL FISHING HERITAGE

Hit the coastal road – two wheels or four – to explore a wild, seafaring landscape dotted with idyllic swimming coves and quaint seaside hamlets built around historic *bagli* (manor houses) and *tonnare* (tuna fisheries). Traditional tuna-fishing villages Bonagia (10km north of Trapani along the SP20) and Scopello (35km east overlooking the Golfo di Castellammare) both explore local history and the ancient custom of *mattanza* used to catch the Mediterranean's prized bluefin tuna in small, evocative museums inside historic buildings.

THE GUIDE

WESTERN SICILY

COUSCOUS FEST

Trapani's beloved local dish couscous is the fun focus of this colourful six-day food fest, celebrated with gusto in the seaside town of **San Vito Lo Capo** during the last week in September. Highlights include cooking shows, workshops, concerts, live music and – drumroll – the Couscous World Championships, in which couscous chefs from 10 countries compete. Throughout the fest, a ticket *degustazione* (€10) gives you access to dozens of different tasting stands around town and on San Vito Lo Capo's famously long and beautifully sandy beach. Buy in advance online or at kiosks in situ during the festival.

GETTING AROUND

Be aware that Tarantola (www.tarantolabus.com) bus services between Trapani bus station and Segesta (40 to 50 minutes) are painfully limited. In Segesta, motorists must park in a purpose-built car park and walk or catch a shuttle bus the remaining 1.5km to the ruins.

In Trapani, to get the funicular up to Erice, take bus 21 or 23 from the western end of Via GB Fardella (immediately around the corner from Piazza Vittorio Emanuele) and get off at the final stop, opposite the lower funicular station.

SELINUNTE

Time travel in western Sicily climaxes atop a windy bluff over-looking the sea. Dating to the 7th century BCE, the majestic ruins of Greek metropolis Selinos (Selinunte) form one of the island's most captivating archaeological sites. Over two and a half centuries it became one of the richest and most powerful cities in the world. Wandering 270 hectares of fields, richly scattered with ruined temples and wildflowers, it's not difficult to imagine the prosperous, temple-laced metropolis of 100,000 people that Selinunte became until the Carthaginians destroyed it in 409 BCE.

So large is this archaeological site that excavations have never really stopped since 1823 when the first metopes were unearthed. As recently as 2022, the largest agora in the ancient world alongside amulets and precious objects equal to finds in Delphi, Greece, were discovered here by a team of international archaeologists from the US and Italy. The work continues.

TOP TIP

Cool down with a sea dip from Lido di Zabbar, the beach hidden below the archaeological site; access it from the beachfront town of Marinella di Selinunte. Feast on fish and overnight 15km east at ravishing hotel and seafood restaurant Da Vittorio in Porto Palo.

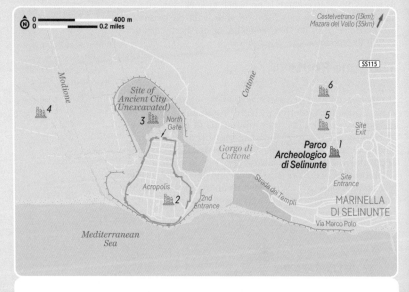

HIGHLIGHTS	SIGHTS	4 Sanctuary of	5 Temple E
1 Parco Archeologico di Selinunte	2 Acropolis	Malophoros	6 Temple G
	3 Ancient City		

Temple C

Ruins Explorer

UNCOVER EUROPE'S LARGEST ARCHAEOLOGICAL PARK

Lose yourself Indiana Jones–style in the temples and acropolis of Ancient Greece's most westerly colony. As you walk from the ticket office, the almost-complete **Temple E** looms large in the Eastern Temples zone. Built in the 5th century BCE and reconstructed in 1958, this is the park's showpiece. The two other temples here, including 6th-century **Temple G** which was one of the largest temples in the Greek world despite never being completed, are piles of rubble.

Explore the **Acropolis** next – the hub of political and social life, about 2km from the entrance – with five temples on a slanted plateau. Sea views are stunning. **Temple C** is the oldest temple and with 14 of its 17 original columns still intact, the most photographed. Smaller **Temple B**, from the Hellenistic period, was possibly dedicated to the Agrigentan physiologist and philosopher Empedocles, whose water-drainage scheme saved the city from the scourge of malaria.

Walk about 20 minutes west next, across the now-dry river Modione and up a dirt path, to the **Sanctuary of Malophoros**. Amid the ravaged ruins of this temple dedicated to Demeter, the goddess of fertility, look for two altars – one was used for sacrifices. End in the **Ancient City**, north of the acropolis on Manuzza hill, where most of Selinunte's inhabitants lived.

SYRACUSE VS. CARTHAGE

Originally allied with Carthage, Selinunte switched allegiance after the Carthaginian defeat by Gelon of Syracuse at Himera in 480 BCE. In 409 BCE the Carthaginians took revenge on its former ally. Troops commanded by Hannibal destroyed the city, leaving only those who had taken shelter in the temples as survivors.

Around 250 BCE, with the Romans about to conquer the city, its citizens were relocated to Lilybaeum (Marsala), but not before they destroyed as much as they could. What they left standing, mainly temples, was finished off by an earthquake in the Middle Ages.

DECORATIVE TREASURES

Enrich your understanding of Selinunte with a half-day at the fascinating **Museo Archeologico Regionale Antonio Salinas** (p76) in Palermo.

GETTING AROUND

Getting around the site on foot requires stamina, especially in summer when water, sun protection and sunhat (even an umbrella to use as a parasol) are survival essentials. Count at least 5km and four hours to walk the entire site. Electric golf carts at the main entrance cut out some of the legwork.

Marsala   Cretto Burri

Selinunte

Beyond Selinunte

Extraordinary land art remembers a settlement destroyed in modern times and age-old vineyards fuel one of Italy's finest sweet wines.

History is equally grand beyond Selinunte and inspires some riveting day trips. A journey inland from the ancient ruins raises the curtain on Sicily's most famous modern ruins, pinpointed on contemporary maps by powerful land art.

An hour northwest along the coast is the ancient town of Marsala, founded by Phoenicians who escaped from Mozia after it was defeated in 397 BCE by an army led by Dionysius I of Syracuse. They settled here on Capo Lilibeo, calling their city Lilybaeum and fortifying it with 7m-thick walls that ensured it was the last Punic settlement to fall to the Romans. In CE 830 it was conquered by the Arabs, who gave it its current name Marsa Allah (Port of God).

TOP TIP

Watch for a future Museo del Vino, with multimedia displays on the culture and history of Marsala winemaking, at Palazzo Rici (funding was finally sorted in 2021).

Via XI Maggio, Marsala

TRABANTOS/SHUTTERSTOCK ©

Cretti di Burri

AN UNFORGETTABLE PIECE OF LAND ART

Modern tragedy oozes out of Cretti di Burri. The sea of lunar white tumbling down a green hillside in the Valle del Belice by Italian artist Alberto Burri (1915–95) is gut-wrenching once you realise that the high-walled alleys cut in the 1.5m-thick cement map out the streets of Gibellina, destroyed by an earthquake in 1968. The rolling hills surrounding the monstrous labyrinth only heighten the drama. After the earthquake, while Burri later buried the ruins in cement, villagers moved 18km west to settle the new town of **Nuova Gibellina**. Visit the latter afterwards to grasp the full horror of the villagers' harrowing story of displacement as they struggled with life in a 'utopian town', void of intimate village piazzas and cafes.

Tasting Wine in Marsala

AN EPICUREAN TOUR

As one of Sicily's viticultural capitals, the handsome old town of Marsala teems with tasting ops. Start on main street Via XI Maggio. Duck beneath the balcony-crowned archway at No 32 to meet local winegrowers, learn about Marsala wine and taste it at the town's municipal *enoteca* (wine bar), run by local wine merchants inside 17th-century **Palazzo Fici**.

Lunch in the company of several Marsala wines and spectacular Sicilian cuisine at Slow Food–endorsed **Ciacco Putia Gourmet**, a five-minute walk southeast along the main street and right onto Via Ciaccoputia. The summertime terrace, on a cobbled fountain-pierced square overlooking the showy baroque facade of 18th-century Chiesa del Purgatorio, is divine – as are Francesco's tastings and creative pairings.

CELLAR ETIQUETTE

Prestigious Marsala wine producers include Florio, Pellegrino, Donnafugata, Rallo, Mavis and Intorcia. Some *cantine* (wine cellars) open their doors to visitors, but strictly by advance appointment only; organised tours advertised must also be booked in advance.

Marsala tourist office has a complete list of cellars, or make a date with **Cantine Florio**. These venerable wine cellars, in a huge walled complex east of the centre and on the seafront since 1833, open their vintage doors to visitors to explain the Marsala-making process and the fascinating history of local viticulture. Afterwards, you can sample the goods in the sharp tasting room: tasting of four wines, accompanied by hors d'oeuvres, is included in the standard 1½-hour tour.

GETTING AROUND

Marsala is easily reached by train from Trapani (35 minutes) and Palermo (3½ to 4 hours), but to visit its out-of-town wine cellars you'll need your own transport. For Cantine Florio, take bus No 16 from Piazza del Popolo.

To find Cretto di Burri, take the Santa Ninfa exit off the A29 and follow brown signs for 'Ruderi di Gibellina' (Ruins of Gibellina) along the SS119. To drive directly to Nuova Gibellina, exit the A29 further north at the Gibellina exit.

FAVIGNANA

When an island idyll beckons, take a slow boat (or speedy hydrofoil) from Trapani or Marsala to the picture-postcard Egadi Islands. The largest, butterfly-shaped Favignana, is a much-loved destination for swimming, snorkelling and slowing right down. Cycling from cove to cove and feasting on swordfish, cuttlefish, tuna and the fertile island's earthy culinary treasures is as energetic as it gets.

The small port town of Favignana, with the fort-crowned peak of Monte Santa Caterina (287m) and historic tuna complex, is an easy place to while away a day. Along the coast, deep square gouges cut in cliffs evoke intense quarrying that occurred from the 17th century until the 1980s. Inland, open quarries where *pirriaturi* (stonemasons) cut blocks of creamy tufa stone by hand now cradle sunken orchards and vegetable gardens or natural swimming pools – all deliciously protected from the salty air and westerly Favonio wind well known for whipping across the island.

TOP TIP

Get up on exhibitions and events at the tourist information desk inside Palazzo Flavio, an elegant Liberty-style mansion between the port and town centre, built in 1876 for local fishing tycoon Ignazio Florio. Its shady, landscaped gardens are picnic-perfect.

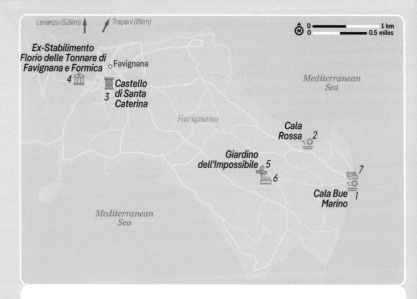

HIGHLIGHTS
1 Cala Bue Marino
2 Cala Rossa
3 Castello di Santa Caterina

4 Ex-Stabilimento Florio delle Tonnare di Favignana e Formica
5 Giardino dell'Impossibile

SLEEPING
6 Villa Margherita
EATING
7 Tunafish Favignana

Cala Rossa

Cala Rossa & Cala Bue Marino

BIKES, BEACHES & FOOD TRUCKS

Rent two wheels – old-school push bike, e-bike or 50cc scooter – at the port and zip along narrow country lanes to a beach. Golden sandy strips lace the island's southern shore (busy, family-friendly **Lido Burrone** is the most developed). But for picture-postcard swimming in clear, deep aquamarine waters and flopping on sun-scorched rocks, leg it to an untamed, rocky cove on the north shore: **Cala Rossa** is a dream.

Or follow signs from here, along a dirt track, to **Cala Bue Marino** on the rocky eastern shore where limestone was mined. Tour boats yo-yo in and out of the famous *grotte* (sea cave) here while street-smart islanders queue for the best *pane cunzato* (open sandwiches) and *panini cu tunno* (tuna sandwiches) on the island from sunflower-yellow food truck **Tunafish Favignana**.

BEST PARTY ISLAND VIBES

Monique Concept Bar
Hobnob over cocktails and craft beers at this lounge bar on the main street.

La Costa Sunset Bar & Bistro
Hit the sand at Cala Trono for drinks, dancing, live music and late-night DJ sets.

Camarillo Brillo
Named after a Frank Zappa song, this downtown bar promises 'cocktails, music, smiles, friends and shots'. Dig the faux-grass-covered bar!

Rest
Join the cool crowd for drinks, food and board games beneath sails strung from pine trees or in a hammock; 3.5km southwest of the port.

 WHERE TO STAY & EAT ON FAVIGNANA

La Casa del Limoneta
An enchanting sunken garden full of centurion lemon trees frames this cosy whitewashed B&B. €€

Villa Margherita
Peace and tranquility reign at this enchanting villa hotel in Favignana's botanical gardens. €€

Osteria del Sotto Sale
The *busiate alla norma* (local pasta with aubergine, tomato and ricotta) at this casual-chic *osteria* is spot on. €€

Giardino dell'Impossible

BOTANICAL BRILLIANCE IN AN ANCIENT QUARRY

It is a scenic, 3km bike ride from the port to this 'Garden of the Impossible' – a vast and incredible Mediterranean garden flourishing in sunken tufa-stone courtyards (some 25m deep), tunnels, caves, grottos and galleries quarried in the 1950s and 1960s. Privately owned, the gardens are the love child of owner and visionary Maria Gabriella Campo, now in her 80s, who personally planted and nurtured most of the 300-odd different flora species – indigenous and exotic – that defiantly thrive in the dusty, tufa-stone landscape. Visits are by guided tour. To experience the incongruous beauty and exceptional serenity of this most odd garden, stay overnight in its upmarket **Villa Margherita** hotel or a self-catering cottage on the estate.

Ex-Stabilimento Florio delle Tonnare di Favignana e Formica

STUDY UP ON TUNA FISHING TRADITIONS

Spend a half-day exploring Favignana's 19th-century tuna cannery – a vast, elegant complex built from local tufa stone overlooking the port. Inside, you can still see the sheds with vintage boats ready to roll out to sea; the terrace where tuna were hung; la batteria de cottura, with a trio of huge red-brick chimneys, where tuna were cooked; and the cavernous hall with the original assembly tables where the cans were filled. Short films document different aspects of the cannery's history and tuna fishing traditions, including the island's famous Mattanza. The *tonnara,* built in 1859 and operational until 1977, was one of many in Sicily to be owned by Favignana's famous Flavio family.

Castello di Santa Caterina

MORNING HIKE WITH ISLAND PANORAMA

Early morning, when the air is cooler, is the best time to tackle the steep footpath – count an hour walking, less running – up to this ruined, 15th-century fort atop Monte Santa Caterina (287m). It was a military observation station during WWII and the 360° panorama of the Egadi Islands is sensational. Pick up the footpath behind Ex-Stabilimento Florio delle Tonnare di Favignana e Formica.

 GETTING AROUND

Make sure you have some form of ID on you (passport, ID card or driving licence) to rent a

bicycle or motorised scooter from one of the many rental outlets at the port.

Beyond Favignana

Offshore from Favignana, a twinset of wild islands languish in the Med. Here, amid whitewashed houses and green mountain peaks, nature is king.

Marettimo

Grotta del Genovese

Favignana

Count a half- or full day each to visit the other two inhabited islands in Egadi's five-island collection. Just 10 minutes by hydrofoil from Favignana, wild and tiny Levanzo seduces with prehistoric cave paintings and pebbly beaches spilling into sparkling turquoise waters..

The wildest, westernmost and least-developed island, Marettimo – 40 minutes by boat from Favignana and 25 minutes from Levanzo – is a huddle of whitewashed cottages overlooking fishing boats bobbing in a little harbour. With the overfishing of tuna affecting fisher's incomes, villagers here are increasingly focusing on tourism to eke out a living. This is the only place you have a chance, albeit very slim, of spotting an endangered Mediterranean monk seal. Come winter, the island virtually shuts down.

TOP TIP

In high season buy tickets in advance for Liberty Lines hydrofoils between Favignana, Levanzo and Marettimo – boats can get full.

Levanzo (p105)

MARCIN KRZYZAK/SHUTTERSTOCK ©

103

ELESI/SHUTTERSTOCK ©

Levanzo

LA MATTANZA

The ancient Egadi Island tradition of the *mattanza* (ritual tuna slaughter) is no longer practised due to the ever-decreasing number of tuna swimming into local waters. Commercial overfishing and climate change disrupting the tuna's breeding and migration cycle are the culprits.

Traditionally, the *mattanza* occurred in late May or early June when shoals of Mediterranean bluefin tuna migrate from the colder Atlantic to western Sicily's warm waters to mate. Fishermen would organise their boats and nets in a complex formation designed to channel the tuna into a series of enclosures, ending with the *camera della morte* (chamber of death). Once enough tuna were imprisoned, the *mattanza* began. It was a bloody affair – with up to eight or more fishermen at a time sinking huge hooks into a tuna and dragging it aboard.

Grotta del Genovese

PREHISTORIC CAVE ART

The journey to Genovese Cave on Levanzo is as memorable as the artistic treasures the *grotta* safeguards. Early islanders scratched or drew with charcoal the Upper Palaeolithic wall paintings and Neolithic incised drawings, discovered in 1949. Most are of bulls, horses and dolphins; later ones include men, women and tuna. Etchings of goats and donkeys reflect farming practices of islanders 12,000 years ago when Levanzo and Favignana were still land-linked.

Cave visits are by guided tour and must be reserved in advance. Transport from the port is by motorboat in good weather – otherwise, it's a 10-minute drive by 4WD, then a steep but staggeringly scenic 700m descent on foot to the cave. Views of the rocky coastline, wild flora and helicoptering sea gulls here are all breathtaking.

 WHERE TO STAY & EAT ON LEVANZO

Albergo Ristorante Paradiso
Ceramic fish and dolphins swim across the facade of this portside cottage, serving traditional dishes with a sea view. €

Panetteria La Chicca
Buy made-to-order *kabbucio* (sandwiches) and artisan biscuits at the village bakery overlooking the port. €

Dolcevita Egadi Eco Resort
Suites with spa baths and spectacular sea views spoil at this adult-only resort, 500m inland from the port. €€€

Island Dips

BEACH-TO-BEACH HIKE

Roll off the boat in Levanzo and up the paved ramp, onto Via Calvario, to buy well-stuffed sandwiches from village bakery Panetteria La Chicca. Then hit the beach. To get to Faraglione, signposted left from the port, walk 1km along the road west of town until you see a couple of rocks sticking out of the water just offshore. Or take a right out of town, along a dirt road and rocky path down to the sea, to Cala Minnola where you can swim in crystal-clear water. The remotest option? A 4km cross-island trail to Capo Grosso on the island's far northern shore.

Slow Going on Marettimo

AN ISLAND FOR WALKING EPICUREANS

With just one road on the island and little traffic bar electric carts, the undeveloped island of Marettimo is paradise for walkers seeking peace and tranquility. From the portside village, trails dive straight into unspoiled nature, climbing up through fragrant pine forests to dramatic coastal lookouts and plunging down to empty pebble beaches: **Cala del Cretazzo** (south) and **Cala Blanca** (northwest) are favourites.

Three of the most popular trails are the hike north from town to the crumbling Norman castle perched on the lonely promontory of **Punta Troia**; the short climb west to **Case Romane** where remains of Roman houses share the stage with a whitewashed Byzantine church; and a longer hike following the island's southwestern shores to the secluded beach at **Cala Nera**. Along every trail, well-placed picnic benches invite hikers to take a shady break. Stock up on artisan cheeses, marinated meats, veg dishes and bread before striding out at gourmet butcher and deli **La Cambusa** (Via Giuseppe Garibalid 5b).

Close the day back on the waterfront with Giuseppe's *zuppa di aragosta* (lobster soup) at **Trattoria Il Veliero** (Via Umberto 22) or a traditional bowl of Paolina's durum-wheat *frascatole* (a type of handmade couscous) in a lobster and cinnamon broth. Order both dishes in advance (☎0923 92 32 74) – the day before for lunch, or in the morning for dinner.

NATURALLY RICH

Given its privileged location in the heart of Europe's largest marine reserve coupled with 600 million years of isolation, Marettimo squirrels away the Egadi's most diverse flora. Slopes richly perfumed with Mediterranean *maquis* (scrub) climb up to Pizzo Falcone (868m), the archipelago's highest point.

Of the 612 flora species found here – including black mulberry and carob trees, bay, myrtle, hollyhock, mastic and an abundance of botanicals – eight are found only on Marettimo. These include the Trapani Widow *(Pseudoscabiosa limonifolia)*, Sea Stork's-bill *(Erodium maritimum)* and pretty-in-pink Dafne olivella.

LA MATTANZA ON SCREEN

Anyone who has seen Roberto Rossellini's classic 1950s film *Stromboli* starring Ingrid Bergman will recall the famous *mattanza* scene. To immerse yourself in the island where the iconic film was set, see p141.

WHERE TO STAY & EAT ON MARETTIMO

Marettimo Residence
This hillside complex draws families with self-catering apartments, pool, playground and barbecue area. €€

Rosa dei Venti
One-stop shop for budget and midrange rooms, many with rooftops and hammock-strung terraces. €–€€

Trattoria Il Veliero
Pasta with sea urchins, fresh tuna and swordfish: every dish is sensational at this waterfront highlight. €€

TYRRHENIAN COAST

BEACHES, FOOD & MOUNTAIN CAPERS

Sybaritic summer playgrounds on the coast and diverse green landscapes in the Madonie and Nebrodi nature parks. There are two ways to go in this richly varied part of the island.

The Tyrrhenian Sea looms large in this northern wedge of Sicily. According to Greek myth, divinity Aeolus stashed away his four mighty winds in cliffs above the this sea. And while it's unclear where these cliffs might be, there's no mistaking the hot southern Sirocco wind when it comes out to play. Raised humidity and mercury levels aside, this wedge of Tyrrhenian Coast spoils with unmatched panoramas of the sea and celestial Aeolian islands beyond from dozens of different hill and rocky headlands. Around Capo d'Orlando, fertile plains perfumed with centurion citrus groves cast hues of delicate white blossom across the majestic tableau. Get set for a spectacular show.

This coastal stretch between Palermo and Milazzo has been a favourite summer holiday destination for aeons. Think Club Med holiday central, with crowded roads and beaches around main coastal towns Cefalù and Capo d'Orlando. Somehow neither this, nor the ever-growing proliferation of concrete buildings marring the coastline, dissuades Sicilians and Italians from holidaying here in August and having a wonderful time.

Two nature parks safeguarding timeless green treasures in the Madonie and Nebrodi mountains reward travellers who head inland. Pristine landscapes enfold hilltop villages where the lifestyle is traditional, the sense of history palpable and the mountain cuisine exceptional. Farmhouse kitchens burst with wild forest mushrooms, *suino nero* (pork from local black pigs) and ricotta straight from the sheep. Take your foot off the gas and slow down.

ANDREW_MAYOVSKYY/GETTY IMAGES ©

THE MAIN AREAS

CEFALÙ
Golden sands and
architecture **p112**

CAPO D'ORLANDO
Rocky coves and
wild outdoors **p120**

Cefalù (p112). Left: Capo Milazzo (p123)

Find Your Way

Its enviable location embracing the beach-bejewelled stretch between Palermo and Milazzo puts the Tyrrhenian Coast right up there with all the chockablock-in-summer hot spots. Meander inland and it couldn't get wilder or more remote.

Alicudi

Tyrrhenian Sea

Cefalù, p112

Beautiful Cefalù offers a rare combination of tourist attractions: one of Sicily's greatest Arab-Norman architectural masterpieces and its finest sandy beach. Panoramic views and dining are equally brilliant.

Golfo di Termini Imerese

Cefalù

Duomo di Cefalù

Capo Cefalù

Castel di Tusa

Termini Imerese

Città Degli Artistico

La Rocca

Mt Calogero

Collesano

Castelbuono

Cerda

Pizzo Carbonara

Pizzo Scalonazzo

Monti Madonie

Tusa

Imera

Parco Naturale Regionale delle Madonie

Polizzi Generosa

Petralia Sottana

Petralia Soprana

CENTRAL SICILY

CAR & MOTORCYCLE

Having your own vehicle is a huge asset, especially in the mountainous interior where countless beautiful back roads beckon. Your own wheels – two (electric-assisted preferably) or four – are indispensable for exploring the scenic Madonie and Nebrodi mountains.

BUS

Buses from coastal hubs like Palermo and Cefalù serve interior towns like Castelbuono, Petralia and Caccamo. But schedules are frustratingly limited, and there's virtually no public transport linking these interior towns to one another once you arrive.

TRAIN

Zipping along the coast between Messina, Milazzo, Cefalù and Palermo, trains are frequent and dependable; buy tickets at train stations or directly online. Head inland, and there's not a train track in sight.

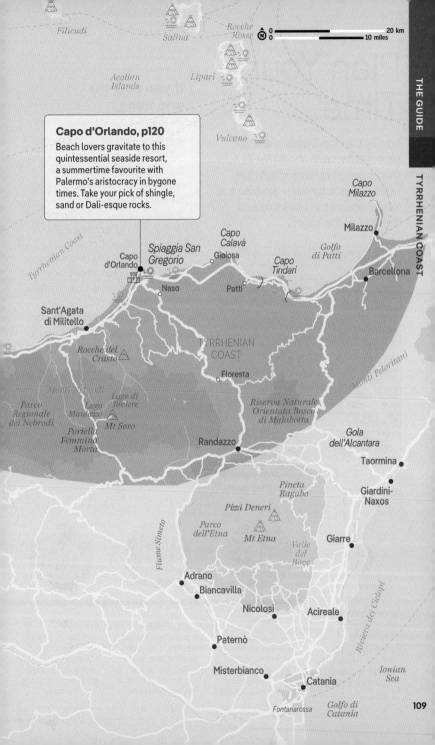

0   20 km
0   10 miles

Filicudi

Salina

Rocche Rosse

Aeolian Islands

Lipari

Vulcano

Capo d'Orlando, p120

Beach lovers gravitate to this quintessential seaside resort, a summertime favourite with Palermo's aristocracy in bygone times. Take your pick of shingle, sand or Dali-esque rocks.

Capo Milazzo

Milazzo

Tyrrhenian Coast

Capo d'Orlando

Spiaggia San Gregorio

Capo Calavà

Gioiosa

Capo Tindari

Golfo di Patti

Barcellona

Naso

Patti

Sant'Agata di Militello

TYRRHENIAN COAST

Rocche del Crasto

Floresta

Monti Peloritani

Monti Nebrodi

Lago di Biviere

Lago Maulazzo

Parco Regionale dei Nebrodi

Mt Soro

Portella Femmina Morta

Randazzo

Riserva Naturale Orientata Bosco di Malabotta

Gola dell'Alcantara

Taormina

Giardini-Naxos

Pineta Ragabo

Pizzi Deneri

Parco dell'Etna

Mt Etna

Valle del Bove

Giarre

Adrano

Biancavilla

Nicolosi

Acireale

Fiume Simeto

Paternò

Riviera dei Ciclopi

Misterbianco

Catania

Ionian Sea

Fontanarossa

Golfo di Catania

Plan Your Time

The Tyrrhenian Coast has a split personality: plan ahead for its busy coastal quarters, but drift without haste through the tranquil mountains of the Madonie and Nebrodi to the south.

La Rocca (p114), Cefalù

If you only do one thing

● Get under the skin of **Cefalù** (p112). Walk up to **La Rocca** (p114), the dramatic promontory above town, before it gets too hot. Devote the rest of the morning to the Byzantine mosaics in the **Duomo** (p113). Lunch at **Tinchité** (p115) then walk to **Capo Cefalù** (p115) for a dip from the rocks and siesta. Join the *passeggiata* crowd for a wander and artisan shopping in the enchanting tangle of back streets. Grab *aperitivo* at **Le Petit Tonneau** (p115) and a seafood dinner at **Cortile Pepe** (p113). End on the sand at **Maljk Beach** (p115) or up high at **V Rooftop** (p115).

Seasonal highlights

Summer on the coast can be crowded and scorching hot. If it all gets too much, retreat to the cooler air and quieter ranks of the mountains inland.

APRIL
Orchids and other wildflowers in bloom carpet slopes in the Madonie mountains, an outdoor-action paradise in springtime.

JUNE
The first beach lovers descend on the coast. Rooftop bars, beach restaurants and sun-lounger rentals usher in the summer season.

JULY
School's out. Prices and temperatures soar. Open-air concerts, film screenings and performances take to the stage.

JAN DANEK JDM.FOTO/SHUTTERSTOCK ©, ANDREI RYBACHUK/SHUTTERSTOCK ©, ANDREI RYBACHUK/SHUTTERSTOCK ©

SVETLAYAT/SHUTTERSTOCK ©

Three days to travel around

● Explore Cefalù the first day and take a road trip into the **Madonie mountains** (p117) the next. Leave the coast early so you have plenty of time for rambling around Castel dei Ventimiglia in **Castelbuono** (p117) and lazing over lunch at Da Salvatore in pretty little village **Petralla Soprana** (p117). End with a dinner to remember – wild boar stew with juniper berries, smoked ham or beef carpaccio and *provola delle Madonie* cheese perhaps – at **Casale Drinzi** (p117); breakfast at the B&B is equally good. Next day, consider a hike in the **Parco Naturale Regionale delle Madonie** (p119).

If you have more time

● Spend three days in and around Cefalù, then head east. If you have a car, devote a day to uncovering contemporary art installations along the Tusa River; pit stop at **Castel di Tusa** (p119) to pick up a Fiumara d'Arte route map. To cool off, end the day in **Capo d'Orlando** (p120) with a sea dip and gelato in **San Gregorio** (p121). Visit **Villa Piccolo** (p121; book in advance) before heading out to town for a coastal stroll on **Capo Milazzo** (p123); bring your bathers for the Piscina Naturale. Spend whatever time you have left getting lost in the **Nebrodi mountains** (p123).

AUGUST
Packed beaches sizzle as summer temperatures peak. Party in Cefalù during its Festa del Santissimo Salvatore on 6 August.

SEPTEMBER
As the scorching sun dissipates and schools return, this month means mellow beach encounters without the high-season crowd.

OCTOBER
Autumn brings wild mushrooms, colourful foliage and harvest festivals in mountain villages. The olive harvest is in full swing.

DECEMBER
Winter blankets Madonie's high mountain plateau of Piano Battaglia in snow.

CEFALÙ

Palermo · Cefalù

It's impossible not to be drawn in by cinematic Cefalù. Offering the rarest of tourist-attraction combos, this handsome town of red roofs by the sea seduces with one of Sicily's greatest Arab-Norman architectural masterpieces and finest sweeps of golden sand. There's no other place on the island you can break a day on the beach with a soul-soaring tour around spellbinding Byzantine mosaics.

Gaudy stalls selling toffee apples, cheap plastic toys and helium balloons on the *lungomare* (seafront promenade) won't be to everyone's taste. But the beachfront hullabaloo is instantly forgotten in the honey-hued medieval town, so postcard-pretty that film director Giuseppe Tornatore set parts of *Cinema Paradiso* (1988) here. On Via Vittorio Emanuele descend curving stone steps leading down to 16th-century washbasins built over an ancient spring, duck down to the water through Porta Pescara, or stare out to sea through the stone arches of 17th-century Bastione di Capo Marchiafava and you too will be instantly snapping away.

TOP TIP

Nothing beats the panorama in August – usually on Saturdays – when the Duomo's roof terrace and towers open from 9pm to midnight. On 5 August, thousands of candles illuminate the cathedral to celebrate the Festa di San Salvatore.

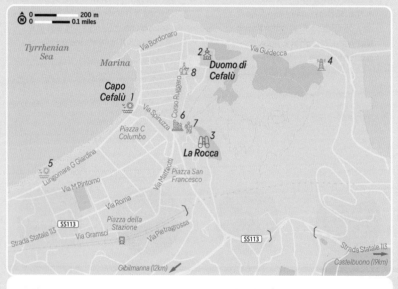

HIGHLIGHTS
1 Capo Cefalù
2 Duomo di Cefalù
3 La Rocca

SIGHTS
4 Capo Cefalù Lighthouse
5 Spiaggia di Cefalù
6 Tempio di Diana

ACTIVITIES, COURSES & TOURS
7 Salita Saraceni

DRINKING & NIGHTLIFE
8 Duomo Gelatieri dal 1952

YURY DMITRIENKO/SHUTTERSTOCK ©

Duomo interior

Step into the Piazza Duomo

CATHEDRAL MOSAICS, GELATO & APERITIVO

You only have to follow the crowd streaming along pedestrian, shop-lined **Corso Ruggero** to Cathedral Square to feel its sacred allure. Go with the flow – and be prepared to stop dead in your tracks at first sight of Cefalù's soaring golden-hued fortress of an Arab-Norman **Duomo**.

Entering on Via Passafiume, climb the spiral staircase at the back of the nave to scale one of the cathedral's twin towers. Bird's eye views of Cefalù's enchanting old town tease as you climb, and the rooftop panorama of town, mountains and Tyrrhenian Sea is quite dizzying.

Back down by the altar, show your ticket to access the privileged viewing point of the cathedral's celebrated mosaics

ARAB-NORMAN GEMS

Cefalù's cathedral is one of nine monuments on Unesco's World Heritage list of Arab-Norman treasures. Duomo di Cefalù is possibly only equalled in magnificence by **Cattedrale di Monreale** (p78) and Palermo's **Cappella Palatina** (p56).

⚒ WHERE TO EAT SEAFOOD

Locanda del Marinaio
Stuffed swordfish rolls and pasta with clams and sea urchins are fishy treats at this old-town seafood restaurant. €

Le Chat Noir
Slow Food gourmets adore The Black Cat; wine lovers, don't miss private dining with tastings in its wine cellar. €€

Cortile Pepe
Multicourse tasting menus at this sublime restaurant naturally include shoals of seafaring epicurean treats. €€€

in the central apse. A towering figure of Cristo Pantocratore (Christ Almighty) is the shimmering focal point of these elaborate Byzantine mosaics – Sicily's oldest and best preserved, predating those of Monreale by 20 or 30 years. Take your time to absorb the scene of a compassionate-looking Christ, holding an open Bible bearing a Latin and Greek inscription. Spot the Virgin with Four Archangels dressed as Byzantine officials. Continue to the sacristy, with an altar in front of a window opening onto the sea; the treasury bursting with 12th- to 19th- century treasures; and a romantic cloister garden with ancient columns supporting graceful Arab-Norman arches.

Back amid the crowds on cafe-clad Piazza Duomo, relax over a morning coffee or *aperitivo spritz* at **Duomo Gelatieri dal 1952**, with terrace tables spilling across the square. Or grab a signature *cannolo* gelato or *affogato al caffè* (espresso with vanilla gelato) to go.

Climb La Rocca

SUNRISE HIKE, RUINS & VIEWS

Looming large over Cefalù, this imposing rocky crag was once the site of an Arab citadel, superseded in 1061 by the Norman castle whose ruins still crown the summit. Climbing its heady heights along **Salita Saraceni**, an enormous staircase that winds dramatically through Aleppo pines and three tiers of city walls before emerging onto rock-strewn upland slopes, rewards with spectacular coastal views.

Below the windy summit, drone-esque views of the cathedral and old-town red rooftops from the castle's old crenellated ramparts are equally dramatic. Lower down again, picnic tables beneath trees by the ruined 4th-century-BCE **Tempio di Diana** (signposted 'Edificio Megalitico') provide a peaceful lunch spot. To access La Rocca, follow Vicolo Saraceni uphill from Corso Ruggero, and expect the hike to take around 45 minutes.

Creative Città Degli Artisti

SCULPTURE, JEWELLERY & FISHING-NET ART

Meet local artists and watch them at work in this 'city of artists'. Footsteps from Porta Ossuna in a cobbled courtyard in the historic old town, Donna Pidda draws inspiration from traditional Sicilian symbols – Palermo's legendary Moor's Head and pine cones symbolising immortality – to craft contemporary

---

 WHERE TO STAY WITH A VIEW

Hotel Turist
Spacious family rooms and Herculean breakfast buffet steal the show at this seafront hotel with private beach. €

B&B Agrodolce
Sunsets over red roofs are a killer at this enchanting, old-town B&B. €

Victoria Palace
Contemporary design woos a flush young crowd to this pool-clad hotel by the sea. €€€

jewellery and accessories. At his bottega artistica at Via XXV Novembre 55, sculptor Roberto Giacchino cuts portrait busts in olive wood, and Michele Valenza sculpts voluptuous nudes in snow-white alabaster in his workshop at Via Vittorio Emanuele 37. For funky lampshades made from recycled fishing nets, walk down the street to No 83.

Escape to Capo Cefalù

LOCAL BEACH LIFE & SNORKELLING

Downtown Cefalù's sweep of action-packed golden sand needs no introduction – crescent-shaped **Spiaggia di Cefalù** is one of Sicily's best sand beaches. To flee the crowd, follow locals to Capo Cefalù, a cape with a vintage lighthouse (1900) and clear, turquoise and emerald waters for snorkelling. From the Duomo, walk downhill along Corso Ruggero then right along Via Porpora until you reach dry limestone walls built by the Greeks in the 4th and 5th centuries BCE. Duck through the *postierla* – a passage cut in the megalithic walls so dwellers could access a fresh spring flowing out of the cliff – to arrive by the sea. Follow the paved path, steps and bridges along rocks to dip in beautiful shallow pools and snorkel in the sparkling big blue.

Celebrate at Festa del Santissimo Salvatore

PARTY WITH LOCALS

Only the sons of local fishers can take part in Ntinna a mari, the grand finale of Cefalù's annual festival on 6 August celebrating its patron saint. The ancestral tradition sees 17 men in swim shorts attempt to walk across a 16m-long pole balanced above the water at il Molo to retrieve a flag of San Salvatore. The narrow pole is greased with fat, assuring hilarity all round.

Traditionally, this four-day fest – ending with midnight fireworks on the beach – is the time to devour Cefalù's signature dish, *pasta 'a taianu*. Derived from the Arabic 'taoi' word for a terracotta dish, it layers two types of shredded meat (beef, lamb or pork meat) with aubergine, tomato sauce and pecorino cheese in a terracotta dish.

BEST PASTA IN A PAN

Tinchité
This on-point *taverna e putia* (inn and grocery store), with foliage-shaded terrace, celebrates local produce and cuisine. Kudos for the backstories on its menu.

La Botte
For over three decades, this family-run restaurant in the old town has served flavoursome local and Sicilian classics.

La Trinacria
Panoramic sea views and top-notch *pasta 'a taianu* justify the 10-minute walk to this clifftop eatery, inside an old pasta factory. Sensational terrace.

 WHERE TO SIP APERITIVO & COCKTAILS

V Rooftop
Sunset sushi, DJs and a party vibe pack out Victoria Palace's sizzling rooftop lounge.

Le Petit Tonneau
Bag the table on the balcony looking out to sea at this traditional *enoteca* (wine bar) with fabulous tasting platters.

Maljk Beach
Sip cocktails with hipsters at this trendy lounge club on the beach; live music and party nights.

Beyond Cefalù

Sun-worshippers who venture inland from Cefalù are swiftly seduced by mountainous landscapes peppered with hilltop villages and ancient forests.

The overwhelming serenity and green riches of the Parco Naturale Regionale delle Madonie, a protected 400-sq-km regional park, is an unmatched antidote to the overdeveloped coast's jostling army of sun-seeking holidaymakers. An outdoorsy paradise well-suited to slow, culturally rich travel, the Monti Madonie (Madonie Mountains) soar up to 1979m some 25km south of Cefalù. From hiking to the top of Pizzo Carbonara – Sicily's highest peak after Mt Etna – to touring tastebuds around village trattorias and making fresh ricotta cheese over an open wood fire with shepherds, this is a part of Sicily where daily life runs in perfect harmony with nature. Simplicity rules, tradition is fierce, and the cuisine is foraged fresh from the forest or farm.

TOP TIP

Eat your way around: think wild mushrooms, *suino nero* (pork from black pigs), pungent local *provola* and sweet manna, made from ash tree sap.

Parco Naturale Regionale delle Madonie (p119)

FERDYNET/GETTY IMAGES ©

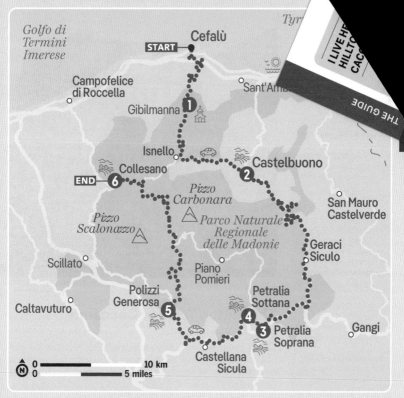

DRIVE FROM CEFALÙ TO COLLESANO

This driving tour (110km) is doable in a day, but warrants one overnight at least. Begin 15km from Cefalù at **1 Santuario di Gibilmanna**, one of Sicily's most important shrines on the slopes of Pizzo Sant'Angelo (1081m). Masterpiece views over the Madonie introduce the protected regional park.

2 Castelbuono, 18km southeast, is dominated by a 14th-century castle. Nip into family-run Pasticceria Fiasconaro for *mannetto* (manna cake), a sweet cake made from the sap of the local flowering ash trees. Follow the winding SS286 to mountain village **3 Petralia Soprana** for a labyrinthine journey past stone houses, wrought-iron balconies brimming with geraniums, and sweeping valley views. Lunch local at Da Salvatore, tucked into a bijou square near Chiesa di Santa Maria di Loreto, or continue to pretty **4 Petralia Sottana**.

It's about 20km to **5 Polizzi Generosa** in the Imera Valley. Named *generosa* (generous) by Frederick II in the 1230s, the village is an excellent trekking base. Sample *sfoglio,* a sweet pastry filled with artisanal sheep's milk cheese, cinnamon, chocolate and sugar.

End in **6 Collesano** 26km northwest, at the eclectic Museo Targa Florio. The village museum documents the Targa Florio, the world's oldest sports-car racing event, dating to 1906 along Madonie's treacherous hairpins. End with the ultimate Slow Food mountain dinner in the hills above Collesano at rustic restaurant-B&B Casale Drinzi.

RE:
P
AMO

Andrew Edwards, co-author of Sicily: A Literary Guide for Travellers shares some favourite places in and around his home in Caccamo.

'Evocatively likened to a folded bird's wing by Carlo Levi, Caccamo spreads along the hillside from the heights of its Norman castle. You can lose hours wandering the lanes, particularly when heading downhill from Piazza Doria. The belvedere by the castle is liberally sprinkled with cafes and eateries, but some of the best food in town is found at La Spiga D'Oro, on Via Margherita at the opposite end of the main street. The *spaghetti cacio e pepe* with local pecorino is definitely worth trying. Just over 30 minutes from Caccamo, on the other side of Lake Rosamarina, is Ciminna. Circle the lake on the landward side and you'll reach this town used by Luchino Visconti in his film of Lampedusa's book The Leopard.'

ECSTKZZ/SHUTTERSTOCK ©

Caccamo

The Hilltop Town of Caccamo

A DAY IN A NORMAN CASTLE

It's all about sausages and swashbuckling Norman knights in Caccamo, possibly Sicily's most handsome hilltop town, on a rocky spur of Monte San Calogero some 45km from both Cefalù and Palermo. With walls and fortifications that originally included ingenious traps for intruders who breached the outer perimeter, **Castello di Caccamo** is an evocative blast to 1093. The ghosts of various broken-hearted souls supposedly haunt the hulk of a Norman fortress, and kings, knights and ladies-in-waiting in period dress fill the castle with historical pomp and gaiety during the Castellana di Caccamo festival. In the old grain stores, glorious mountain and river views unfold from the restaurant terrace of **A Castellana**. Sink your teeth into a meaty *salsiccia pasqualora di Caccamo* here or head into town to historical butcher's shop **Antica Macelleria Canzone** at Via XII Novembre 11 where the town's famous pork sausages are still cut and ground by hand.

 WHERE TO STAY IN AN AGRITURISMO

Antico Feudo San Giorgio	**Casale Villa Rainò**	**Azienda Agrituristica Bergi**
Eat and sleep on a farm estate producing organic olives, grain, beef and wine; 30 minutes from Polizzi Generosa. €	Baronial villa-turned-*agriturismo* with 14 rooms, by the medieval town of Gangi. €	Just south of Castelbuono, this family-friendly *agriturismo* is surrounded by olive groves and mountain vistas. €

Fiumara d'Arte Art Trail

ART IN THE WILD

Take an artistic spin along the banks of the Tusa River with this open-air museum showcasing sculptures and contemporary art installations in the wild. Following the course of the Tusa's *fiumara* (riverbed), **Fiumara d'Arte** is a dramatic art-nature mashup – best explored in a day. Kick off your art tour on the coast in **Castel di Tusa**, 25km east of Cefalù. Grab a map of the artworks – marked up with the best route for art enthusiasts in cars, on bicycles and on scooters – at funky art hotel-museum **Atelier Sul Mare** and hit the road.

Feast on Funghi

PICK, EAT & CELEBRATE MUSHROOMS

Join fungus fans in Castelbuono in October at the epicurean town's annual mushroom festival. Main square Piazza Castello, in front of the 14th-century castle soaring above Castelbuono's golden patchwork of houses, is the focal point for three days of foodie fun. Rev up tastebuds for tastings, cookery workshops, live cooking and foraging for wild mushrooms – including the prized *basilisco* – in chestnut and manna ash forests.

Should you be in the Madonie another time of year, experience Castelbuono's mushroom magic at **Ristorante Nangalarruni** where chef Giuseppe Carollo seduces epicureans with *funghi di bosco* (fresh mushrooms) in every guise: *insalatini di funghi* (salad) with locally sourced veg and *burratina*, *zuppa di funghi* (soup) laced with saffron flowers, *funghi gratinati* (gratin) with smoked *caciocavallo* cheese, wild boar with *salsa di funghi,* orange-laced duck with mushrooms and black-pork bacon. Extraordinary wines accompany the unforgettable funghi feast.

The Hilltop Village of Gratteri

FOLKLORE & MEATBALLS

Hunting down a hidden hilltop village more handsome than the last quickly becomes an impossibly addictive pastime in the Madonie mountains. If you stumble upon Gratteri, in the hills 15km south of Cefalù, you might well call it a day. Folkloric tales of monsters, petrified shepherds et al shroud its 13th-century castle, cluster of medieval churches and cave-riddled **Parco della Grotta Grattara** in mystery. Taste the village's traditional *purpietta c'addauru* – meatballs served on laurel leaves – at its Sagra dà Purpietta c'addauru festival in August.

BEST HIKES IN THE PARCO NATURALE REGIONALE DELLE MADONIE

Pizzo Carbonara
Classic ascent of Monti Madonie's highest peak (1979m), on a 6km loop (3hr) from Piano Battaglia.

Pizzo Caterineci
Enjoy clear-day views of Pizzo Carbonara and Mt Etna on this loop above Petralia Soprana (5hr); guide required.

Vallone Madonna degli Angeli
Spectacular views on this 8km (2.5hr) loop; the signposted trailhead is 7km southwest of Piano Battaglia, along the SP119.

SALSICCIA PASQUALORA

Named after the ancient custom of preserving some of the pork from the family pig slaughtered before Pasqua (Easter) to eat later in the year, the *pasqualora* sausage is a Sicilian icon. Caccoma's are among the island's best. See The Food Scene (p32) for more.

WHERE TO EAT LOCAL & EXCEPTIONALLY WELL

A Fuoco Lento
Intimate stone-walled address in Cipampini, 10km south of Petralia Soprana. €€

Da Salvatore
Salvatore Ruvutuso, his wife Maria and two children run this Slow Food–acclaimed trattoria in Petralia Soprana. €

Ristoro dello Scioattolo
Cosy up by the fireplace or enjoy panoramic views from the outdoor deck at this Piano Battaglia favourite, at 1600m. €

CAPO D'ORLANDO

The coast's busiest resort town after Cefalù, Capo d'Orlando was founded – so legend says – when one of Charlemagne's generals called Orlando stood on the *capo* (headland) and declared it a fine spot to build a castle. In 1299 Frederick II of Aragon was defeated here by the rebellious baron Roger of Lauria, backed up by the joint forces of Catalonia and Anjou. Modern-day rebels include the town's shopkeepers and traders, who made a name for themselves in the 1990s with their stand against the Mafia's demands for *pizzo* (protection money).

Fortress ruins still dot the headland and a climb up rewards with a panorama of the town and its sandy and shingle beaches; those to the east, with enchanting views of the Aeolian Islands, are the best for swimming. Northwards are green sweeps of citrus groves, cultivated by lemon and lime farmers on the fertile alluvial plain here since the 1890s and celebrated for their exceptional quality of fruit.

TOP TIP

To explore afloat, rent stand-up paddle boards from the Sunset beach club, midway along the main beach. New Happygo, by the beachfront tourist office at Lungomare Andrea Doria 15, rents bicycles, 50cc scooters and four-wheel pedal carts.

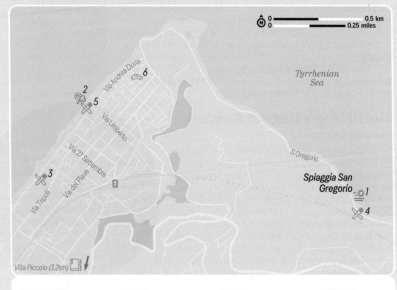

HIGHLIGHTS	SIGHTS	EATING	SLEEPING
1 Spiaggia San Gregorio	**2** Sunset Beach Club	**3** Doria 66 **4** Gelateria Sapore di Sale **5** Sunset	**6** New Happygo

REDA&CO/GETTY IMAGES ©

Spiaggia San Gregorio

Charming Spiaggia San Gregorio
SWIMMING, SNORKELLING & TOMBSTONING

Hang out for the day with one of the most charmed spots on the entire Tyrrhenian Coast. From the seafront in Capo d'Orlando, it's a half-hour walk north along Lungomare Andrea Doria and past the lighthouse on the windy cape to quaint seaside hamlet San Gregorio. En route, steps cut down from the coastal road to a succession of teeny shingle beaches. Framed by Dali-esque rocky outcrops and spoiling with unmatched views of the Aeolian Islands, these hidden beaches promise romance in spades – Spiagge 8, 10 and 15 are extra gorgeous.

The Fantastical Villa Piccolo
FOIBLES OF THE ECCENTRIC ARISTOCRACY

Learn what made Palermo's aristocracy tick at this whimsical 19th-century summer villa which the Piccolo di Calanovella family – cousins of novelist Giuseppe Tomasi di Lampedusa – moved to in 1930. Much of its belle époque interior remains unchanged and a guided tour (booking required; www.fondazionepiccolo.it) unveils black-and-white photographs, ceramics, paintings and furnishings celebrating each family member's brilliant eccentricity. Esoteric artworks by painter Casimiro Piccolo, who wandered the grounds at night in search of fantastical elves and fairies; and the pet cemetery, created by keen botanist Agata Giovanna for the family's beloved dogs and cats, are colourful highlights. Watch for summertime jazz concerts in its gardens, bursting with rare flora.

WHEN LIFE GIVES YOU LEMONS

Take part in the olive harvest, hone your lemon-picking skills and learn precisely how to taste olive oil at family-run **Azienda Agricola Paparoni Agricontura** (www.vacanzecapodorlando.com). A 15-minute drive inland from the Capo d'Orlando beachfront, this dreamy *agriturismo* (farmstay) is organic and encourages sustainable living in its six self-catering cottages on the estate. Guests can buy farm veggies, eggs, Smeraldo di Contura olive oil and other produce, and lend a hand on the farm – different varieties of lemons are harvested all year. The farm, dating from the 1950s, uses solar energy to irrigate its 35 acres of citrus groves and olive trees – 7000 trees in all.

 WHERE TO EAT & DRINK IN CAPO D'ORLANDO

Sunset
Poke bowls, wraps, sushi, DJ sets and cocktails match every mood at Capo d'Orlando's best beach club. €

Dorio 66
Impeccable service and excellent fish and seafood pack out Capo d'Orlando's top seafront restaurant. €€

Gelateria Sapore di Sale
Linger over coffee and saffrn-spiced amaretto gelato at this nautical-styled gelateria in San Gregorio.

Beyond Capo d'Orlando

A hilltop castle looking out to sea and a clandestine collection of mountain villages await those who linger around Capo d'Orlando.

From Capo d'Orlando, the train line zips along the coast east to Milazzo and beyond. For most visitors, the prime reason for setting foot in the busy port town is to sail to the dreamy Aeolian Islands from swanky hydrofoil docks. But away from its refineries and industrial port development, Milazzo soothes and surprises with its unassuming small-town vibe, magnificent hilltop castle and pretty Borgo Antico (Old Town) dotted with small shops and family-run eateries. Inland, nature lovers and outdoor-action fiends can hit the road running in the Monti Nebrodi (Nebrodi Mountains) – an exquisite wilderness of spectacular landscapes, moody peaks and largely forgotten villages where time really does stand still.

TOP TIP

In the rural Nebrodi, opt for an *agriturismo* (farm stay) – the glimpse of rural life and farm-fuelled homemade cooking is priceless.

View from Santuario Rupestre di Sant'Antonio da Padova

MARCO CRUPI/SHUTTERSTOCK ©

Walk the Capo Milazzo

CAPE TO CASTLE URBAN WALK

If you don't have a car, take a taxi north along Strada Pan-oramica to Capo Milazzo, the isthmus that juts out north of town. Park on Piazza Belvedere and continue on foot, past hedgerows of prickly pears and weathered dry stone walls, towards the lighthouse. After an olive grove the footpath narrows and plunges down to rock-fringed pool **Piscina di Venere**. Separated by a small ring of rocks from the ultra-marine Mediterranean, this much-romanticised shallow pool is a popular swimming spot, but sunbathing on the rocks is shadeless and bum-numbing.

Returning to Piazza Belvedere (20 minutes), admire the evocative remains of 13th-century church **Santuario Rup-estre di Sant'Antonio da Padova**, clinging to the cactus-covered hillside overlooking Capo Milazzo's crystal-clear waters. San Antonio da Padova sought refuge here after a shipwreck in 1221.

Allow an hour for the 5km walk back to town. The inland SP72 brings you directly to **Castello di Milazzo**. Frederick II built the enormous fortress in 1239 and Charles V of Ara-gon expanded it to fit in the entire town. Clamber around its crumbling fortifications and exhibition halls, drinking in dreamy views of the bay and the Aeolians at sea.

Into the Nebrodi Mountains

A TASTE OF MOUNTAIN ADVENTURE

Several routes wind across the Nebrodi ranges, weaving through tiny mountain hamlets and steep, forested slopes. The SS116 starts on the coast at Capo d'Orlando and climbs to **Floresta** (1275m), the highest village in the park, where you can stop for local olives, cheeses and meats at **Alimen-tari Giuseppe Calabrese** on the main square. From here, the road makes a spectacular descent to **Randazzo**. Views of Mt Etna are unforgettable.

PARCO REGIONALE DEI NEBRODI

The lovely, off-the-beaten-track Nebrodi Regional Park, traversed by the 70km-long Dorsale dei Nebrodi hiking trail, constitutes Sicily's largest forested area. Its undulating landscape shelters the remnants of Sicily's wildlife: porcupines, San Fratello horses, wildcats and birds of prey. Bird-watchers can peacefully observe herons and stilts on back-country Lago di Biviere, and the occasional golden eagle, peregrine falcon and griffon vulture circling the park's highest peak Monte Soro (1847m). Lower pastures hide a handful of remote, traditional villages where agricultural communities harvest mushrooms and hazelnuts, churn out creamy ricotta and graze cows, sheep, horses, goats and Nebrodi's signature black pig.

GETTING AROUND

Milazzo train station is in the sticks 3.5km southeast of the port and town centre. The few buses linking the two don't tally with train times; budget €15 for a taxi and hardball if drivers try to charge you more.

Buy tickets for the Aeolian Islands in advance, particularly in high season when hydrofoils and ferries fill up fast. Main operators Liberty Lines and Siremar have ticket desk inside Milazzo's port building on Via dei Mille.

Don't even consider exploring the Nebrodi mountains without your own wheels (or serious hiking boots) and a stomach of steel.

Lipari (front; p130) and Vulcano (behind; p136). Right: Pollara (p138), Salina

AEOLIAN ISLANDS

SLOW ESCAPES & OUTDOOR ADVENTURES

Rising from blue seas off Sicily's northeastern coast, the Unesco-protected Aeolians are a slice of paradise. Think relaxation, outdoor fun and restorative exploration in pristine nature.

Boats yo-yo across the big blue from Milazzo to this seven-island archipelago year round. But it's May to September that visitors seeking la dolce vita flock to this prized part of Sicily in droves. With its gin-clear waters, whitewashed villages and honey-sweet wine, life doesn't get much sweeter than this.

The largest island, Lipari, is the springboard for island-hopping, and each island has its own character and quirks. Boat-tour operators at Lipari's main dock tout one-day excursions taking in multiple islands – resist the urge to dash around and devote the time you have to exploring one or two islands properly. With its lush vineyards, caper fields and island-sourced eco-kitchens, Salina entices gourmets and famously spectacular sunsets in fishing hamlet Pollara. Vulcano is an excellent introduction to the archipelago's volcanic heritage, and to really get away from it all, head to Filicudi or Alicudi.

This ancient archipelago of submerged volcanoes bares its soul around Stromboli. Legend has it that wind god Aeolus and other mythological deities had a hand in the Aeolian's marvellous creation. But a guided hike up charred, blackened slopes on Stromboli cuts straight through the postcard gloss. Overcoming volcanic explosions, fire, floods and mudslides is part of everyday life for islanders from these fragile lands whose extraordinary resilience, endurance and creativity becomes all too apparent when you spend more than a few hours here.

THE MAIN AREAS

LIPARI
Lively port, island-hopping paradise p130

STROMBOLI
Volcanic adventure and wild nature p141

Find Your Way

Rising out of cobalt-blue waters off Sicily's northeastern coast, this seven-island volcanic archipelago peppers 1600 sq km in the Tyrrhenian Sea. Most arrive from Milazzo on the Sicilian 'mainland'. Getting around is an ode to slow travel.

AEOLIAN ISLANDS

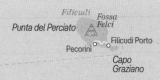

Filicudi *Fossa Felci*

Punta del Perciato

Filicudi Porto

Pecorini

Capo Graziano

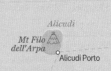

Alicudi

Mt Filo dell'Arpa

Alicudi Porto

Tyrrhenian Sea

BOAT

Liberty Lines (www.libertylines.it) runs frequent hydrofoils connecting all seven islands; cheaper, slower ferries ply the same routes. Services are most frequent June to September and reduced in winter, when heavy seas affect schedules and sensitive stomachs. Island boat taxis are handy for accessing remote beaches and caves.

BUS & TAXI

Lipari, Vulcano and Salina are the only islands with significant road networks; local buses can help you explore, but services are limited. On car-free Stromboli and Panarea, vintage three-wheeled vehicles called Apes and nippy electric golf carts provide an efficient taxi service.

CAR & SCOOTER

Book rental cars and scooters (50cc and 125cc) on Lipari and Salina well in advance to ensure you bag wheels; helmets are provided but locals don't necessarily wear them. Car rental can be pricey.

Stromboli, p141

Black beaches and
sunset volcano hikes
entice nature lovers
to this captivating,
resilient island where
daily life is tough.
Manicured, fashionista
Panarea is a boat ride
away.

Stromboli ○☼ San Vincenzo
○ (Stromboli Town)

Ginostra

*Tyrrhenian
Sea*

Basiluzzo

Punto del San
Corvo Pietro
Panarea
Punta Milazzese

Salina Capo
Malfa Faro
Valdichiesa Santa Marina Salina
○Leni
inella ○ Lingua

Acquacalda
Quattropani ○ ○Porticello
Lipari
○Canneto
Belvedere ⚲Lipari Town
Quattrocchi 🏛 Castello
Spiaggia di Lipari
Valle Muria

Capo Grosso ○Porto di Levante
Capo Grillo
Mt Rosso
Capo Secco ○Piano
○Gelso
Vulcano

Lipari, p130

A perfect island-hopping base, the
Aeolian's largest, liveliest island is
an easy sell: pebble beaches, tasty
dining, attractive shopping and a
rugged hinterland to explore on foot.

Capo
Milazzo

⊕ 0 ___ 10 km
N 0 ___ 6 miles

● Milazzo

Plan Your Time

This archipelago is all about feasting on ridiculously good-looking coastal views, remote beaches and seafaring home cooking. Finding a view, meal or strip of sand better than the last can become an obsession.

Lipari (p130)

If you only do one thing

● Devote the day to **Lipari** (p130), which mixes small-town attractions with hidden beaches and caves evoking the islands' sought-after escapism vibe. Alighting at Marina Lunga, grab a coffee at historic **Pasticceria Subba** (p133), then hit the hilltop **Castello di Lipari** (p131) and **archaeological museum** (p131) – superb bilingual displays provide the best introduction to island history, geology and volcanology. Grab lunch at **Gilberto e Vera** (p132) and spend the afternoon on **Spiaggia Valle Muria** (p132). Shop for souvenirs on Corso Vittorio Emanuele II during a late-afternoon *passeggiata,* before *aperitivo* at waterfront **D'Ambra** (p133) and dinner at **Kasbah** (p134).

Seasonal highlights

Summer is sizzling hot and can be uncomfortably humid. Spring and summer's tail end are ideal for hiking, swimming and diving.

MARCH

Candlelit processions, a crucifixion re-enactment, barefoot penitent parade and fireworks mark Easter in Lipari.

APRIL

The first capers are hand-picked on the islands of Salina and Filicudi; the harvest continues until August.

MAY

Perfect hiking on Aeolian trails, with sunny, breezy days and exuberant wildflowers. Wild orchids pepper trails on Lipari.

Three days to travel around

● Spend your first day in **Lipari** (p130), and then take a hydrofoil to **Stromboli** (p141); overnight at **Hotel Villaggio Stromboli** (p142). Explore the volcanic island's **black beaches** (p142) by day, with lunch at **Punta Lena** (p143) or **TerraNera** (p143). Later, shop for an evening picnic at **La Bottega del Marano** before hooking up with Magmatrek for a guided trek to the volcano's **Sciara del Fucco Viewpoint** (p142) at 400m. Third day, sail to **Panarea** (p145) for a dose of fashionista island life – bring your swimmers for the coastal walk to the **prehistoric village** (p145) vestiges above Cala Junco.

When you have more time

● After three days on Lipari and Stromboli, sail to the Aeolians' greenest island, **Salina** (p137). Spend a morning in beach hamlet **Lingua** (p138), tasting the island's sweet dessert wine with the Hauner family at their winery and scoffing some of Sicily's best *granita* and brioche at **Da Alfredo** (p138). End the day with a hot-spring soak in a traditional adobe-walled steam house at **Hotel Signum** (p136), followed by dinner in its Michelin-starred, zero-km restaurant. If you have the time (and leg power), don't miss the seriously steep but spectacular hike up the steps on old-world **Alicudi** (p140).

JUNE
Flowering caper bushes colour rocky plains and cliffs with bursts of purple and white. Midsummer means extra-long days.

JULY
Eco-fest Festa di Teatro Ecologico takes to the stage on Stromboli: 10 days of theatre, dance and music using no electricity.

AUGUST
Holidaying Italians arrive. Salina's grape harvest begins and wild fennel, oregano, basil, mint and rosemary perfume kitchens.

SEPTEMBER
Balmy weather for swimming, with still-warm seas and no crowds. This is the best month for volcanic walks on Stromboli.

LIPARI

Home to some 12,000 islanders year-round – double in summer – lively Lipari is the Aeolians' largest and most accessible island. For first-time visitors, stepping off the boat from the Sicilian 'mainland' in bijou port Marina Lunga is a relaxing introduction to laid-back island life. If you're returning from the outer Aeolians, the intrusive din of screeching *motorini* (scooters) and shouting street touts at the harbour pushing boat trips is reminiscent of landing in a big city.

Lipari town was settled by the Greeks and destroyed by an earthquake in 365 CE. Its pastel-coloured waterfront and car-free main street today belies its standing as the archipelago's transport hub. A dozen volcanoes sculpted the island's windswept highlands, precipitous cliffs and rugged Mediterranean *macchia* (scrubland), and many islanders still mete out a living selling pumice stones and jewellery embedded with glassy deep-black obsidian extracted from ancient volcanic deposits on the island's northeastern coast.

TOP TIP

A tour of the island takes about an hour by rental car or scooter. With more time, hike or use buses and private minivans: check bus schedules, including for pebble beaches on the island's northeast coast such as Spiaggia di Canneto at the port.

HIGHLIGHTS
1 Belvedere Quattrocchi
2 Castello di Lipari
3 Osservatorio Geofisico
4 Spiaggia Valle Muria

SIGHTS
5 Cattedrale di San Bartolomeo
6 Museo Archeologico Eoliano
7 Pianoconte
8 Quattropani

ACTIVITIES, COURSES & TOURS
9 Nesos

EATING
10 Pasticceria Subba

Shopping
11 Fratelli Laise

130

Cattedrale di San Bartolomeo

Historic Castello di Lipari

FIVE MILLENNIA OF ANCIENT HISTORY

After 'red beard' pirate Barbarossa rampaged through Lipari in 1544, murdering most of the town's menfolk and enslaving its women, the island's Spanish overlords sensibly fortified the settlement. It is in their impressive clifftop citadel Castello di Lipari (1556) that island history comes alive.

Approach the citadel on **Via del Concordato**, a steep photogenic stairway that climbs up from central Via Garibaldi (opposite No 104) to **Cattedrale di San Bartolomeo**. A beautiful example of 17th-century baroque architecture, the Aeolians' 'mother church' replaced the 11th-century Norman cathedral also destroyed by the ruthless Barbarossa. Head next door to 18th-century Palazzo Vescovile (Bishop's Palace), home to the prehistory section of the top-drawer **Museo Archeologico Regionale Eoliano**. Unravel Lipari's intriguing backstory, from early Neolithic settlers to Roman Lipára, through trichrome painted pottery, copper and bronze artefacts, lava-stone votive offerings, marble carvings and finely sculpted tools handcrafted from obsidian.

THE LIPARI PAINTER

In the ancient Greek empire, prized pottery came from Lipari. Vases containing jewellery, cosmetics and other grave goods to be placed in the sarcophagus with the deceased were formed in terracotta and painted with increasingly intricate patterns. By the 4th century BCE ceramists were illustrating sophisticated stories of the deceased (always female) preparing for the marriage of their soul to a divinity. One such master was the Lipari Painter who, between 300 and 260 BCE, painted elaborate compositions on ceramics in rich earthy colours. His signature was an egg-shaped motif, from which laurel branches burst forth. His pupils – the Dove Painter, the Falcone Painter, the Swan Painter – in turn each had their own distinctive trademarks.

 WHERE TO STAY IN LIPARI TOWN

Grand Hotel Arciduca & Residence Villa Fiorentina
Tranquillity is assured at this pool-clad twinset with lush garden. €€

Hotel Villa Augustus
Vintage photos and knick-knacks evoke island life in the 1950s at this flower-festooned old-timer near the port. €

Casajanca
Boutique hotel with 10 rooms and natural thermal water pool, by Canneto beach. €€

HOLGS/GETTY IMAGES ©

Corso Vittorio Emanuele II

BEST DIVING SPOTS

Punta della Castagna
A spectacular dive with a 10m white pumice platform interrupted by multicoloured channels (difficult; depth 10m to 40m).

Pietra Menalda
See the homes of octopuses, eels, groupers and other sea critters on the southern side of the island (medium; depth 18m to 40m).

Pietra del Bagno
Circumnavigate the Bagno rock, while witnessing colourful rock surfaces and sea life (all levels; 20m to 40m).

La Parete dei Gabbiani
A black-and-white dive: black lava rock streaked with white pumice stone, cracks in which are home to lobsters (medium; 20m to 45m).

The archeological museum romps through six further citadel buildings. Shipwrecked amphorae, the world's largest collection of miniature Greek theatrical masks and exquisite painted ceramics from the Greek necropolis of Lipari steal the show in the Sezione Classica. A riveting portrait of the Aeolians' oldest industries – the extraction of sulphur on Vulcano and of alum, pumice and obsidian on Lipari – and its volcanoes unfolds in the Sezione Vulcanologica. Break between sections in the tree-shaded archaeology garden, littered with remounted sarcophagi from the 4th and 5th centuries BCE. Catching a summer performance with sea view at the open-air amphitheatre here is a treat.

Swim at Spiaggia Valle Muria

A DAY AT THE BEACH

Cradled by cliffs and sun-spangled emerald waters, this pebbly beach on Lipari's southwestern shore is a dramatically beautiful swimming and sunbathing spot. The journey is also memorable. The signposted turn-off, 3km west of Lipari town, is easily reached by car or scooter, but it's far more fun to bus it there and sail back. From the road, the final leg

 WHERE TO EAT IN LIPARI TOWN

Osteria Liparota
Tuck into burrata with island figs and anchovies or seared tuna at this jovial *osteria* with tables in a line on the street. €€

L'Anfora
Don't miss the sea-fresh specials – any dish starring Mazara prawns is superb – at this alley-hidden *ristorante*. €€

Gilberto e Vera
Well-stuffed *panini* named after customers embrace every mood at this family-run icon near Marina Corta. €

down to the beach is a steep, 25-minute downhill hike through a rugged landscape of long grass, wildflowers and cacti. Return by sea with local boat captain Barni – find him at the beach kiosk – or another boat taxi; there are always several on the quays at Lipari's Marina Corta (book ahead). Navigating the *faraglione* (rock towers) of the island's western shore at sunset, with Vulcano's crater smoking on the horizon, is unforgettable.

The Osservatorio & Quattrocchi Viewpoints

ISLAND PANORAMAS AT SUNSET

Near Lipari's southwesternmost tip, observation platform **Osservatorio Geofisico** commands unparalleled views south to Vulcano and Mt Etna, and west into a dizzyingly steep ravine backed by Alicudi and Filicudi at sunset. Park at the end of the road and follow the dirt path onto the headland. On the road to Pianoconte, celebrated viewpoint **Belvedere Quattrocchi** (Four Eyes) cooks up giddying views of cliffs plunging into the sea, while smoke plumes rise from the dark heights of neighbouring Vulcano in the distance. Sunset at either is celestial.

A Lipari Passeggiata

CAKES, CAPERS, WINE & JEWELS

Around 4pm when the beach crowd rolls back into town and shops reopen after the lunchtime siesta, join the crowds on pedestrian Corso Vittorio Emanuele II for a traditional *passeggiata*. Cafe terraces buzz with holidaymakers sipping spritz and spooning mulberry *granita,* and locals chinwag over coffee and *dolci* at 1930s **Pasticceria Subba** (No 90). Buckets of salt-preserved *capperi* (capers) and *cucunci* (caper flowers) tempt at **Fratelli Laise** (No 118); sweet Malvasia wines, grappa and Aeolian *limoncello* inside the vintage grocery-deli are equally irresistible.

Islanders have carved obsidian – nicknamed 'black gold' but actually volcanic glass formed by solidifying magma – into knives and utensils since prehistoric times. Head east along Via Maurolico onto shop-lined Via Giuseppe Garibaldi where Francesco Bertè at **I Gioelli del Mare** sets obsidian in exquisite jewellery pieces. The artisan goldsmith also smelts gold in lava rocks at over 1000°C to create unique handmade Aeolian pendants and rings.

BEST APERITIVO BARS

D'Ambra
Live music and tiered cake stands of complimentary snacks pack Marina Corta's most fashionable waterfront bar.

Giardino di Lipari
Fairy lights between trees add late-night magic to this trendy walled-garden lounge.

Cafè La Precchia
Breakfast to nightcaps, this people-watching address buzzes all day long.

Club White Beach
Hit pebble beach Spiaggia di Bianca, a taxi-boat ride away, for daytime chilling, happy-hour drinks and discos on the sand.

E Pulera
A serene garden setting, tile-topped tables and exquisite traditional cuisine assure romance in spades. €€

Trattoria del Vicolo
Chef Giuseppe cooks up a top-notch *busiate* with swordfish, aubergine and mint at this gourmet trattoria. €€

Filippino
Going strong for over a century, this glass pavilion is widely considered the island's finest restaurant. €€

WANDER AEOLIAN PATHWAYS

Centuries-old mule tracks, steep footpaths and dry-stone walls stray across the island's rugged interior. Where only farmers once trod to reach isolated vineyards, terraced olive groves and caper fields, hikers now explore. Signage can be erratic and it's best to walk with a naturalist guide or conservation biologist from Nesos (www.nesos.org). The local environmental organisation sells the excellent hiking guide 15 Best Walks in the Aeolian Islands (€7) and arranges guided bird-watching and botanical walks, archaeology treks and mountain-bike tours (minimum five people, reserve in advance).

Shop at Mollo Tutto

BEEN THERE, BOUGHT THE ECO T-SHIRT

Buy a T-shirt or hoodie at the flagship store of Lipari designer Natalie Rossi's wildly popular sustainable fashion brand at Corso Vittorio Emanuele II 83. Born from a desire to *'mollare tutto'* or 'drop everything', Mollo Tutto captures the Aeolians' carefree lifestyle in tops blazing liberating mottos like *'Mollo tutto vivo in barca'* ('Drop everything live on a boat'). Fabrics are made from recycled fishing nets and the brand collaborates with Italy's marine-environmental non-profit Marevivo to clean beaches and recuperate discarded fishing materials.

Vibrant Via Nuovo

STREET ART & CREATIVE GARDEN CUISINE

Cut from snippets of magazines from the 1920s to 1950s, the retro street collages of Sicilian street artist Demetrio Di Grado (b. 1976) are easy to identify: he blots out the eyes of his bold, often life-sized or larger figures with a hashtag-on-black reflecting his social or political message. You can find a couple at Marina Corta, but Di Grado's finest pieces colour narrow Via Nuovo. This tiny alley also squirrels away the garden entrance to candlelit **Kasbah**, another superb artwork with wine bottles in buckets strung from the bamboo awning and mismatched tableware from yesteryear. The trendy kitchen's shared cheese and salami chopping boards, wood-fired pizzas, pasta and dishes incorporating local swordfish (fresh between May and September) are equally creative.

Pianoconte to Quattropani

VILLAGE TO VILLAGE HIKE

From the village school in Pianoconte, 5km west of Lipari town, pick up the trailhead for this scenic, three- to four-hour hike – strenuous climbs and steep descents reward with spectacular views of the big blue and outer Aeolians from coastal bluffs on Lipari's western shoreline. As you descend from Pianoconte towards the sea, spot the old Roman baths of San Calogero, famous in antiquity for the thermal spring that flowed at a constant temperature of 60°C. Climbing up to the village of Quattropani, you'll also pass the visible remnants of an old kaolin mine in the scarred hillside.

 GETTING AROUND

Many hotels outside of Lipari town include transfer from the port in their rates; if they don't, they can arrange a minivan pick-up. Beach restaurants and bars can give you the name and mobile telephone number of taxi boats they work with; otherwise find taxi boats at Marina Corta and Molo di Canneto. Book ahead by phone.

March to October, a lineup of kiosks at Marina Lunga and numerous agencies in town sell tickets for organised day trips to other Aeolian islands. It's also easy to DIY: buy tickets at least a couple of days ahead in high season, either online or at the Liberty Lines ticket office at Marina Lunga.

Download the smartphone app to buy tickets for local Urso buses (www.ursobus.it).

Beyond Lipari

Island-hopping around the western Aeolians is a treat for seafaring adventurers sailing off into the Tyrrhenian Sea.

TOP TIP

Reserve scooters, rental cars and taxis before arrival. Few outlets stock bikes; where roads exist, they're steep and perilously narrow.

While the island of Lipari has a generous share of crystalline waters and beautifully remote beaches, most visitors can't resist a boat trip to another Aeolian island. Salina (20 minutes north by hydrofoil) and Vulcano (10 minutes south) are each close enough to fit into separate half-day jaunts from Lipari – although both warrant far longer. Compact Alicudi and Filicudi, far-flung in the west and about 30 minutes apart by boat, make an obvious pairing for a one-day excursion. Wherever you choose to sail to, set your compass for spectacular vistas and whitewashed villages, dazzling black-sand beaches, naturally sustainable marine cuisine and a privileged sprinkling of offbeat adventure.

Pollara (p138), Salina

ANTONIO BUSIELLO/GETTY IMAGES ©

GIUMA/SHUTTERSTOCK ©

Pozza dei Fanghi, Vulcano

AEOLIAN ECO-PADDLES

Explore Aeolian coastlines, caves and beaches from a different perspective – afloat a sea kayak or stand-up paddleboard, during the day, at sunset or by night. From his home base on Vulcano, passionate kayaker, guide and eco-warrior Eugenio Viviani at **Sicily in Kayak** leads half-day, day and multiday expeditions around the different islands. Sea adventurers eager to dip, duck and dive can combine paddling with swimming, snorkelling and coasteering (rock scrambling, climbing and diving) on a sit-on-top kayak trip. If you're an eco-paddler, sign up for one of Eugenio's beach cleanups by kayak – he organises four full weekends a year dedicated to cleaning up beaches in Vulcano and Lipari.

Scoot Around Vulcano

TWO-WHEEL ROAD TRIP

Stepping off the hydrofoil at the port, the overpowering bad-egg reek instantly makes you question the wisdom of a day trip to this volcanically active island. Rest assured, away from the hydrofoil dock the vile pong of sulphurous fumes emanating from the island's dramatically smoking crater dissipates.

Head south along the waterfront, past kiosks selling boat tours to iridescent sea cave **Grotta del Cavallo** and natural swimming pool **Piscina di Venere**. Turn right along Via Provinciale to rent wheels at **Luigi Rent** (www.nolosprintdaluigi.com). The island is only 20.9 sq km but surprisingly hilly, so you're probably best with a classic Italian, Hepburn-style scooter or e-bike (Luigi's open-sided Mini Mokes are hot too). If you've forgotten your snorkel, hiking boots or want to dump your rucksack for the day, this is the place.

Hit the main road south, cruising sinuously uphill for 7km to **Capo Grillo**. The island panorama from this breathtaking viewpoint – of Lipari and Salina, with Panarea, Stromboli and Filicudi floating in the distance – is unmatched. Continue south to the minuscule fishing port of Gelso. Lunch on the

 WHERE TO STAY & EAT ON SALINA

Hotel Ravesi
Family-run hotel on Malfa's town square with a grassy lounge-bar area and an infinity pool overlooking the sea. €€

Hotel Signum
Michelin-starred eco-dining and sensational spa make this Malfa retreat the island's top boutique address. €€€

Agriturismo Al Cappero
Simple rooms on a caper farm in Pollara, with terrace serving Sicilian home cooking and sensational sunset views. €

morning's catch at family-run **Trattoria da Pina** and enjoy a siesta and afternoon swim on black-sand **Spiaggia Cannitello**. Returning north to Porto di Ponente, taste island wine with passionate winemaker and artist Giuseppe Livio at **Soffio sulle Isole**. Sunset *aperitivo* at this beautiful vineyard estate, glass of volcanic red or sweet Malvasia in hand, is out of this world.

Dine at Il Cappero

GASTRONOMY WITH A VIEW

Reserve a table well in advance at gastronomic hot spot Il Cappero, inside five-star Therasia Resort on Vulcano's northeastern coast. This is a rare spot in the archipelago where you can admire all the other islands in a single panorama. A 10-course menu celebrating island produce by Michelin-starred, Palermo-born chef Giuseppe Biuso only heightens the excitement.

Hike the Volcanic Island Vulcano

WHITE PUMICE & BLACK SAND

Explore Vulcano on foot and get a sense of daily life for the 700 Vulcanari living on the Aeolians' southernmost island. The smoking volcano towering over their island's northeastern shores last erupted in 1890. 'Gas hazard' street signs – instructing what to do should you stumble upon a dead animal or toxic gas leak – are a stern reminder that the volcano is alive and kicking. Hiking on 391m Fossa di Vulcano, both to its crater and on its lower slopes, is forbidden.

From the port, walk west past the *faraglione* (rock spire) to **Pozza dei Fanghi**. Once the island's favourite beauty and bathing spot, the abandoned pool of coffee-coloured mud and adjacent hot springs bubbling up from the sea are now too hot to dip in. Ten minutes' walk beyond is **Spiaggia Sabbie Nere**, with snack bars on its black sand. From the beach, follow the road across a small isthmus to **Vulcanello** (123m), a bulb of land spewed out by a volcanic eruption in 183 BCE. Count 1.8km – the final 600m up a spectacular white pumice-dust footpath – to the belvedere (viewpoint). Or continue north to **Valle dei Mostri** (Valley of the Monsters), a grotesque group of wind-eroded dark rocks.

Taste Produce in Salina

SALINA CAPERS & HONEY-SWEET WINE

Salina's good fortune is its freshwater springs. It is the only Aeolian island with significant natural sources and

PANE CUNZATO

To taste the best *pane cunzato* in the Aeolian archipelago, reserve a table at **Malvasia**, hidden on a mainly residential street on Vulcano. Charismatic owner Maurizio Pagano spent years selling open-faced sandwiches from a pushcart near the port before opening the legendary garden restaurant. And the plate-sized bread, baked in a wood-fired oven, soaked in island olive oil and piled high with tomatoes, capers, tuna, buffalo-milk mozzarella, local ricotta and other seasonal produce, is well worth the 10-minute walk from the port. If you fall head-over-heels for the handmade tableware, stroll five minutes down the street to Mare del Sud Resort where Sicilian pottery Acitavoli has its boutique.

MALVASIA IN MILAZZO

If you have a hankering for a repeat *pane cunzato* after leaving the island of Vulcano, take heed: there is a second Malvasia, equally memorable, in **Milazzo** (p123).

Nni Lausta
Grape must and Malvasia wines feature on the veggie-rich menu at Santa Maria Salina's most creative table. €€

A Quadara
Seasonal specials and enticing local recipes bag a loyal following for this authentic Aeolian kitchen in Malfa. €€

A Cannata
Fresh seafood, home-grown veggies and herbs at this family-run trattoria steps from Lingua's beachfront. €€

residents on this green, twin-peaked island have put them to good use: they produce their own style of wine, Malvasia, and – as proud Salinari will tell you – the archipelago's finest capers (caper rivalry between islands is fierce).

From port town **Santa Marina Salina**, bus it to the seaside hamlet of **Lingua**, 3km south. Handwritten signs outside islanders' homes advertise homegrown capers, *caperoni* (caper berries), *curcuma* (turmeric) and oregano for sale. Next to the bus stop, look for the trailhead to the Aeolians' highest point **Monte Fossa delle Felci** (962m; 2.5hrs). On lower slopes the trail passes the pea-green vineyards of **Azienda Agricola Carlo Hauner**. Call ahead (☎ 339 7213713) to arrange a winery tour and guided tasting of its classic reds, whites and signature Malvasia delle Lipari Passito DOC with Carlo, Andrea or another family member. Grandfather and painter Carlo Hauner nurtured the first vines in the late 1960s and also painted the original wine-bottle labels – miniature works of art evoking traditional island architecture, the startling greens of Salina's verdant vegetation, sea blues and sunsets. Estate-grown capers and other delicious nibbles accompany tastings – forget dinner afterwards (catch sunset in **Pollara** instead).

Granita Legends

STAY COOL ISLAND-STYLE

If you're on Salina with kids, it's not only the shallow pools formed by the concrete breakwaters on Lingua's Spiaggia Biscotti that will ensure you love this family-friendly island. Across the street from its pebble beach is the lavender-blue terrace of **Da Alfredo**, famed across Sicily for its *granite*. Flavours handcrafted from fruits of the land include pistachio, watermelon, lemon, fig and mulberry. Go local with glass beakers of blackberry *granite* and a basket of brioche – rip off chunks of the sweet bread and dunk in the crushed ice.

The sublime ricotta *granita* with candied capers and toasted capers at **Pa.Pe.Ro** is reason enough to visit bijou fishing hamlet Rinella, on Salina's southern coast.

Villaggio Preistorico di Capo Graziano

HIKE UP TO BRONZE AGE FILICUDI

Among the least developed of the islands, snail-shaped Filicudi is also one of the oldest, with tectonic activity dating

NECTAR OF THE GODS

It is thought that the Greeks brought Malvasia grapes – a name derived from greek city Monemvasia – to Salina in 588 BCE, and the wine is still produced using traditional techniques. Malvasia and Corinto Nero (Black Corinthian) grapes are harvested in mid-September when the grapes are picked and dried in the sun on *cannizzi* (woven reed mats) for 15 to 20 days. This drying process is crucial: the grapes must dry out enough to concentrate the sweet flavour but not too much, which would caramelise them. The result is a sweet, dark-golden or light-amber wine that tastes, some say, of honey – 'nectar of the gods' for the Greeks. The sweet dessert wine is usually drunk in very small glasses and pairs well with cheese, sweet biscuits and almond pastries.

 WHERE TO STAY & EAT ON VULCANO

Hotel Faraglione	**Therasia Resort**	**Mari del Sud Resort**
Location alone renders this two-star, portside hotel exceptional value. €	Dreamy, luxurious resort with utterly divine sea views and exceptional dining. €€€	Four-star resort with expansive Mediterranean gardens and chic rustic interior with decorative ceramics. €€€

EUGENIA STRUK/SHUTTERSTOCK ©

Filicudi

SAVING THE AEOLIAN WALL LIZARD

Common wall lizards are easy to spot on the sun-bathed Aeolians – on hikes you'll see them slinking across your path on numerous occasions. The same cannot be said for the Aeolian wall lizard, indigenous to the island but now critically endangered and reduced to tiny populations on pockets of Vulcano and uninhabited islets offshore from Salina and Filicudi. Similarly sized to a common wall lizard, you'll know if a rare Aeolian wall lizard cross your path – these lizards are black.

back 700,000 years. From the minuscule port on its southeast shore, follow the main road 10 minutes uphill towards Capo Graziano. At the bend, veer off left along a signposted footpath to the cape's *villaggio preistorico* (prehistoric village).

A stiff 20-minute walk rewards with the evocative, lichencovered stone foundations of 27 Bronze Age huts from 1700 BCE, uncovered in 1952 on a terraced hillside. Bilingual signs provide historical context, and the dramatic sea and island views are hypnotic. When you finally manage to tear your eyes away, trace the rocky path back downhill and take the fork through sun-blazed scrub to Filicudi's only real beach **Spiaggia del Porto**. A big smooth pebble affair (highly challenging for sunbathers), this is the easiest swimming on the island – to dip elsewhere, clamber down jagged rocks or rent a boat. South around the cape, sunken wrecks of nine ancient Greek and Roman ships entrance divers in the underwater **Museo Archeologico Sottomarino**.

VOLCANIC TOURISM

Rising temperatures, higher gas emissions and violent storms have all impacted visitor access to the Aeolians' two active volcanoes in recent years (p264) – check updated rules when planning your trip.

La Forgia Maurizio
Sicilian cuisine gets a dash of world spice at this devilishly good restaurant near the port. €€

Trattoria da Pina
Two local men do the fishing and their families do the cooking at this seaside trattoria in Gelso. €€

Maria Tindara
This family-run restaurant 7km south of port is a pleasant antidote to Porto di Levante's tourist-thronged eateries. €€

Pecorini Mare

FISHING-VILLAGE IDYLL ON FILICUDI

If it's an off-grid escape you desire, peppered with sea swims and salt-of-the-earth seafood, Pecorini Mare ticks all the boxes. Colourful fishing boats sit on the pebbly shore of this old-world seaside hamlet on Filicudi's often-overlooked western shore. On the waterfront time appears to stand still. Check into one of five rooms at vintage *pensione* La Sirena and reserve a table on its restaurant terrace – an on-point mix of traditional majolica tiling, flea-market furnishings and contemporary art – just steps from the sea.

Alicudi

ISLAND OF STEPS

Magical and mesmerising, the Aeolians' second-smallest island feels like a mischievous afterthought on the map. As isolated a place as you'll find in the entire Mediterranean basin, the 5.2-sq-km island has no roads – just a relentless succession of time-wizened, volcanic-stone steps staggering mercilessly up to **Monte Montagnola** (675m). This is the kind of place where you have to ask around for rooms or a boat taxi, where you whittle away hours watching fishers unload and clean fish. Old-timer donkeys and mules, boats and wheelbarrows are the only means of transport and lugging stuff around.

Stepping off the hydrofoil at the sleepy port, simply head uphill. Count two hours along the **Filo dell'Arpa** trail of steps to reach Alicudi's central peak; **Chiesa di San Bartolo** marks the hike's midpoint. At the T-intersection up top where the trail dead ends at a stone wall, turn left to circle the crater of the extinct volcano or right to continue to dramatic cliffs at Alicudi's western edge. Near the summit look for Timpone delle Femmine, huge fissures where women are said to have taken refuge during pirate raids. The sea views are beyond heavenly. Back down at the port, cool off in the crystal-clear sea – either from the pebble beach right by the hydrofoil dock or from rocks immediately south.

GETTING AROUND

Of the seven Aeolian islands, Vulcano is closest to mainland Sicily, meaning that Liberty Lines' hydrofoil services are especially frequent: all Lipari-bound boats from Milazzo and Messina stop here first.

When sailing to Salina, check which ferry port you want – the island has two. Boats to Stromboli and Panarea typically stop at Santa Marina Salina (eastern shore); boats from Lipari to Filicudi and Alicudi stop at Rinella (southern shore).

Private boat taxis operated by individual boat captains operate on every island, and are eminently useful for accessing more remote beaches and caves. Call their mobile numbers to reserve.

STROMBOLI

There is something strangely hypnotic about this intoxicating island. Stromboli conforms perfectly to one's childhood idea of a volcano, with its symmetrical, smoking silhouette rising dramatically from the sea. Trekking halfway up the volcano at sunset to watch its nightly firework show makes it a popular day-trip destination. To really appreciate the raw beauty, languid pace and harsh reality of island life here, stay a couple of days.

Volcanic activity has scarred and blackened much of the island, but the northeastern corner is inhabited. It's here you'll find the famous black beaches, whitewashed village squatting along the volcano's lower slopes and family-run kitchens cooking up *spaghetti alla stromboliana* (with wild fennel, mint, anchovies, cherry tomatoes and breadcrumbs). Despite the picture-postcard gloss, life is tough: food and drinking water are ferried in, there are no roads across the island, and electricity only arrived in Ginostra – the diminutive second settlement on Stromboli's west coast – a few years ago.

TOP TIP

Book guided volcano treks to 400m (any higher is off-limits) well before arrival. Weather conditions change quickly and tour details can change last minute. Rent walking boots (you need them), head torch, rucksack and other equipment from Totem Trekking.

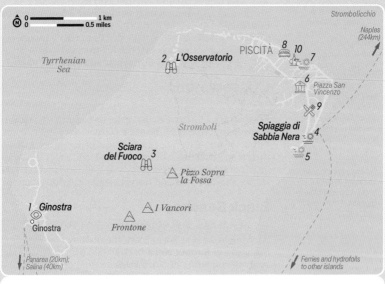

HIGHLIGHTS
1 Ginostra
2 L'Osservatorio
3 Sciara del Fuoco
4 Spiaggia di Sabbia Nera

SIGHTS
5 Forgia Vecchia
6 Red House
7 Spiaggia di Ficogrande

SLEEPING
8 Hotel Villaggio Stromboli

EATING
9 Il Canneto

DRINKING & NIGHTLIFE
10 La Tartana Club

Mario Pruiti,
experienced
volcanologist guide
and Magmatrek co-
founder, was born in the
Nebrodi mountains and
moved to Ginostra on
Stromboli's unexplored
western shore over 30
years ago. He shares
his top tip for island
explorers.

'In Ginostra we have a
beautiful sunset and in
Stromboli, a beautiful
sunrise. In winter there
is more sunshine in
Ginostra – by 3pm in
Stromboli in winter the
sun is gone. The best
spot to watch sunset in
Ginostra is next to the
church or on Punta dei
Corvi. A footpath leads
here from the village to
a beautiful viewpoint,
about 5km away, where
you can see the sunset
and the volcano's
explosions after dark.
Many people come to
Ginostra for a sunset
aperitivo. In winter
about 35 people live in
Ginostra, in summer, it's
about 400.'

Sciara del Fuoco Viewpoints

SUNSET HIKES & CRATER FIREWORKS

The force of nature doesn't get mightier or feel closer than from the nighttime slopes of Stromboli's beloved volcano. Sit on a rock or stand at one of two viewpoints on the lower slopes of the 924m-high volcano to watch spectacular fireworks explode from the hidden crater. The show is more dramatic some nights than others – during active periods, explosions occur every 20 minutes or so and are preceded by a ferocious belly-roar as gases force hot magma into the air. The occasional cascade of red-hot rock crashing down the lava-blackened mountainside into the sea below is breathtakingly spectacular. Linger past nightfall when the volcano's vivid, fire-orange glow burns brighter.

Two viewpoints facing the Sciara del Fuoco – the blackened laval scar running down Stromboli's northern flank – are accessible on foot from Stromboli village. You can hike up to the 290m platform alone, but to access the 400m viewpoint, you need a guide. Informative, small-group treks (8km, five hours) led by a volcanologist guide depart from **Magmatrek**, on Via Vittorio Emanuele near the church, two or three hours before sunset and return around 10pm. Bring a picnic to enjoy at the viewpoint and a torch (flashlight or head torch) for the return hike.

If you plan to DIY to 290m, check the current trail route with local guides. **Stromboli Adventures** (Via Roma 17) also provides a visitor information service, with a family-friendly exhibition on one of the world's most active volcanoes. Volcanic activity is monitored by Florence University's Laboratory of Experimental Geophysics (LGS) in Stromboli; download its View Stromboli app for daily reports and real-time images.

L'Osservatorio

PIZZA & NOCTURNAL FIREWORKS

Feast on pizza by candlelight against a backdrop of volcanic fireworks at Stromboli's favourite garden restaurant. Squatting at the foot of the volcano, 3km west of the village, L'Osservatorio was shut down by flooding and mud slides in August 2022, but at time of writing plans were underway to rebuild the single-lane dust track and footpath leading to the restaurant.

Black Beaches

SEA DIPS, SUNBATHING & LATE-NIGHT COCKTAILS

Arriving by boat at Porto Scari, the inviting black sands of **Spiaggia di Sabbia Nera** beckon. To swim at leisure and sunbathe on a mix of black volcanic sand and pebbles, hit black sand 300m south at **Forgia Vecchia** or 1km north on

 WHERE TO STAY & EAT ON STROMBOLI

Hotel Villaggio Stromboli
A 1950s icon. Rooms with
ceiling fans open onto a
sea-facing courtyard. Private
beach and rooftop terrace. €€

B&B Il Giardino Segreto
The sweet scent of lemon trees
complement sea and volcano
views at this hillside B&B with
'secret garden'. €€

L'Angolo del Pesce
Raw fish spot with party vibes
after dark: sushi burgers, poke
bowls and savoury doughnuts
in a garden of fairy lights. €

Sciara del Fuoco

the island's biggest black beach **Spiaggia di Ficogrande**, with wooden beach huts selling renting sunloungers and parasols. At the beach's northern end, Stromboli's beautiful people hobnob over breakfast coffee, casual lunches and signature cocktails at illustrious piano bar and club **La Tartana**.

Movies Beneath the Stars

STROMBOLI ON THE BIG SCREEN

Explore Stromboli's silver-screen heritage. Ingrid Bergman and Roberto Rossellini lived together in an ochre-red house at Via Vittorio Emanuele 22 while filming Stromboli, Terra di Dio in 1949. Their liaison sparked scandal in the film world – both were married to someone else at the time – and while the house can't be visited, it's fun to see where their illicit affair happened.

Nearby, superb black-and-white photographs of the actors from the 1940s hang on walls in the breakfast room at vintage **Hotel Villaggio Stromboli**. In summer this enchanting, 1950s seaside hotel screens films on its rooftop Terrazza La Dolce Vita. Or make a date beneath the stars with local island hipsters at La Libreria sull'Isola, a bookshop-cum-trendy bar, lounge garden and stage to open-air film screenings, music gigs and other events against a backdrop of Stromboli's volcano.

WHY I LOVE STROMBOLI

Nicola Williams.
@tripalong

Each Aeolian island has its own distinct personality, but it's Stromboli that intrigues the most. Islanders here share a raw, ancestral relationship with their volcano. They live at its ruthless mercy, and it's impossible not to feel its primeval force sizzling off every last volcanic rock and grain of black sand. Stromboli is an island where it's easy to identify locals: barefooted, they stroll nonchalantly across sun-blazed beaches as hot as coals and taxi drivers trundle around in three-wheeled Apes (there are no cars) without shoes.

Il Canneto
This locally loved cafe-*pasticceria*, with elevated terrace on Via Roma, buzzes non-stop. €

Punta Lena
For romance with unmatched sea view, dine on local fish at this sustainably responsible, upscale restaurant. €€

TerraNera
Chef Francesco Tovini heads up Stromboli's classiest dining address, fuelled with island and sea produce. €€€

Beyond Stromboli

The yin to Stromboli's yang, the contrast of glitzy Panarea is wild. Enjoy the difference.

Two islands cut from the same volcanic block couldn't be more different. Panarea, flung in the eastern Aeolians a 30-minute hydrofoil ride from rough-cut Stromboli, is the archipelago's smallest island: it's only 3.34 sq km. It's also the priciest and most densely populated in summer when international jet-setters, Milanese fashionistas and Parisian influencers pour in for an exclusive taste of Sicilian *dolce far niente* (sweet nothing). Luxury yachts fill the tiny harbour and day-trippers pack the whitewashed streets of port town San Pietro to bursting. Visit out of season and you'll be hard-pushed to spot a local, let alone one of the zippy electric golf carts that tear around the island, terrorising any mortal who dare walk two footsteps.

TOP TIP

Car-free Panarea is a strictly summer-only destination. Arrive between November and Easter and you'll find most places closed.

Villaggio Preistorico, Panarea

FRANK LAMBERTI/SHUTTERSTOCK ©

Climb up to Punta del Corvo

WALK IN THE WILD

Don your hiking boots to uncover the less-manicured face of Panarea. Two trails (marked 1 and 2 on local maps) wind past ancient olive groves and dry-stone walls to converge at rocky outcrop Punta del Corvo (421m). Dominating volcanic cliffs on the island's western coast, this is the highest point of the island and views of all six of the neighbouring Aeolian islands are spectacular. Combine both trails to make a scenic full-day walk in the wild. Allow around four hours for the round trip, and be prepared for steep, rocky climbs and descents.

Keep your eyes peeled for springtime candytuft, Boccone's fennel (named after 17th-century Sicilian botanist Paolo Boccone from Palermo) and rare violet Silene hicesiae pushing up between rocks. The latter, endemic to Panarea and Alicudi, was discovered in the 1980s. In spring and summer Eleonora falcons and other raptors helicopter wildly overhead.

The Headland of Punta Milazzese

BRONZE AGE PANAREA

Arriving at the port, bear left along the waterfront and up the stone ramp towards San Pietro's village centre to pick up ceramic wall signs for Panarea's **Villaggio Preistorico** – archaeological vestiges of a prehistoric village dramatically built on a cliff-like headland in the 15th century BCE. The 45-minute walk – via **Spiaggetta Zimmari**, the island's only sandy beach – is a great excuse to peek over high whitewashed walls into manicured villa gardens; watch for speeding golf-cart taxis. Midway, break at ochre-cottage **Museo Diffusio** to explore a terraced Mediterranean garden perfumed with fig, olive and carob trees. Directly below the prehistoric village, steps head down to **Cala Junco**, a gorgeous little cove with a rocky beach and aquamarine waters.

BEST FASHIONABLE STOPS & PHOTO OPPS

Basiluzzo
Charter a private boat to visit this uninhabited islet, given over to caper cultivation.

Dattilo
Drop anchor at this dramatic islet's southwestern tip to dip in pretty swimming spot of Le Guglie.

Buganville
Chic boutique to pick up must-have Borsalino sun hats, Castañer espadrilles and handmade Sicilian straw bags.

Bridge Ammare
Ultimate beach-chic lounge bar and restaurant, this shimmering white villa gazes out – shades on – over Baie Zimmari.

Il Bar del Porto
A chic young crowd pack out the terrace of this portside bar, the place to be seen.

 WHERE TO EAT IN PEACE IN PANAREA

Da Francesco
At the port, this is a laid-back trattoria with fish-focused menu and Stromboli views from its upstairs terrace. €€

Trattoria La Sirena
Away from the glitzy port crowd, enjoy drinks, *panini* and *granite* beneath a bamboo awning in a peaceful garden. €

Cusiritati
Since 1970, three generations of women from the same family have run this classy spot. Phenomenal seafood. €€€

IONIAN COAST

BETWEEN MYTH & HISTORY

Vibrant cities, hillside villages, magnificent nature, myths and history: experience the unforgettable energy of the Ionian coast.

The Ionian coast is awash with some of Sicily's most impressive places. Our journey begins at the Strait of Messina overlooking a sea full of myths. Here lived the fearsome Scylla and Charybdis who swallowed passing ships. Around Messina you'll find magnificent nature and ancient villages where life still flows to the rhythms of the past.

Mighty Mt Etna watches over the inhabitants of the coast and is considered a benevolent mother who makes the soil fertile and, at the same time, an evil stepmother who could destroy everything (for local people, Etna is female). If you're lucky, you'll be in the area during an eruption – don't worry, it's all spectacle. Enjoy a climb to the craters or a walk through woods interrupted by ancient lava flows. Exceptional wines are produced on the volcanic soil, so be sure to take a wine tour to taste them all.

There is a spectacular view of Etna from the sun-drenched clifftop resort of Taormina. After a walk through the town's narrow streets, take the cable car to the beach and enjoy a dip in the sea. The vibrant city of Catania has abundant baroque architecture, a lively fish market and buzzing nightlife. As you stroll along its lava-stone streets, you'll discover your own special places to visit.

WESTEND61/GETTY IMAGES ©

THE MAIN AREAS

MESSINA	TAORMINA	CATANIA
Gateway to the island p152	Sicilian dolce vita p157	Lava-stone architecture p164

Taormina (p157). Left: Buildings in front of Mt Etna

Find Your Way

While travelling along the Ionian coast to discover the historical gems, cultural heritage and natural treasures of eastern Sicily, you will be constantly accompanied by the volcano on one side and the sea on the other.

Messina, p152

Overlooking the strait that separates Sicily from the rest of Italy, it was devastated by an earthquake in 1908 and rebuilt in a belle époque style.

Taormina, p157

On the top of a cliff with a stunning view on Mt Etna. Do not miss the ancient Greek theatre or the chance to take a refreshing dip in front of Isola Bella.

10 miles

20 km

Tyrrhenian Sea

Straits of Messina

Villa San Giovanni

Santissima Annunziata dei Catalani

Messina

Milazzo

Marina di Patti

Riserva Naturale Orientata Bosco di Malabotta

Parco Regionale dei Nebrodi

Randazzo

Gole dell'Alcantara

Riserva Naturale Fiumedinisi

Roccalumera

IONIAN COAST

Taormina

Pineta

Greek Theatre

CAR

Hitting the road is the best way to explore the Ionian coast. Parking is free almost everywhere and it's easy to find. In Taormina, a car park is connected to the centre by shuttle.

BUS

Buses are not the best way to explore this part of the island, however you can use them to reach Taormina from Catania or Messina. Connections between smaller towns are less frequent.

TRAIN

Cities and towns between Messina and Catania are connected by trains (Trenitalia) that run along the coast with breathtaking landscapes. On Thursdays and Saturdays a special train (Ferrovia Circumetnea) will take you to the wineries on the slopes of the volcano.

Catania, p164

The beating heart of eastern Sicily with Roman ruins, baroque buildings, boisterous markets and an energetic nightlife scene.

Giarre

Acireale

Catania

Roman Amphitheatre

Mt Etna

Deneri

Parco dell'Etna

Fiume Simeto

Fiume Dittaino

Lago di Lentini

Augusta

Plan Your Time

Start at the Strait of Messina and pass by hill villages and volcanic gorges on your way to the luxury resort of Taormina and the Unesco-listed buildings in the city of Catania.

Corso Umberto I, Taormina (p157)

A. KOLOS/SHUTTERSTOCK ©

Pressed for time? Taormina and around

● Spend a morning diving into the **Gole dell'Alcantara** (p162) or take a quad bike ride along the river immersing yourself in the magnificent natural landscape created over the millennia by the volcano Mt Etna, which is always in sight. Head to **Taormina** (p157) and treat yourself to an unforgettable *cannolo* before strolling around Corso Umberto and its surrounding alleyways. Take the cable car to **Isola Bella** (p159) at sunset or climb along an old path that connects Taormina with **Castelmola** (p161) and sip local almond wine on a terrace. In the evening, attend a night show at the **Greek theatre** (p159).

Seasonal highlights

Summer on the Ionian coast is never too hot thanks to the sea breezes, while winter is always very mild and less crowded. This is a region you can enjoy all year round.

JANUARY
This is the ideal month for skiing on the volcano along the snow-covered slopes of Mt Etna.

FEBRUARY
From 3 to 5 February a million people follow a reliquary through the streets honouring St Agata, patron saint of Catania.

MARCH
The Carnival of Acireale is one of the oldest in Sicily and is considered the most beautiful.

SPELORITANO/SHUTTERSTOCK ©, WEAD/SHUTTERSTOCK ©, SOLOSERGIO/SHUTTERSTOCK ©

Three days to travel around Catania

● **Catania** (p164) is a city that's risen from its ashes, offering vibrant nightlife, a baroque city centre, one of the largest monasteries in Europe and two unmissable markets. Take time to discover them as you get lost in the city's lava-stone streets. Spend a full day exploring the **Riviera dei Ciclopi** (p169): the Norman castle in Acicastello, the seaside village of Aci Trezza and the beautiful **Acireale** (p169). Hike the slopes of **Mt Etna** (p169) to the summit craters. Alternatively you can hop on a train and visit **foothill villages** (p171) to see the volcano from another point of view.

If you have more time: six days along the coast

● Start discovering **Messina** (p162) with a full-day walking tour, then immerse yourself in the unspoiled nature on a hike in the enchanting **Valle degli Eremiti** (p156). End the second day with a short road trip among the hillside villages of **Savoca, Casalvecchio Siculo and Forza d'Agrò** (p156). Continue towards **Taormina** (p157), also known as The Pearl of the Ionian Sea. The day after, get on the small train called *littorina* from Riposto to the medieval town of **Randazzo** (p163) and travel the wine route around Etna. **Catania** (p164) deserves at least a full day to explore its baroque wonders and it's worth dedicating another day to the **Riviera dei Ciclopi** (p169).

JUNE
Marranzano World Fest is a four-night music festival held in the courtyard of the Monastero dei Benedettini in Catania.

JULY
In summer the Greek theatre of Taormina hosts Taormina Arte, a mix of concerts, dance, opera and plays.

AUGUST
Between 14 and 15 August (Ferragosto) on the Ionian coast many people spend the night with friends around a bonfire.

SEPTEMBER
During grape harvest season do not miss the traditional Festa della Vendemmia in Piedimonte Etneo.

MESSINA

Messina's ancient name was Zancle (sickle) due to the shape of its port. It has always been a safe haven for people of different backgrounds, helping to create the rich cultural life you see today.

Before the 1908 earthquake that razed it to the ground, Messina had always been a powerful and proud city that stood up to the Angevins, who tried to conquer it in 1282, and the Spaniards, who ruled Sicily from 1516. Between 1674 and 1678 Messina rose up, determined to make itself independent from Spain, and became a sort of maritime republic similar to Genoa and Venice.

The richest families of the city took great pride in the palaces built in the 1910s and 1920s to show how the city rose again after the disaster. Do not miss the buildings designed by Gino Coppedé, the same architect who created the Coppedé neighbourhood in Rome.

Today Messina is an airy city with belle époque vibes. Finish your visit along the coastal road that leads to Ganzirri lake and Torre Faro – here you can take a dip where two seas mix together and dine on locally farmed mussels.

Palermo   Mes

TOP TIP

From Torre Faro you will have the most beautiful view of the strait between Sicily and Calabria. Sicilians call it the Eiffel Tower of the Strait: it's a 232m-high steel pylon on the easternmost tip of Sicily where the Ionian and Tyrrhenian seas meet.

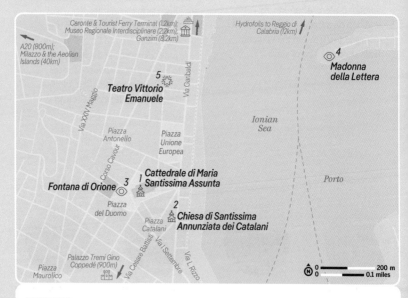

HIGHLIGHTS

1 Cattedrale di Maria Santissima Assunta

2 Chiesa di Santissima Annunziata dei Catalani

3 Fontana di Orione

4 Madonna della Lettera

5 Teatro Vittorio Emanuele

Churches, Palaces & Views

TRACKING A PROUD PAST

Start from the church of **Santa Maria Alemanna**, a rare example of Gothic architecture in Sicily, then proceed to **Santissima Annunziata dei Catalani**, which survived the 1908 earthquake. The **Cattedrale di Maria Santissima Assunta** did not have the same luck. Over the centuries its Norman structure has been destroyed by fires, earthquakes and Allied bombs. On the same square is the Fontana di Orione with its statue of the Greek god who founded Messina. At midday the cathedral's bell tower comes to life. After the show, climb the stairs to the **Santuario di Montalto** where in 1282 the local heroines Dina and Clarenza saved Messina from the Angevins, led by Charles of Anjou, by throwing stones at enemy soldiers and ringing the bells to wake up the whole city.

Enjoy the view over the golden statue of the Madonna della Lettera from the **Sacrario di Cristo Re**. This was the former site of the medieval castle Roccaguelfonia. Returning towards the sea, stop at **Teatro Vittorio Emanuele**, where a painting by Renato Guttuso shows the myth of Colapesce, who is said to support Sicily on his shoulders. Note the 19th- and 20th-century buildings lining the avenues, especially Palazzo Zanca and Palazzo del Governo in front of the statue of Neptune made by Montorsoli, pupil of Michelangelo.

Nearby is the church of **San Giovanni di Malta**, once a huge Benedictine complex. Finally, visit the **Museo Regionale**. Its collection includes works by Antonello da Messina and Caravaggio.

A PAINTER TO DISCOVER

Visit Villa Cattolica in Bagheria (p81), near Palermo, to see other works by Renato Guttuso.

Visit an Art Gallery by Tram

ILLUSTRATED HISTORY

In 2015 the tram stops were decorated by street artists and photographers featuring stories, legends and characters of the city. Other murals can be seen in the port area. The stories are often linked to the area where the stop is located. The journey runs from Piazza Cairoli up to **MuMe** (Museo Interdisciplinare Regionale di Messina) and lasts 25 minutes.

I LIVE HERE: BEST LOCAL TREATS

Messina is famous for its pastry. **Adriana Cannaò,** Messina-born art expert, recommends some unmissable places.

Puleo
As soon as you enter this unassuming place you discover a world of delights. Try a *lulù,* a puff filled with cream.

Bar Torino
The best Sicilian *granita* is coffee flavoured and served with cream and a fluffy brioche.

Ragusa
Here the Sicilian pastry tradition is handed down from father to son. Taste the *pignolata,* shortcrust pastry balls fried and covered with chocolate.

GETTING AROUND

Most of the city's attractions are within walking distance, but be prepared to face many stairs: Messina is built on the sea but rises on the hills that surround it. It is always worth the climb, as the view of the strait from above is phenomenal.

You can also count on an electric tram (line 28) running along the coast. Use it to reach the Museo Regionale, switching to the bus (with the same ticket lasting 100 mins) to head to the beach in Torre Faro.

If travelling by car, note that street parking streets is often metered (blue lines denote meter parking). Check the back streets too; if you are lucky you can park for free. Parking around the train station and the port is easier.

Messina

Riserva Naturale
Fiumedinisi

Peloritani Mountains

Casalvecchio Savoca

Forza d'Agro

Beyond Messina

Exploring the Messina region means
entering another time while wandering
through woods, castles, Byzantine churches
and villages perched on the rock.

Messina's surroundings are among the most beautiful but
also the most underrated in Sicily. Here you'll find long beaches overlooking the Ionian Sea dotted with fortified castles
that defended the area from Arab raids, as well as stunning
natural scenery between the Peloritani mountains and the
sea, particularly in the wild and unspoiled Riserva Naturale
Fiumedinisi. Get a sense of the most authentic Sicilian villages in atmospheric Savoca and Castelvecchio Siculo, and don't
miss the tiny village of Forza D'Agrò where you can have an
unforgettable dinner on a terrace with a view. Watch out for
the many traces that still remain of the area's Byzantine settlements: ancient churches and monasteries to be discovered along the way.

TOP TIP

Late spring it the best
time of the year to enjoy
the surroundings of
Messina, when nature
is at its best and the
castles built on the rocks
guarding the sea are
surrounded by the most
luxuriant flowering.

Savoca (p156)

ANNA LURYE/SHUTTERSTOCK ©

Fiumedinisi

EXCURSIONS ON PELORITANI MOUNTAINS

If you are an experienced trekker you can join the path along the Valle degli Eremiti to climb Mt Poverello (1279m). From the top you will have a spectacular view of two seas: on one side the Tyrrhenian Sea with the Aeolian Islands in the distance, on the other the Ionian Sea. It's a 13km round trip. **Camminare i Peloritani** organizes excursions all year round, both on Peloritani and Nebrodi. The most recommended is the Sentiero dei Due Mari, a 15km circular route (5–6 hours) mainly running along a ridge.

Wild Riserva Naturale Fiumedinisi & Monte Scuderi

UNFORGETTABLE HIKES & LANDSCAPES

This is still a wild area crossed by impetuous streams, including the Fiumedinisi, whose name is linked to the Greek colony Nisa founded nearby. Back then, the river was called Chrysorroas (golden stream) due to its yellow rocks. Visiting Mt Scuderi, at 1253m above sea level is a wonderful experience well worth the climb. From the A18, exit at Itala Marina and follow SP30 to Itala Superiore (45 mins). Park a few kilometres outside the town and start following the path. The hike to the top takes around two hours and you'll pass many *fosse delle nevi* – holes in the ground used for storing ice before the fridge was invented. In good weather, you can see the outlines of Mt Etna and the Aeolian Islands. This place is linked to the legend of *truvatura,* a treasure hidden in the depths of the mountain that can only be found by those who overcome many challenges.

 WHERE TO EAT IN SAVOCA, CASALVECCHIO & FORZA D'AGRÒ

Pipispezzi
Traditional cuisine with a modern twist in an enchanting location with breathtaking views €€

Donna Giosina
Have lunch in the countryside. Homemade bread, macaroni and local meat. €

Osteria Agostiniana
Local ingredients and seafood specialties: taste true Sicilian dishes. €€

CASTLES WITH A BREATHTAKING VIEW

Castello Belvedere
Not far from the town of Fiumedinisi. Only ruins remain but it offers a magnificent panorama.

Castello Rufo Ruffo
Dip into history with a view at this worthwhile stop along the A18, exit Scaletta Marina.

Castello Pentefur
On one of the two hills on which Savoca stands, this fortress guarantees a spectacular view as far as the sea.

Castello Pentefur

The Ancient Valle degli Eremiti

ALONG A NARROW CANYON

The enchanting Valle degli Eremiti (Hermits' Valley) is a 2km-long canyon covered with dense vegetation where you can still see the caves inhabited by hermits in ancient times as well as the ruins of a shrine and a convent. From the town of Fiumedinisi follow the signpost to Gole della Santissima. The terrain is quite easy to walk but stony, so wear sturdy shoes. Return to the starting point the same way you came.

Discover a Basilian Monastery

DIVE INTO THE MIDDLE AGES

The **Monastero della SS Annunziata** dates back to 1100 when Count Roger, after having expelled the Arabs from Mandanici, donated a church and an abbey to the Greek monks of San Basilio. The complex has been remodelled during the Baroque period but retains Arab-Norman elements. It took on great importance in the Middle Ages, supporting the economic, religious and cultural development of the whole Valley of Olives.

Savoca, Casalvecchio & Forza D'Agrò

ROAD TRIP THROUGH A HISTORIC VALLEY

Start your road trip from **Savoca** (A18 exit Roccalumera), where Francis Ford Coppola filmed part of *The Godfather* (1972). One of the film's locations, Bar Vitelli, stands at the village entrance near a terrace with a magnificent view over the valley. Behind, the little village hidden in the hills has gated walls, haunting churches surrounded by olive groves and streets decorated with artistic ceramic panels made by local artisans. Explore the churches of San Michele, San Nicolò and the Mother Church, climb up to the castle of Pentefur and discover that Savoca also had an ancient synagogue. Do not miss the catacombs beneath the 17th-century Capuchin monastery.

Then head to the nearby **Casalvecchio Siculo** to visit SS Pietro e Paolo, a fortress-like church 10 minutes' drive from the tiny village. Built by Roger II of Sicily in 1117 and originally part of a Basilian monastery, its style mixes Arab, Byzantine and Norman elements, reflecting the heterogeneity of 12th-century Sicily.

Your last stop is **Forza D'Agrò**. End the day with a stroll around its cobbled streets and dinner with a view of the coast.

GETTING AROUND

Exploring the area around Messina requires a car. Hitting the road is the only way to reach the Fiumedinisi nature reserve 45km from Messina. Take the A18 toll road or the SS114 towards Catania, exit at Itala Marina and then follow the signs to Itala Superiore.

Savoca is just 18km from there. Leave your car at the entrance to this small village if you want to avoid navigating its narrow streets – it's relatively easy to explore on foot.

Casalvecchio is not far along the SP19, but the church of SS Pietro e Paolo is outside the village. A narrow road with many curves takes you there, so drive cautiously. The road that leads to Forza D'Agrò is full of bends too, but it's much wider and has a spectacular view over the coast below.

TAORMINA

Despite being one of the busiest and most expensive destinations in Sicily, Taormina retains its charm. Founded in the 4th century BCE, it reached its peak splendour during the Greek and Roman times, then passed through periods of Arab and Norman rule. It became a popular tourist destination during the 18th century when European travellers visited on the Grand Tour. Many fell in love with Taormina and stayed for years, or even for a lifetime.

Since then, Taormina has been a destination for the rich and famous. The European aristocracy came here to spend their holidays in the 1920s and '30s, and in the '50s and '60s movie stars loved sunbathing on its beaches and dancing all night in its clubs. Taormina is still an unmissable stop on your visit if you want to taste the Sicilian dolce vita.

TOP TIP

The best spot to photograph Mr Etna standing over the bay of Taormina is the Villa Comunale, once Lady Trevelyan's private garden and now municipal park. From the entrance on Via Roma, go straight to the balcony overlooking the sea.

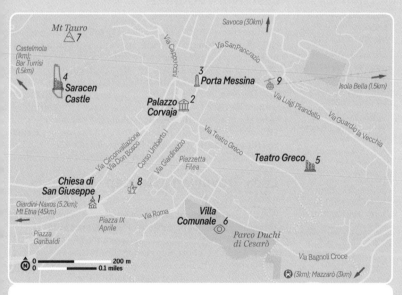

HIGHLIGHTS		SIGHTS	DRINKING & NIGHTLIFE
1 Chiesa di San Giuseppe	4 Saracen Castle	7 Mt Tauro	8 Morgana
2 Palazzo Corvaja	5 Teatro Greco		TRANSPORT
3 Porta Messina	6 Villa Comunale		9 Funivia

BEST BEACHES NEAR TAORMINA

Isola Bella
A small pebble beach with crystal water, connected to an island by a thin sand isthmus.

Mazzarò
North of Isola Bella, one of the best-loved beaches of the area.

Giardini-Naxos
A stretch of coast south of Taormina alternating golden sand and pebbles.

Spisone
Well-equipped sandy beach with stone islets poking up from the water.

Mazzeo
Between Mazzarò and Letojanni, this is a wider beach with finer sand.

Palazzo Corvaja

Discover Taormina

STROLL ALONG CORSO UMBERTO I

Starting from Porta Messina, follow Corso Umberto I past the 10th-century **Palazzo Corvaja**, the church of **Santa Caterina** built on a Greek temple with a little Odeon right behind it, then head to **Piazza IX Aprile** for a spectacular view of the bay. Facing the square is the church of San Giuseppe. Walk by the 12th-century clock tower and head up to **Piazza Duomo** with its baroque fountain. Take a look at the 13th-century cathedral and admire the buildings along the way, including the 14th-century **Palazzo Ciampoli** and the 13th-century **Palazzo Duca di Santo Stefano**. Get lost in the side alleys too, full of tiny churches and narrow streets decorated with ceramics.

Lady Trevelyan's Garden

A WHIMSICAL PLACE

When a green oasis of calm beckons, make your way to the stunningly sited public gardens of **Villa Comunale**. Created by Englishwoman Florence Trevelyan in the late 19th century, this is a wonderful place to escape the crowds, with tropical plants, delicate flowers punctuated by whimsical follies and breathtaking views of the coast and Mt Etna.

 WHERE TO EAT IN TAORMINA

Osteria Rosso DiVino
On a romantic and intimate staircase, serving excellent fish cuisine with a good wine list. €€€

Bam Bar
Best *granita* in town, no wonder it is constantly busy. Try a fruit-based seasonal flavour. €

Pasticceria D'Amore
Do not leave without tasting the freshly filled *cannoli*. €

Showtime at a Greek Theatre

TWO SHOWS IN ONE

Gorge on sensational Etna views from Taormina's remarkable clifftop **Teatro Greco**. Built in the 3rd century BCE and still in use, this horseshoe-shaped theatre between sea and sky is the world's most dramatically situated Greek theatre and Sicily's second largest (after Syracuse). Bag a gold-dust ticket for a summer concert and enjoy the thrilling double act: the performance on the stage and the fire-red flow of erupting Etna beyond.

Ascent to Mt Tauro

A CHURCH INSIDE A GROTTO

Climb to the top of Mt Tauro to discover the **Saracen Castle**, once an ancient Greek acropolis. From Via Circonvallazione take the stairs up to the **Santuario Madonna della Rocca**, built in 1640 inside a grotto. It was here that, according to legend, the Virgin Mary appeared to a shepherd. The path is uphill but not too taxing, and your reward will be a heavenly view over Taormina and the Ionian Sea. the whole climb is 800m and takes about 20 minutes, but it's worth giving it a couple of hours to admire the scenery from above, take photos and visit the church and the ruins of the castle.

Nature Reserve at Isola Bella

VILLA CARVED INTO THE ROCK

In 1806 King Ferdinand I of Bourbon gifted Isola Bella to Taormina; in 1890 it was acquired by Lady Florence Trevelyan, who built a house where she planned to spend the hottest hours of the day. After her death, the island was abandoned for decades until it was bought by the Bosurgi family, citrus-processing magnates from Messina, who dug new rooms and a swimming pool following the shape of the rock. Now the island is a protected nature reserve open to visitors. While you are here, take a boat ride to the nearby caves. Just ask on the beach.

Dip in the Sea

TAKE THE PATH OR CABLE CAR TO THE BEACH

Do you feel like taking a dip? Take the *funivia* (cable car) to reach the pebble beach or choose the 1km walking path that takes you straight to Isola Bella from Belvedere on Via Pirandello. The path is only partially shaded so in summer it might be better to go later in the day when the sun isn't as strong. The *funivia* entrance is on Via Pirandello 22, about 200m from Porta Messina. It's only a three-minute ride but the view is spectacular.

THE GUIDE

IONIAN COAST

BEST NIGHTLIFE IN TAORMINA

Morgana
This lounge bar's decor changes every year and the menu contains drinks that you can only taste here.

Daiquiri
Delicious cocktails and good vibes on a staircase in the heart of Taormina, near Piazza Duomo.

Re di Bastoni
Try Pan, a brown ale with Nebrodi hazelnuts, while enjoying live jazz.

Daiquiri

GETTING AROUND

Taormina is definitely best explored on foot. Its historic centre is entirely pedestrianised and made up of stairs and alleys too narrow for cars. Parking here can be a nightmare too, as the rare spaces in the centre are almost entirely reserved for residents. If you are staying in town ask your host, who may have reserved places for guests.

The nearest car park to the city centre is Porta Pasquale, but it is quite small, so aim to arrive early. At the opposite end of Corso Umberto is the Parcheggio Porta Catania, just 250m from the main street. Parcheggio Mazzarò is downhill.

Gole
dell'Alcantara
Randazzo   Castelmola
Taormina

Beyond Taormina

Taormina attracts all the attention but allow
yourself to leave the usual routes and discover
what the surroundings hide.

TOP TIP

Dying to buy all the
delicious Etna wines you
have tasted on a wine tour
but luggage limits don't
allow it? Several wine
producers are able to
ship them home at quite
reasonable prices.

Taormina is undoubtedly the star of the area but its surroundings reserve many surprises. Just 4km away is the cute village of Castelmola, which can also be reached on foot with
a pleasant walk through nature and history. About 25km
away are the Gole dell'Alcantara, amazing volcanic gorges
created by lava over millennia. The surroundings are dotted with delightful villages and wine lovers may want to follow the Strada del Vino wine route. There's also a train that
runs along a unique railway line circumnavigating the volcano. The final stop is the medieval town of Randazzo, right
on the slopes of Mt Etna.

Sentiero dei Saraceni

ORIETTA GASPARI/GETTY IMAGES ©

MAREMAGNUM/GETTY IMAGES ©

Gole dell'Ancantara (p162)

Walk the Sentiero dei Saraceni to Castelmola

STROLL TO THE VILLAGE IN THE SKY

A path has connected Taormina to **Castelmola** since prehistoric times and it takes around 45 minutes to walk it (3km). The starting point of the **Sentiero dei Saraceni** (Path of the Saracens) is on Via dei Saraceni, a street near Piazza Goethe. On the way up you can see fields of prickly pears, water wells from the Roman era, an Iron Age necropolis and a wall gate through which the Arabs entered Taormina in 902 CE, not to mention the magnificent view. Shortly before reaching Castelmola, you'll come across the small church of San Biagio whose original building dates back to the 1st century CE. A few steps away is a mulberry tree to refill your energy.

With a single glance from this delightful town perched high above the sea you can see the whole Ionian coast, from the Strait of Messina down to Syracuse. Castelmola, crowned by the ruins of a Norman castle, has a majestic belvedere in Piazza Sant'Antonio and an old *taverna* founded by monks in 1700, still open today as Caffè San Giorgio. It's here that Don Vincenzo Blandano created his almond wine in 1907.

SICILY'S ALMOND WINE

During the Greek period it was customary to add food to wine to flavour it. Don Vincenzo Blandano took up that ancient tradition in 1907 to create his almond wine Blandanino, which he used to offer to travellers. Among the famous travellers who visited here to taste this speciality was German photographer Baron Von Gloeden, who sat in the square enjoying the view and sipping a glass of wine or a sour cherry with herbs.

The almond wine has a dark amber color, an intense scent of Sicilian almonds and a liqueur-like consistency. Taste it here accompanied by Sicilian amaretti (almond-based biscuits) or buy a bottle to take home.

WHERE TO EAT IN RANDAZZO

Gli Antichi Sapori
This family-run place is a must if you are looking for traditional flavours. €€

San Giorgio e il Drago
Typical cuisine of Etna and Nebrodi in front of the ancient convent of San Giorgio. €€

Pasticceria Musumeci
Right in front of the Santa Maria church. Ask for the special Pirandello ice cream. €

Discover the magnificent **Mother Church of San Nicolò di Bari** built in 1934 on the site of a 16th-century church. You can trace the different styles used here: Arab, Norman, Romanesque and Gothic. Do not miss its terrace overlooking Mt Etna. From sacred to profane, a few steps away is **Bar Turrisi**, full of phalluses of all materials and sizes, symbols of abundance according to Greek tradition.

Climb Gole dell'Alcantara

VERTIGINOUS LAVA GORGES

Enjoy an unforgettable swim in the icy waters of the Alcantara river, whose name derives from the Arabic *al qantara,* meaning bridge. It flows inside the lava gorges created over the millennia by the volcano. This place is unique due to the basalt rocks formed from lava flowing into the water. It is just 15km from Giardini-Naxos, open from April to October.

Make your way from the free car park to the bottom of the gorges by lift or on foot. Be prepared to go down (and climb back!) 224 steps. The wonder will be worth the effort. You can simply splash around and enjoy half a day here or stay longer and try canyoning and body rafting. Explore the river from above too, walking the 3.5km nature trail above the gorge.

Swim at Le Gurne dell'Alcantara

PONDS & WATERFALLS

Much less crowded than the gorges are the ponds and waterfalls of Gurne dell'Alcantara, located further upstream. To get there follow the SS185 and turn left just before reaching the town of Francavilla di Sicilia. A path runs along the river. Dive into the ponds between the waterfalls and bring food with you to enjoy in the nearby picnic area.

Visit Volcanic Wineries

WINE ROUTE ON THE RAILS OR ROAD

On Thursdays and Sundays you can travel the **Strada del Vino dell'Etna** (Etna Wine Road) by train travelling along the Ferrovia Circumetnea, one of the most unique railways in the world, which climbs the volcano and passes through foothill villages. The route starts from Riposto and tickets include the train ride, a guide and a special wine bus that takes you around vineyards and cellars. Many wineries are located inside sumptuous noble villas. Taste Etna wines and find out how they are produced on the volcanic soil. Book your wine tour on the website (www.stradadelvinodelletna.it); They are

River Alcantara

WHERE TO HAVE A DRINK IN CASTELMOLA

Antico Caffè San Giorgio	**Bar Turrisi**	**La Caverna**
On the square overlooking the bay. Order almond wine and bruschette with aubergine. €€	Ask to sit on the top floor to enjoy the sunset while having a drink. €	Taste local wines accompanied by cheeses and charcuterie in this bar in a cave. €

Chiesa di San Nicola, Randazzo

BEST WINERIES NEAR MT ETNA

Donnafugata Randazzo
Taste amazing wines, walk through the vineyards and visit the *barriquerie* (barrel stores), all with a stunning view towards Mt Etna.

Tenuta di Fessina
An abandoned village transformed into a winery. You can also stay overnight.

Cantine Palmeno Costanzo
Located on an old lava flow from 1879, it stands between the yellow of the brooms and the green of the vineyards.

usually half-day tours starting at 9 am but on request you can book a full-day tour (9am to 4pm, including lunch).

You can also choose to travel by car exploring the wineries along SS120 between Passopiasciaro and Rovittello. Start from Antichi Vinai, continue towards Tenuta Tascante and Cantine Patria, then head to Tenuta Fischetti and Torre Mora. End the tour by visiting **Castiglione di Sicilia**, listed among Italy's Most Beautiful Villages (www.borghipiubelliditalia.it), with a Byzantine castle and cobblestone alleys.

Randazzo

A MEDIEVAL GEM ON MT ETNA

Randazzo has a special charm due to its medieval past. Enter its defensive walls and explore its main churches corresponding to the three ancient districts of the city: **Santa Maria** (Latin Quarter), **San Nicola** (Greek Quarter) and **San Martino** (Lombard Quarter). Up until the 16th century, three different languages were spoken here. Cross the beautiful Via degli Archi and look for the mullioned windows here and there, as on Palazzo Clarentano. The Swabian castle, part of the city walls, now houses an archaeological museum. The royal palace was built by the last Norman kings and housed the likes of Charles V.

GETTING AROUND

Castelmola can be reached on foot from Taormina on the Sentiero dei Saraceni (45 mins), by bus (15 mins, Pirandello bus terminal) or by car (10 mins via SP10). Park up in the small car park or on the road into town and enjoy the cobbled streets on foot.

Driving is the best way to get to the Gole dell'Alcantara, which has a large car park (free). A car is also useful to get to Randazzo, stopping at the wineries along the way. Parking in Randazzo is not a problem even in the centre, except on 15 August when there is the Feast of the Madonna. Alternatively, take the train (Ferrovia Circumetnea) from Riposto, Giarre or Piedimonte Etneo, admiring the sea on one side and the volcano on the other.

Palermo

Catania

IA

...proximity to Mt Etna, Sicily's second-biggest city ...dealt with devastating volcanic activity on numerous occasions. It was engulfed by boiling lava in 1669, and in 1693 an earthquake hit the region. On Catania's Porta Ferdinandea city gate, an inscription reads 'Melior de cinere surgo' (I rise stronger from the ashes), summing up Catanians' pride in their rebuilt, Unesco-listed city. Over the centuries Greeks, Romans, Byzantines, Arabs, Normans, French, Aragonese and Spaniards have passed through here and the city's impressive black-and-white *palazzi* and dizzying domes, towering over grandiose baroque piazzas and vivacious street life, continue to attract a huge mix of admirers today.

TOP TIP

Cool down in summer at a 19th-century *chiosco* (drinks kiosk) – order a *seltz limone e sale* (sparkling water, lemon juice and salt) or sweet *mandarino verde* (with green tangerine syrup). Costa near Piazza Stesicoro and Giammona on Piazza Vittorio Emanuele III are Liberty-era favourites.

Tour the Resurrected City

SOAK UP BAROQUE ARCHITECTURE

STOP AT A CHIOSCO

Since the 19th century the *chiosco,* or drinks kiosk, has been part of the city's heritage. Catanians stop at the *chiosco* for a refreshing drink during the hottest hours of the day and at the end of a night out with friends. Historic examples in the city centre include Costa, a footstep from Piazza Stesicoro, and Giammona on Piazza Vittorio Emanuele. Stop here to drink a *seltz limone e sale* like a local. It is an invigorating mix of seltzer water and freshly squeezed lemon juice. Also taste *mandarino limone* with tangerine syrup added or *mandarino verde* with green tangerine.

Keep your head up so as not to miss any of Catania's magnificent, Unesco-listed baroque buildings crafted in black lava and white limestone. Begin on **Piazza del Duomo** with the city symbol: U Liotru in local dialect, aka **Fontana dell'Elefante** (1736), a lava-stone elephant surmounted by an obelisk. The splash-happy waters of 19th-century **Fontana dell'Amenano** pour into the underground River Amenano, which once ran above ground. The piazza star is **Cattedrale di Sant'Agata**, dedicated to the city's patron saint, celebrated on 5 February with one of Sicily's largest festivals. World-famous Catanian composer Vincenzo Bellini rests here. Next door, the concave-convex facade of **Chiesa della Badia di Sant'Agata** is an architectural masterpiece by Giovanni Battista Vaccarini.

Walk along Via Etnea to reach Piazza Università, framed by **Palazzo Sangiuliano** and **Palazzo Università**, with a beautiful cobblestone courtyard designed by Vaccarini. Turn left to follow Via Alessi up to **Via Crociferi**, a triumph of baroque: visit **Chiesa di San Giuliano** and **Arco di San Benedetto**, and walk to the opposite end of the street to admire Vaccarini's **Villa Cerami** (today the university's law faculty). Return to Via Etnea via Via Penninello, and at the **Quattro Canti** intersection walk east along Via Sangiuliano to neo-baroque **Teatro Bellini**. The theatre was inaugurated in 1890 with the opera *Norma,* which inspired *pasta alla Norma* (pasta with basil, aubergine, ricotta and tomato). End with a look around nearby **Chiesa di San Placido** and memorable *cannoli* at neighbouring **I Dolci di Nonna Vincenza**.

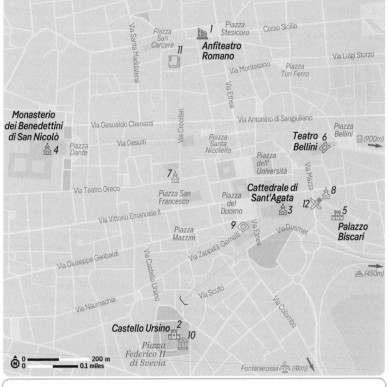

HIGHLIGHTS
1 Anfiteatro Romano
2 Castello Ursino
3 Cattedrale di Sant'Agata

4 Monasterio dei Benedettini di San Nicolò
5 Palazzo Biscari
6 Teatro Bellini

SIGHTS
7 Chiesa di San Benedetto
8 Church of San Placido
9 Fontana dell'Amenane

10 Museo Civico
11 Villa Cerami

EATING
12 I Dolci di Nonna Vincenza

Amphitheatres & Roman Baths

ROMAN CATANIA

Catania retains traces of its ancient past. Much of its huge **Anfiteatro Romano** was buried by lava centuries ago, but snatches of the ruined Roman amphitheatre are visible below street level on Piazza Stesicoro. On the southern side of Piazza Duomo, the **Museo Diocesano** safeguards excavated ruins of 5th-century Terme Achilleane, one of several baths in the Roman city. In the Byzantine era, a frescoed church was built atop the ruins of nearby **Terme della Rotonda**.

 WHERE TO STAY IN CATANIA

Asmundo di Gisira
Designer rooms with artworks inspired by mythological figures and Grand Tour travellers. €€€

Habitat
A late-19th-century factory turned boutique hotel just a footstep from Teatro Massimo. €€

Casa d'Aria
Apartments with unique interiors. Close to Catania but in a quiet neighbourhood. €

The most impressive Roman ruins rub shoulders with 18th-century *palazzi* in the **Parco Archeologico Greco Romano** on Via Vittorio Emanuele: what's left of a 2nd-century Roman Theatre and its small rehearsal theatre, the Odeon, are evocatively sited in the thick of a crumbling residential neighbourhood, with vine-covered buildings that appear to have sprouted organically from the sunken stage. Come here at night, after the rain, to admire twinkling city lights reflected in the water-submerged stage.

I LIVE HERE: BEST PLACES TO EAT IN CATANIA

Ivan Nicosia, licensed tour guide, shares his dining recommendations for authentic local cuisine in Catania.

Canni e Pisci
Loved by locals and tourists, Canni e Pisci serves excellent fish and meat dishes.

Vuciata
Nice atmosphere and delicious food. Try the *sarde a beccafico* (stuffed sardines), although everything on the menu is good.

Scirocco
Order fresh and crisp fish *fritture* (batter-fried seafood) served in a paper cone, to eat while strolling around.

Piazza Scammacca
Four thematic restaurants, a pastry shop, a cocktail bar, a wine shop and an exhibition space for contemporary art.

Monastero dei Benedettini di San Nicolò

ONE OF THE LARGEST IN EUROPE

Founded in 1558, the original structure of Monastero dei Benedettini di San Nicolò was modified by the 1669 lava eruption and the 1693 earthquake. Enjoy the richly decorated baroque facade, a grand staircase with marble and stucco, long corridors, peaceful cloisters, a garden built on lava, frescoed rooms and a stunning library. At the end of June the four-night Marranzano World Fest is held in the courtyard. Join a guided tour to access parts of the monastery not otherwise accessible, such as the kitchens tiled with Sicilian majolica and the magnificent Roman domus in the basement, as this was the ancient acropolis of Catania. Do not miss the nearby church of **San Nicolò l'Arena** with a historical organ and the Ursino Recupero library.

A Piscaria & A Fera o Luni

VISIT THE MARKETS

Tables groan under the weight of decapitated swordfish, ruby-pink prawns and trays full of clams, mussels, sea urchins and all manner of mysterious sea life at Catania's raucous fish market, **La Pescheria** or A' Piscaria in local dialect. Visit early morning – it opens at 7am – to grab the best of the action and morning catch. Look for stalls offering tastings and restaurants cooking up fresh fish. For seasonal fruit, veg, spices, clothing, all sorts, continue to **Fera 'o Luni**, a morning market around since the Middle Ages and filling Piazza Carlo Alberto with the din of hawking vendors since 1832.

Palazzo Biscari

18TH-CENTURY NOBLE PALACE

For centuries Palazzo Biscari has been, and still is, the residence of the noble family Paternò Castello, princes of Biscari,

 WHERE TO HAVE A DRINK IN CATANIA

Mercati Generali
The place to spend the night dancing or listening to live music while having a drink. €€

Fud Off
One of the coolest spots for casual bites with cocktails. €€

Vermut
Budget-friendly and good vibes. Cocktails, wines and beers accompanied by charcuterie. €

Castello Ursino

BEST VIEWPOINTS IN CATANIA

Chiesa della Badia di Sant'Agata
Swoon over a 360-degree panorama of the city's rooftops, domes and a brooding Mt Etna to the north from the church's terrace.

Ostello degli Elefanti
Enjoy an *aperitivo* at sunset in the rooftop bar of this popular hostel, in a 17th-century palazzo a stone's throw from the cathedral.

San Nicolò l'Arena
Spiral up 141 steps to the roof of the church, with striking unfinished facade, in the Benedictine monastery complex on Piazza Dante – the panorama is top-drawer.

which no traveller on their Grand Tour could miss. Built over a stretch of the 6th-century city walls, this is a Sicilian baroque jewel with frescoed halls and a stunning ballroom. If you are lucky, you will be guided by the heir who will share nice family anecdotes with you.

Castello Ursino

LANDLOCKED CASTLE

When it was built in the 13th century, the Swabian castle of Castello Ursino stood on a promontory overlooking the sea. In 1669 the lava flow reached the water changing the landscape. Today the castle is landlocked but still has a strong visual impact. It houses the Museo Civico and the Biscari's archaeological collection, admired by Goethe during his trip to Sicily.

GETTING AROUND

Catania airport is 7km southwest of town, with frequent train and bus (Alibus) connections to Catania's central train station. From the latter, it's a 20-minute walk or short metro ride (alight at the Piazza Stesicoro stop) to the historic centre – compact, walkable and hilly in places. To zip around swiftly, use the local e-scooter sharing system; download Helbiz, Dott or Lime apps to locate and rent wheels. Think twice before renting a bicycle – road traffic is chaotic and lava-stone pavements can be a bone-rattling challenge.

A hop-on hop-off panoramic bus departing from Piazza del Duomo loops around the main sights in the centre. Take Catania's one-line metro from the Giovanni XXIII stop (across the street the central train station) to the Cantania Borgo stop, where you can pick up the Ferrovia Circumetnea train encircling Mt Etna.

Bronte Mt Etna
La Timpa Nature Reserve
Riviera dei Ciclopi Acireale
Catania

Beyond Catania

A mythical coastline much-loved by Homer and the hissing craters of brooding Mt Etna usher in outdoor adventure in spades.

TOP TIP

Walking on Mt Etna is best in April, May, September and October. Even when it's hot at lower altitudes, it's windy up top and temperatures can dip below freezing. Bring walking shoes, wind jacket, warm headgear, gloves and sunglasses. Rifugio Sapienza , next to the lower cable-car station, rents kit.

The names of Acireale, Aci Castello and Aci Trezza, 30 minutes from Catania, are linked to a legend. It is said that the young shepherd Aci was in love with the water nymph Galatea. Unfortunately Polyphemus, who lived in a cave on Etna, also fell in love with her, but she refused him. The Cyclops decided to take revenge, killing Aci by throwing lava stone at him. The Gods took pity on Galatea's despair and transformed Aci into a river.

After emerging from this cobalt-coloured mythical sea, explore the seaside villages along the coast and climb the magnificent volcano where you can hike, mountain bike, ski or explore the caves, including a stunning ice cave.

Carnival float, Acireale

SOLOSERGIO/SHUTTERSTOCK ©

Riviera dei Ciclopi

ROCKY BEACHES & FISHING VILLAGES

The coastal stretch north of Catania is called Riviera dei Ciclopi due to the Greek legend involving Polyphemus throwing rocks to stop Odysseus escaping. The **Norman castle** in Aci Castello, 10km from Catania, looks like a stone ship. It was built in 1076 on a lava stone outcrop above a pre-existing Roman fortification. Right in front of the port of **Aci Trezza** (5 mins by car, 25 mins walking) are the *faraglioni* (rock towers) created by prehistoric submarine eruptions. Visit the Casa del Nespolo, a mid-19th century Sicilian house reproducing the one described by Giovanni Verga in the novel *I Malavoglia*.

Acireale

TOWN OF 100 BELL TOWERS

Acireale is known as the town of 100 bell towers due to its many churches. The most imposing are the **Cattedrale di Maria Santissima Annunziata** and the **Basilica dei Santi Pietro e Paolo** on Piazza Duomo, near the baroque town hall. A short distance away is the **Basilica di San Sebastiano** with a facade combining multiple orders. The town is also known for its carnival held in February or March, when huge papier-mâché caricatures and decorated floats created by artisans are paraded through the town. The event dates back to the 16th century, but probably derives from the ancient Roman Saturnalia games.

La Timpa Nature Reserve

THE VOLCANIC COAST

Just below Acireale is the nature reserve La Timpa, a cliff overhanging the Ionian Sea. A path starting from the church of Santa Maria del Suffragio connects Acireale to the village of Santa Maria La Scala through seven little squares *(chiazzette)*. The best way to enjoy it is a boat tour along the 20km volcanic coast and the marine protected area around the Cyclopean Islands. It departs from Aci Castello.

Hiking Mt Etna's Lower Slopes

WILD LAVA TRAILS ON AN ACTIVE VOLCANO

Explore Mt Etna's lower slopes on foot. While many dramatic hiking trails can be tackled independently, it is forbidden to trek above 2450m without a professional guide; recommended trekking companies include Guide Vulcanologiche

BEST GRANITA IN ACIREALE

Caffè Cipriani
Fabulous location right in front of the church of San Sebastiano. Taste the *babà* (rum) flavour.

Bar Al San Domenico
Said to be the best *granita* in the Catania area. Best flavour: pistachio.

Pasticceria Condorelli
Tasty traditional *granita*. Try almond, pistachio and Etna's flowers.

 WHERE TO EAT AROUND ACIREALE

La Bettola dei Marinai
Excellent food on a terrace overlooking the sea in the village of Santa Tecla. €€

Il Moro di Trezza
Great seafood in a rustic building with a veranda in front of the sea. €€€

Trattoria La Grotta
In Santa Maria la Scala dug in a grotto. Tables outside in summer. Book ahead. €€

VOLCANO BY TRAIN

You can also hit the volcano's northern slope by taking the train from Riposto up to Randazzo along the wine route **Strada del Vino dell'Etna** (p162).

Etna Nord and Etna Exclusive Guide. From the **Rifugio Sapienza** car park on the southern slope – the closest to Catania, an hour by car or two by bus – it's a five-minute walk to the lower crater of inactive **Crateri Silvestri**, dating to an eruption in 1892, and 20 minutes to the upper crater along an easy, signposted footpath.

With more time and energy on your hands, pick up the two-hour **Schiena dell'Asino** trail (5.5km) not far from the car park. Easy but uphill, it edges along the Valle del Bove where lava flows collect. Birds of prey in the sky above and great views of Catania and the Ionian Sea keep you company along the way.

On Etna's eastern slope in the fertile Val Calanna, the **704 path** (two hours, 4km) tangoes between woods and lava (dating from eruptions between 1991 and 1993 that completely swamped the valley) to the top of Mt Calanna. Find the trailhead in Piano dell'Acqua in **Zafferana Etnea**. This town is the place to taste local honey and Sicilian pizza, aka fried calzone filled with *tuma* (cheese) and anchovies.

Summiting Mt Etna

CLIMB TO 3000M WITH A GUIDE

Park in **Piano Provenzana** (1800m), a small ski station and gateway to Etna's quieter northern slopes. From here, join a 90-minute 4WD guided tour with Etna Freedom (www.etnafreedom.it) up to the **Observatorio Volcanologico** (Volcanic Observatory) looking out across the Valle del Leone at 2900m. Volcanologist guides point out lava flows and extinct craters en route up the mountain and take you on a short half-hour walk around the observatory to unravel the extraordinary view before driving back down.

Summit seekers can book an add-on guided hike from the observatory up to 3300m; count four to five hours walking. Buy tickets for both tours in advance online or at Etna Freedom's ticket office in the Piano Provenzana car park.

To summit Etna from the south, ride the **Funivia dell'Etna** cable car from **Rifugio Sapienza** up to Montagnola (2500m). Clamber aboard a 4WD jeep operated by Star (buy tickets in situ) and continue to **Torre del Filosofo** (2920m). From here, you can continue on foot with a guide hired at a small wooden hut by Torre del Filosofo.

For an unforgettable experience, catch the last cable car up to 2500m, revel in the glorious sunset, and walk back down by moonlight. You can't get lost: cable-car pylons guide you.

WHERE TO STAY ON MT ETNA

Il Ginepro dell'Etna
You can rent the entire chalet for up to six people. Fully equipped kitchens, a sauna and great views. €€

Bosco Ciancio
Set in a chestnut forest, the building dates back to the 18th century. Wood-beamed ceilings and a pool. €€

Rifugio Sapienza
Right next to the cable car. You can stay overnight, eat, rent a bike or book a tour. €

Volcano Villages

GREAT VIEWS & DELIGHTFUL PLACES

Don't feel like getting too close to the craters? Enjoy the volcano by train (Ferrovia Circumetnea) starting from Catania (stop Borgo). Do not miss the medieval city of **Adrano** with a fortress, Greek ruins, beautiful churches and palaces. Stop in **Bronte** to taste the famous pistachio grown on the lava soil and still harvested by hand.

Skiing on the Volcano

SKI RESORTS ON ETNA

The Sicilian volcano might not be the first thing that comes to mind when you think of skiing destinations but Etna has two main ski resorts, **Piano Provenzana** and **Nicolosi**, providing downhill slopes and ski lifts all with the backdrop of scenic landscapes. You can also enjoy cross-country skiing. Skis, snowshoes and snow sleds are available to rent at both ski resorts.

Subterranean Etna

EXPLORING LAVA TUNNELS & CAVES

Delve into Etna's hidden underworld, a labyrinth of tunnels and caves sculpted by lava flows and used as burial places, shelters and storage spaces for snow and ice in ancient times. Grotta del Lamponi (Raspberry Cave) extends for 700m and Grotta del Gelo (Ice Cave), carved by a 17th-century eruption, is considered Europe's most southern glacier. Uncover both on a challenging day hike (20km, eight hours) through pine forest and lava flows from Piano Provenzana. Trekking company **Gruppo Guide Alpine Etna Nord** arranges guided hikes to both.

WHERE TO EAT PISTACHIO IN BRONTE

Pasticceria Gangi
Best pistachio ice cream in Bronte. The pistachio *arancino* is also highly recommended.

Bar Conti Gallenti
Finger-licking pastries and jars of pistachio pesto that you can buy to take home.

L'Angolo dei Sapori
Pastry shop selling freshly made pistachio treats. Don't miss the pistachio *granita*.

Protosteria
Nice location and good food. Everything is pistachio-based, from starters to desserts.

Pepe Rosa
Extremely welcoming staff and good food. Try the pistachio bruschetta.

 GETTING AROUND

You can get to Aci Castello and Aci Trezza from Catania by bus (534 AMT) or hopping on the panoramic bus tourist service starting from Via Vittorio Emanuele right next to the cathedral. Acireale is just a 30-minute drive. You can also get there by train but the station is quite far from the centre and there is no transport connection: the walk takes 30 minutes.

Etna is not well connected by public transport. Only a bus departing from Catania train station (AST) leads up to Rifugio Sapienza on the southern slope. To reach other sides of the volcano you need a car unless you book a tour departing directly from Catania (www.excursionsetna.it).

You can also get to Etna by train (Ferrovia Circumetnea) starting from Catania (stop Borgo) up to Adrano and Bronte. Along the way enjoy views of the stunning landscape, which get even better at the summit.

Palazzolo Acreide (p186). Right: Necropoli di Pantalica (p185)

SYRACUSE
& THE SOUTHEAST

ANCIENT & DAZZLING LANDSCAPES

An ever-changing landscape: crystal sea, white beaches, deep canyons, olive groves, prehistoric tombs, Greek ruins and baroque cities.

It is easy to fall in love with Sicily's southeast and the great variety of landscapes and wonders it can offer. Here you will find the most luminous baroque towns such as Noto and Ortygia, built with golden stone shining in the sun, and the stunning Greek theatre in Syracuse where classical plays are still staged in an inexhaustible dialogue between past and present. Ragusa and the nearby Comiso, Modica and Scicli are a real feast for the eyes as for the palate, thanks to their culinary delights.

In the wetlands of the Riserva di Vendicari migratory birds find their paradise while a few steps away a crystalline sea caresses sweeping white beaches, dotted with old crumbling *tonnare* (tuna fisheries). One of the southeastern beaches became famous thanks to the Italian TV show *Inspector Montalbano,* partly filmed at a house at Punta Secca.

The countryside is olive-laden as far as the eye can see and bordered by low pale-stone walls, typical of the rural landscape of the area. Mysterious canyons (called *cave*) in Pantalica and Cava d'Ispica hide ancient prehistoric civilizations and their necropolises. You can also discover the Greek past of Palazzolo Acreide, the medieval one of Buccheri, the old Sicilian peasant civilization in Buscemi.

And if you are looking for a bit of magic, dive into the emerald lakes of Cavagrande del Cassabile.

ERIK VAN DE LEUR/SHUTTERSTOCK ©

THE MAIN AREAS

SYRACUSE	NOTO	RAGUSA
Greek and Roman ruins p178	Baroque at its peak p188	A city with two souls p196

Find Your Way

Exploring the Val di Noto, which extends from Syracuse down to Ragusa and onwards to the tip of southern Sicily, means opening your eyes in wonder at beautiful landscapes along the way.

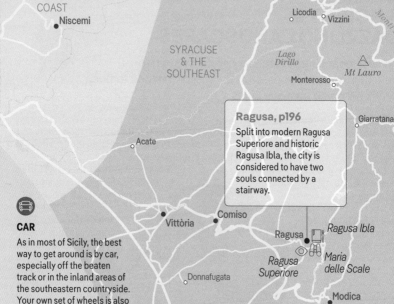

MEDITERRANEAN COAST

Niscemi

SYRACUSE & THE SOUTHEAST

Sco

Militello

Francofo

Licodia   Vizzini

Monti Ible

Lago Dirillo

Mt Lauro

Monterosso

Giarratana

Acate

Ragusa, p196

Split into modern Ragusa Superiore and historic Ragusa Ibla, the city is considered to have two souls connected by a stairway.

Comiso

Vittòria

Ragusa · *Ragusa Ibla*

Ragusa Superiore · *Maria delle Scale*

Donnafugata

Modica

Santa Croce

Scicli

Pozzallo

Marina di Modica

Mediterranean Sea

CAR

As in most of Sicily, the best way to get around is by car, especially off the beaten track or in the inland areas of the southeastern countryside. Your own set of wheels is also recommended for reaching seaside resorts.

BUS

Buses connect Catania airport to the main cities of Syracuse (Etna Trasporti), Noto (AST) and Ragusa (Interbus). They are frequent, reliable and faster than the train. It is more difficult to reach smaller towns by public transport.

TRAIN

Train connections are very good between Catania and Syracuse and between the cities around Ragusa (Modica, Comiso and Scicli). However, getting to other destinations can mean a long and uncomfortable journey.

0   10 km
0   6 miles

Syracuse, p178

Syracuse has two hearts: the Greek one beats in the archaeological park of Neapolis; the Sicilian one lies in the sea on the island of Ortygia.

Noto, p188

Among Sicily's most beautiful baroque cities, in the centre of the Val di Noto, Noto was rebuilt after the 1693 earthquake. Its red-gold buildings glow at sunset.

Lago di Lentini

Lentini

Carlentini

Brucoli

Augusta

Melilli

Priolo Gargallo

Mt Santa Venera

Sortino

Solarino

Floridia

erla

Mazzolo reide

Mt Grosso

Canicattini Bagni

Parco Archeologico della Neapolis

Catacombe di San Giovanni

Syracuse   Ortygia

Duomo   Teatro dei Pupi

Ciane

Passo Ladro

Riserva di Cavagrande del Cassibile

Fontane Bianche

Noto Antica

Mezzo Gregorio

Avola

San Carlo al Corso   Noto

Noto Marina

Rosolini

pica

Riserva Naturale di Vendicari

Ionian Sea

Pachino

Isola Capo Passero

Capo Passero

Isola delle Correnti   Capo delle Correnti

Anapo

Valle dell'Anapo

175

Plan Your Time

The Val di Noto lies between Syracuse, Noto and Ragusa in the southeastern corner of Sicily: let yourself be seduced by the beautiful island Ortygia, the golden Noto and the narrow streets of Ragusa.

Museo Archeologico
Paolo Orsi (p182), Syracuse

If you only do one thing

● Head to **Syracuse** (p178) to discover one of the most powerful cities that rivalled Athens in ancient times. Spend the morning wandering the archaeological site **Neapolis** (p181) to see a magnificent Greek theatre, ancient quarries on a cathedral scale and the famous Ear of Dionysius. If it gets hot, take refuge at the **Museo Archeologico Paolo Orsi** (p182), one of Sicily's most prominent museums.

● After lunch with a view in **Ortygia** (p179), stroll around the island, a labyrinth of narrow streets, centuries-old palaces and baroque churches. End your day at a traditional puppet show at the **Teatro dei Pupi** (p181).

Seasonal highlights

The best times to enjoy the southeast are late spring and summer until early October. But the mild climate in winter makes a holiday unforgettable here even between November and March.

MAY
Noto hosts the flower festival Infiorata and Scicli celebrates the Madonna delle Milizie, a warrior Madonna on horseback.

JUNE
From end of May to early July classical plays are staged in the Greek theatre of Syracuse.

JULY
Ortygia hosts Ortigia Sound System, an electronic music festival mixing Mediterranean rhythms and new musical trends.

JANNHUIZENGA/GETTY IMAGES ©, DUCHY/SHUTTERSTOCK ©, VLADIMIR HODAC/SHUTTERSTOCK ©

Three days exploring baroque beauty

● After a full day in Syracuse browsing baroque churches and palaces, drive towards **Noto** (p188), stopping by for a sunset swim along the coast. Spend the following day exploring the town known as the Garden of Stone due to its astonishing buildings of golden stone that glow at sunset.

● On your third day head to **Ragusa** (p196) and fall in love with Ragusa Ibla and its maze of narrow streets, the baroque gems among them and the famous Piazza Duomo with the church of San Giorgio in the background.

Five days around the southeast

● Start from Syracuse. Wander its archaeological site and stroll around the lovely island of Ortygia, then head to Noto to discover the Val di Noto's shining star. Spend the third day relaxing on a wild beach in the **Vendicari nature reserve** (p193) and enjoy a magical dinner by the sea in the lovely fishing village of **Marzamemi** (p194).

● Along the road towards Ragusa, stop for a walk in the underrated but beautiful **Ispica** (p200) and then reach **Modica** (p200), a maze of staircases and winding alleys, hidden wonders and a surprisingly crumbly local chocolate. End your tour in Ragusa or spend a day discovering **Scicli** (p202).

AUGUST
Historical parade, juggling, shows on stilts and medieval drums – MedFest is held in Buccheri during the third week of August.

SEPTEMBER
Marzamemi hosts the Festival del Cinema di Frontiera. Movies are shown on the square and in the old *tonnara* (tuna fishery).

OCTOBER
The streets and stairs of the historic centre of Ragusa are the setting for a buzzing event celebrating Sicilian food.

DECEMBER
Devotees follow the relics of Santa Lucia on 13 December shouting *Siracusana jè!* (she is a Syracusan!).

SYRACUSE

se was the most important city in the
r than Athens both in size and status.
It was founded by Corinthian colonists in 734 BCE on the
island of Ortygia. Later, they built a new city on the mainland, called Neapolis, where you can still witness a glorious
past. Now it is one of Sicily's greatest archaeological sites
with impressive caves on a cathedral scale and a theatre still
in use. Over centuries, takeovers and makeovers by Romans,
Byzantines, Arabs, Normans and others left their traces in-
fluencing art, culture and cuisine.

Today's Syracuse is an incredible mix of wonders from different eras and styles, constituting the true distinctive soul
of the city. The main attraction is the historic centre on Ortygia island, a maze of narrow streets with the blue sea peeking
out at the bottom, centuries-old palaces, baroque churches
and a promenade all around its perimeter.

TOP TIP

To escape from the tourist
crowds, explore the
mesmerising maze of La
Giudecca, Ortygia's old
Jewish quarter, around the
old guild neighbourhood
on Via della Maestranza
and the Via della Giudecca
Jewish ghetto. Accessed by
Ponte Umbertino or Ponte
Santa Lucia, the area is best
explored on foot.

HIGHLIGHTS
1 Catacombe di San
Giovanni
2 Duomo
3 Ortygia
4 Parco Archeologico
della Neapolis
5 Teatro dei Pupi

SIGHTS
6 Basilica di Santa Lucia
al Sepolcro
7 Castello Maniace
8 Fontana di Diana
9 Galleria Regionale di
Palazzo Bellomo
10 Museo dei Pupi

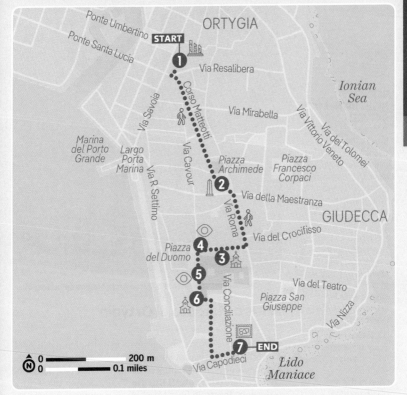

A WALKING TOUR IN ORTYGIA

Cross Ponte Umbertino and admire the ruins of Sicily's oldest Doric temple, **1 Tempio di Apollo**. Walk south along Corso Matteotti to Giulio Moschetti's **2 Fontana di Diana** (1906–07) on Piazza Archimede. The fountain's leading lady is Artemis, goddess of hunting, who transformed her handmaiden Aretusa into a spring to protect her from the advances of pesky river god Alpheus.

Continue south along Via Roma and turn right onto Piazza Minerva. Observe the Doric columns of the 5th-century BCE temple to Athena on which Syracuse's 7th-century cathedral was built. Before entering the **3 Duomo**, contemplate Syracuse's showpiece square and its sweep of baroque, pale golden-stone *palazzi* that appear to be built from light. Spot the signature stone lizard of Spanish architect Juan Vermexio on the left corner of the cornice at **4 Palazzo**

Municipale (1629). Opposite, 17th-century **5 Palazzo Arcivescovile** hosts the Biblioteca Alagoniana with rare 13th-century manuscripts. In **6 Chiesa di Santa Lucia alla Badia**, uncover a nuns' parlour with beautiful blue majolica floor. Before leaving Piazza del Duomo, sit and watch the world go by – children playing, musicians busking – over pistachio *granita* from Bar Condorelli at No 16 on the square.

Or walk five minutes south to 13th-century Catalan-Gothic *palazzo* **7 Galleria Regionale di Palazzo Bellomo**, stopping at Cannoli Del Re en route for typical Sicilian *cannoli* in a cone instead of the traditional shell. Among the gallery's collection of early-Byzantine to 19th-century art, *Annunciation* (1474) by Sicily's greatest 15th-century artist, Antonello da Messina, is a highlight.

BEST LATE-NIGHT DRINKS IN ORTYGIA

Boats
Despite a nautical-themed decor, Boats stands for 'Based on a True Story'. A good drinks list, guest barstaff and a great vinyl collection.

Muciula
Good vibes and a great place for *aperitivo* with a huge platter of street-food nibbles while listening to live music on the Piazzetta San Rocco.

Cortile Verga
Enjoy drinks and chilled music in an 18th-century courtyard at one of Ortygia's top cocktail bars.

Orecchio di Dionisio (p182), Parco Archeologico della Neapolis

Antico Mercato di Ortygia

FOODIE FINDS AT THE MARKET

Ortygia's open-air market sets up shop by the Tempio di Apollo every morning except Sunday. Weave your way through the kaleidoscope of stalls selling seafood, fruit, veggies, herbs and cheeses to reach **Fratelli Burgio**. Take a pew on the terrace, order a charcuterie board and glass of wine, and enjoy the dress-circle spectacle of vendors shouting and gesticulating to catch shoppers' attention. Freshly shucked oysters and giant *panini* prepared in front of you with locally sourced products are the star attraction of legendary **Caseificio Borderi**. If fish rocks your boat, hit **La Lisca** for red tuna tartare spiked with *friggitelli* (sweet chilli pepper).

The Ortygia Loop

WALK THE ISLAND'S PERIMETER

It should take less than an hour to walk a complete loop of Ortygia along its handsome perimeter. Start at **Forte San Giovannello**, part of the island's 16th-century fortification system, and drink in perfect views of modern Syracuse on the mainland. Continue along Lungomare di Levante to **Forte**

WHERE TO STAY IN ORTYGIA

Algilà Ortigia Charme Hotel
In a baroque palace with a 14th-century courtyard. Cool design balancing Arab heritage and contemporary comforts. €€€

Alla Giudecca
In a restored 15th-century building, above an ancient Jewish ritual bath. Gorgeous courtyard. €€

Hotel Gutkowski
Simple yet chic mix of vintage details and industrial vibes. Book in advance for a sea-view room. €

Vigliena – snap photos of waves crashing against the crenellated fort walls. Visit 13th-century **Castello Maniace** on the island's southern tip, host to July's electronic-music festival Ortigia Sound System. Don't miss the castle's vaulted central hall. Continue your walk along the western shore to **Fonte Aretusa**, the legendary spot where goddess Artemis transformed Aretusa into a bubbling spring, now a pretty pond of papyrus plants. End on the pedestrian jetty – a magical place to enjoy sunset.

La Giudecca

EXPERIENCE JEWISH ORTYGIA

Jewish people are thought to have been part of the Syracusan cultural patchwork at least as early as the 1st century CE. Ortygia's Giudecca (Jewish Quarter) used to have 12 synagogues, until Spain, which ruled in Sicily, expelled the Jews from its domain in the 15th century. Giudecca is a labyrinth of narrow stone-paved alleys still revealing the ancient Jewish presence: a star on a facade, an inscription in Hebrew on the church of **San Giovannello**, which once was a synagogue, and a medieval tombstone displayed in the museum at Palazzo Bellomo. You can also visit the most ancient *miqweh* (Jewish ritual bath) in Europe. It was discovered while converting a palace into hotel **Alla Giudecca** – underneath the courtyard hid an underground chamber brimming with fresh water. You can see another *miqweh* under the church of **San Filippo**, 18m below street level.

Act Out at Teatro dei Pupi

KNIGHTS, ROYALTY & MONSTERS

Sicily has a rich tradition of puppet theatre enacting old tales of knights, royalty and monsters that need defeating. You can attend a show at the **Teatro dei Pupi** every afternoon except Sunday, and visit the small **Museo dei Pupi** nearby to learn the history of Sicilian puppet theatre.

Parco Archeologico della Neapolis

ANCIENT GREEK DRAMA ON AND OFF STAGE

It's pretty wild to think you can sit in the very theatre – potentially even the same seat – where ancient Greek playwright Aeschylus watched his tragedies unfold on stage for the first time. Syracuse's 16,000-capacity **Teatro Greco**, dating to the 5th century BCE and rebuilt two centuries later, remains one of Sicily's most prestigious theatres and watching a summertime play here is unforgettable. Mid-May to early July, during the Festival del Teatro Greco, Syracuse's INDA (National

BEST PLACES TO SWIM IN ORTYGIA

Forte Vigliena
Right next to the fort, metal stairs lead to the rocks below. Space is limited but the water is deep enough for diving. In summer there is an additional wooden platform.

Cala Rossa
For those that prefer a proper beach there is a sandy crescent below the walls. It's very small so it can be crowded in summer.

Zefiro Solarium
Just below the Arethusa spring there is a wooden platform offering sunbeds, parasols, music and drinks. In the evening it turns into a lounge bar, a lovely spot to enjoy a sunset.

Forte Vigliena

WHERE TO EAT IN ORTYGIA

A Putia delle Cose Buone
Lovely atmosphere, great home-style food, generous portions. A nice lunch stop; reserve for dinner. €€

Schiticchio
Cosy place serving innovative pizzas prepared from high-quality Sicilian ingredients. Try the Levanzo. €€

Siculish United Tastes of Sicily
Excellent food, broad selection of Sicilian wines. Don't miss: seared tuna with pistachios. €€

WHY I LOVE SYRACUSE

Sara Mostaccio.
@fritha

The first time I set foot in the archaeological park of Neapolis, in Syracuse, I was seven years old on a school trip. The Ear of Dionysius impressed me but what really hit me was the ancient Greek theatre. It seemed immense to me. During high school I kept coming back, summer after summer, to attend the classical plays staged here by INDA Fondazione. It is still a ritual I maintain to this day. Every single time I attend performances speaking of universal human values the magic happens and I feel catapulted back in time. Those ancient tragedies still have a message to deliver.

Institute of Ancient Drama) – the only school of classical Greek drama outside Athens – stages classical Greek plays (in Italian). Bag tickets in advance online (www.indafondazione.org) or from the ticket booth outside the theatre.

Pre-performance, time-travel to ancient Greek Syracuse with an evocative amble around the archaeological park. Beside the theatre, the mysterious **Latomia del Paradiso** is a precipitous limestone quarry from which stone for the ancient city was extracted. Riddled with catacombs and perfumed with citrus and magnolia trees, this is where 7000 survivors of the war between Syracuse and Athens in 413 BCE were imprisoned. The tyrant Dionysius eavesdropped on his prisoners from the entrance of **Orecchio di Dionisio**, a grotto with perfect acoustics, 23m high and extending 65m back into the cliffside.

Up to 450 oxen could be killed at one time on the 3rd-century-BCE **Ara di Gerone II**, a monolithic sacrificial altar to Hieron II, and gladiatorial combats and horse races provided entertainment at the 2nd-century **Anfiteatro Romano**. End at the **Museo Archeologico Paolo Orsi**, a one-stop shop covering Syracuse's backstory from prehistory to Roman times.

Basilica di Santa Lucia al Sepolcro

PATRON SAINT & CARAVAGGIO

This 17th-century church is dedicated to Syracuse's patron saint, Lucia, a noble girl martyred on 13 December 304 CE. On that day, the silver statue of Lucia wends its way from the cathedral in Ortygia to this church, followed by devotees yelling *'siracusana jè!'* (she is a Syracusan). Beneath the church lie early-Christian catacombs. On the altar you can see the *Seppellimento di Santa Lucia* (The Burial of St Lucia) by Caravaggio, who arrived in Syracuse in 1608 after having escaped from prison in Malta.

Catacombe di San Giovanni

TOUR LARGE CATACOMBS

San Giovanni Evangelista is a stunning open-air church hiding an underground treasure: a painted crypt dedicated to Syracuse's first bishop St Marcian, flogged to death in 254 CE, and the largest catacombs in Syracuse. A path will lead you along a sacred labyrinth of tunnels carved into the limestone, where silence rules.

 GETTING AROUND

Most of Ortygia is restricted to resident motorists only. Find two paying car parks (Marina and Talete) at the entrance of the island.

Arriving by train is only really convenient from Catania – from elsewhere, take the bus. Count 20 minutes on foot from Syracuse train station to Ortygia, or 10 minutes by electric minibus 1. To reach the Parco Archeologico della Neapolis, take minibus 2 from Molo Sant'Antonio (just west of the bridge to Ortygia). Buy bus tickets on board. Siracuse Tour Bike (www.siracusatourbike.it) rents bicycles and organises city bike tours.

Gole della
Stretta
Buccheri
Sortino
Buscemi
Pista Ciclabile
Rossana Maiorca
Palazzolo
Acreide
Syracuse
Area Marina Protetta
del Plemmirio

Beyond Syracuse

History and nature have never been so intertwined as in the Syracuse area. Discover all their unexpected connections.

If you don't plan to extend your trip to Sortino, where you can taste the traditional *pizzolo* born here, don't worry, you can find it throughout the Syracuse area. Each pizzeria has at least one *pizzolo* on its menu.

Imagine exploring sea caves, ancient *tonnare* and golden cliffs riding along a former railway line transformed into a nature trail. Consider traveling in the distant past and discovering a prehistoric necropolis carved into the rock of a gorge. Visualise diving into the emerald water of a small lake set in white rock. Think about walking through the stone streets of a medieval village perched on a hill surrounded by nature as far as the eye can see. You are picturing the surroundings of Syracuse, rich in natural and historic beauties all waiting to be explored: the Plemmirio nature reserve; the necropolis of Pantalica in the Anapo valley; the villages of Palazzolo Acreide, Buscemi and Buccheri; and the lakes of Cavagrande del Cassibile.

Area Marina Protetta del Plemmirio (p184)

FILIPPNG/SHUTTERSTOCK ©

BEST BEACHES NEAR SYRACUSE

Arenella
Sandy beach 10km south of Syracuse. It also offers clubs, bars and handy parking areas.

Ognina
Rocky cliffs, sea caves and sandy coves lapped by crystal waters 13km from Syracuse. Swim to reach the deserted island offshore.

Fontane Bianche
The beach takes its name, which means white fountains, from several fresh water springs flowing from the seabed. It's 18km from Syracuse.

Necropoli di Pantalica

Area Marina Protetta del Plemmirio

PROTECTED MARINE RESERVE

There is a protected marine area 10km south of Syracuse that you can explore as a diver, trekker or mountain-biker. Along the rocky peninsula you'll find several coves perfect for swimming; rent a bike or an e-bike in Syracuse or book a tour (www.siracusatourbike.it) and cycle the full route (25km). You can also reach the area by car and then continue on foot along the Sentiero della Maddalena from Punta Castelluccio to Capo Murro di Porco (10km). There are several great spots for photos including Pillirina beach, Punta del Gigante, Punta Tavernara, Scoglio dell'Elefante and the lighthouse at Capo Murro di Porco. To explore the seabed – with caves, stalactites, arches and rich marine life – book a dive at Ortigia Diving (www.ortigiadiving.com).

Syracuse by Boat

EXPLORE GROTTOS

Boat tour bookings are available from many stands around the port of Ortygia. Go out to sea and explore the caves along

 WHERE TO STAY IN PALAZZOLO ACREIDE

Domus Hyblaea Resort
Rooms, suites and villas in an idyllic setting. Restaurant, sun terrace and outdoor pool. €€€

Feudo Bauly
Former noble residence surrounded by countryside, a few minutes' drive from Palazzolo Acreide. €€

Dimora Bennardo
Located in the historic centre, fully equipped apartment with stone walls and modern design. €

the coastline, including the heart-shaped Lovers' Grotto. Tours last between two and four hours, and from May to September you can dive off the boat for a swim.

Pista Ciclabile Rossana Maiorca

RIDE ALONG A FORMER RAILWAY

A former railway track 2km north of Ortygia opened in 2008 exclusively for cyclists and pedestrians extending for 6.5km from Piazza Cappuccini to Targia. Rent a bike in Ortygia as there are no rental facilities near the start of the track. Along the way you can see the rock Due Fratelli, dramatic cliffs, an abandoned railway station, an old *tonnara,* the gulf where the Greeks built the port of Trogilo, Greek-era stone quarries and WWII bunkers.

Sortino

CITY OF HONEY

There are three great reasons to visit Sortino, a 40-minute motor northwest from Syracuse: it's a delightful baroque village; you can taste authentic native *pizzolo* (pizza); and the town's *fascitrari* (beekeepers) produce excellent honey, hence its 'city of honey' nickname. Wander its streets, not missing Chiesa di Santa Sofia dedicated to the town's patron saint, and the dazzling baroque gem of Chiesa di Monevergine. Traditional Sicilian puppetry comes alive in the small Museo dell'Opera dei Pupi and beekeeping paraphernalia fills house-museum Casa ro Fascitraru.

Tombs at Necropoli di Pantalica

TREK THE ANAPO VALLEY

The largest Mediterranean necropolis includes over 5000 tombs and dates back to the 13th century. The necropolis is on a plateau surrounded by the river Anapo and the Calcinara stream. At the highest point are the ruins of Anàktoron, the Palace of the Prince. The main path (13km) along the Anapo's valley follows a railway built in the early 1900s but there are many other trails you can walk either independently or accompanied by a guide (www.scopripantalica. it). Start from Sortino (45 mins from Syracuse), follow the signs for Pantalica and leave your car at the entrance. Along the path you can see the necropolis, the **Anàktoron** and the Byzantine village of **San Micidiario**. You can also start from Ferla, the opposite side of the valley, leaving your car at Sella di Filiporto.

TRY PIZZOLO DI SORTINO

Typical Syracusa *pizzolo* (local pizza) originates in Sortino. Scraps of leftover bread dough were traditionally used in family kitchens to make focaccia rounds spiced with thyme, salt and oil. Today *pizzolo* is topped with an additional layer of dough to resemble a pizza sandwich stuffed with cheese, oregano, pepper and whatever else the *pizzarolo* chef chooses to add. La Castellina and Le Monache in Sortino both cook up some wild combos. Sweet variations ooze ricotta and honey – sample for dessert at La Pizzoleria.

Pizzolo

 WHERE TO EAT A PIZZOLO IN SORTINO

La Castellina	Le Monache	La Pizzoleria
The specialty is *ruccoletta* with rocket pesto, red wine reduction, buffalo mozzarella, parmesan flakes and lard. €	Try the *nfigghiulato,* a dough stuffed with catmint, *stracciatella* cheese, sausage, dried figs, tomatoes and olives. €€	A *pizzolo* as a dessert? Try the one filled with ricotta and honey. €

BEST RESTAURANTS IN PALAZZOLO ACREIDE

Trattoria del Gallo
Excellent food, from appetizers to desserts. Try Palazzolo's traditional sausage or the pork shank. Usually full of locals.

Scrigno dei Sapori
Let Lidia advise you on what to taste but you can't go wrong, everything is exquisite. Don't miss her pistachio tiramisu.

Al Punto Giusto
Hidden from the main street but worth a visit. Good regional dishes, a wide selection of wines and great Sicilian hospitality.

Walk through Palazzolo Acreide

3000 YEARS OF HERITAGE

The Greeks founded the city of Akrai here in 664 BCE. Later, the Normans called it Palatiolum. It was rebuilt after the 1693 earthquake and today is a Unesco-listed baroque city 40km from Syracuse called Palazzolo Acreide. Begin your visit from Piazza del Popolo, lined by the **Palazzo del Comune** and the **Chiesa di San Sebastiano** with a spectacular staircase. Take Corso Vittorio Emanuele and admire **Palazzo Judica** and **Palazzo Pizzo**. At the end of the street is the **Chiesa dell'Immacolata Concezione** with a convex facade. It houses a marble Renaissance masterpiece, *Madonna col Bambino*. A little further on is the **Chiesa di San Michele Arcangelo** with a hexagonal bell tower.

Keep on walking and you'll find the **Casa Museo di Antonino Uccello**, an ethno-anthropological museum on Sicilian popular culture. From here you will soon reach the **Mother Church** and the remarkable **Basilica di San Paolo** with a baroque tower facade. The destroyed castle nearby offers a panoramic view over the Anapo valley. Returning towards the centre, admire the balconies of the 18th-century **Palazzo Zocco** and go ahead to the **Chiesa dell'Annunziata** with its spectacular portal with four twisted columns. Now take Via Garibaldi to see the 18th-century **Palazzo Lombardo** with a stunning balcony and the **Palazzo Ferla di Tristaino**. In a nearby street admire **Palazzo Cappellani**, now an archaeological museum. The **archaeological area** is 1km away from the centre. Behind the 2nd-century Greek theatre, you can see the remains of the 6th-century temple of Aphrodite, and not far away is the sanctuary dedicated to the goddess Cybele.

Drive to Buscemi, Buccheri & Gole della Stretta

ROAD TRIP THROUGH HISTORY

Buscemi stands on a hill of the Hyblaean plateau about 50km from Syracuse. Its name dates back to Arab rule when it was Qal'at Abî Sâmah meaning "the fortress of Abû Sâmah" (an epithet of the prophet Muhammad) due to its high-up position. Over time, Abî Sâmah became the town of Buscemim which is today known as a Paese Museo (country museum) thanks to an interesting ethno-anthropological itinerary through the whole town, called I luoghi del Lavoro Contadino. Walking around the streets you can visit a mill, a traditional farmer's house, the blacksmith's workshop, the shoemaker's shop and more, discovering how people lived and worked in Sicily until the mid-1900s.

 WHERE TO EAT IN BUCCHERI

Osteria U Locale
Here you can try all the local specialties, including the traditional *pani cu pipi*. €€

Da Antonio
Eat well for less at this pleasant restaurant among olive groves. Try the pasta with asparagus, mushrooms and speck. €

La Zafferaneto
A traditional *masseria* (farm) offering very good cuisine and cooking classes. Saffron is grown here too. €€€

Chiesa di San Sebastiano, Palazzolo Acreide

BEST THINGS TO EAT IN BUCCHERI

Funciddi
Delicious mushroom-shaped biscuits made with toasted almonds and hazelnuts.

Krocos
Saffron grown in the Buccheri area is used to make a liqueur called *krocos*.

Local olive oil
Buccheri has become the capital of extra virgin olive oil, winning several awards. Its production is based on Tonda Iblea, an indigenous olive.

Pani cu pipi
A Buccheri peasant tradition, once eaten at breakfast. It's bread baked with tomato extract, garlic and chilli.

Favi liezzi
A delicious broad bean soup with oregano, extra virgin olive oil, chilli and vinegar.

Buccheri is 10 minutes away along the SS124 located on the slopes of Mt Lauro. The Normans colonised the territory, building a two-tower castle on the hill. The **Chiesa di Sant'Antonio** was founded in 1212 while the **Chiesa di Santa Maria Maddalena** dates back to the 15th century. In the third week of August, Buccheri hosts MedFest, a medieval re-enactment with a drum competition, performances and medieval cuisine. Buccheri is known throughout Sicily for its local specialties, so you can enjoy its culinary delights any time of year.

On a hillock west of the town stands the small but charming **Santuario della Madonna delle Grazie**, once a hermit monastery. About 2km north of the village is the frescoed cave church of **San Nicola**. The path is often overgrown but it is worth it. North-east along the SP5 for 8km is the **Chiesa di Andrea** built in Gothic style in 1225. From here you can quickly reach the **Gole della Stretta**, an impressive gorge created by the San Leonardo rover.

GETTING AROUND

You can still reach the coast from Syracuse by bus (lines 21, 22, 23 to the beaches) or by bike (rentals are available along Corso Umberto), but to explore the inland area a car is essential.

Ride along the coast north of Syracuse by bike on an easy cycle path. The Plemmirio peninsula, south of the city, is also good to explore on two wheels. If you do prefer driving, you can get there in about 20 minutes.

Reaching Sortino and Pantalica requires a car. Parking in Sortino is easy. At Pantalica, park at the entrance and follow the path. Parking is more difficult in Palazzolo Acreide's centre. Follow the SS124 from Syracuse and aim for Parcheggio Fontana Grande south of the city centre.

Driving the narrow streets of the villages of Buscemi and Buccheri, 50 minutes from Syracuse, is a challenge; park up and walk.

NOTO

An earthquake in 1693 razed Noto to the ground, but a grander legacy arose from the tragedy. Unesco-listed Noto is an elegant baroque beauty, dubbed 'garden of stone' for its flamboyant *palazzi*, churches, bell towers and balconies strung with sculpted masks and cherubs. At sunset the city really works its magic: limestone buildings glow honey-gold.

The Noto you see today dates from the early 18th century, but a town called Netum existed here for centuries before. You can visit Noto Antica, the ruined medieval city, a short drive from the city centre. It was perched on a plateau overlooking the Asinaro valley full of almond, olive and citrus groves.

TOP TIP

Listen to Sicily (www.listentosicily.it) offers a nice multilingual audio guide (English included) to learn the history of Noto while walking around the city. The entire package of four audio guides costs less than €2. You can also choose a Baroque or Unesco themed audio tour.

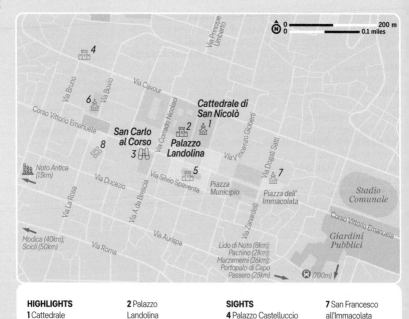

HIGHLIGHTS
1 Cattedrale di San Nicolò
2 Palazzo Landolina
3 San Carlo al Corso

SIGHTS
4 Palazzo Castelluccio
5 Palazzo Ducezio
6 San Domenico
7 San Francesco all'Immacolata
8 Teatro Tina di Lorenzo

Basilica Cattedrale di San Nicolò

A Walk into the Baroque

GARDEN OF STONE

Plunge through Porta Reale into Noto's beautiful historic centre. Walk west along main street Corso Vittorio Emanuele to 18th-century **Chiesa di San Francesco d'Assisi all'Immacolata** and **Basilica del Santissimo Salvatore**, adjoining a Benedictine convent. Spot the ornate original portal of **Chiesa di Santa Chiara**, made redundant after the street was lowered in the 19th century. The church's elliptical interior is awash with whimsical stuccowork and stars one of Noto's finest baroque altars, but it's the rooftop terrace with soul-soaring view that steals the show.

The peachy dome dominating the skyline is that of **Basilica Cattedrale di San Nicolò**, a renovated baroque beauty. In front of the cathedral, **Palazzo Ducezio** is now the town hall, with a Versailles-style Hall of Mirrors. **Palazzo Landolina** and **Palazzo Nicolaci di Villadorata**, wrought-iron balconies propped up by grotesque figures, boast two more fantastical facades flanking architectural jewel box Piazza Municipio. Continue west along Corso Vittorio Emanuele to **Chiesa di San Domenico**, one of Noto's finest baroque

SWEET OR SAVOURY? TREATS IN NOTO

Caffè Sicilia
Order an almond *granita*, a *saccottino* pastry filled with ricotta or a Montezuma ice cream.

Dolceria Costanzo
Treat yourself with a *cassata* (sponge cake, cream, marzipan, chocolate and candied fruit) or a pistachio ice cream.

Pasticceria Mandolfiore
A brioche filled with ice cream or a *cannolo*? You can't go wrong either way.

Putia del Coppo
Cones full of fried fish and veggies. Don't miss the calamari.

Panificio Maidda
Taste *sfincione* (a spongy, oily pizza topped with onions and *caciocavallo* cheese) or a *scaccia* (filled pancake) with onions at this tiny bakery.

Pani Cunzatu
Affordable yet delicious salads and sandwiches combined with tasty local beer.

WHERE TO HAVE A DRINK IN NOTO

Anche Gli Angeli
Have an *aperitivo* while you browse books or a late-night drink while listening to live music in this old church. €€

Il Brillo Parlante
A family-owned wine bar. Local cheeses and good Sicilian wines. Let Giuseppe, the sommelier, guide you. €€

Il Libertyno
The perfect spot to have a good beer or a cocktail accompanied by Sicilian tapas. €€

buildings, designed to a Greek-cross plan by baroque architect Rosario Gagliardi, who is reputedly buried here. Duck a block north to uncover a bounty of noble, 18th-century *palazzi* on Via Cavour.

BEST RESTAURANTS IN NOTO

Manna
In a former prince's wine cellar, this is the best restaurant in town. Sicilian cuisine with contemporary flair.

Dammuso
Cosy seafood restaurant. Try the tuna in pistachio crust, *sarde a beccafico* or a grouper tartare.

Trattoria Giufà
Loved by locals. The rabbit cooked in red wine and the squid meatballs with sultanas and toasted almonds are both excellent.

Crocifisso
Michelin-starred restaurant. Tasting menus available or order à la carte. Extensive wine list.

Campanile di San Carlo
PERFECT PHOTO SPOT

To get a sense of a place it helps to get up high. In Noto that means scaling the bell tower of **San Carlo al Corso**. The church is dedicated to San Carlo Borromeo and is part of a Jesuit convent. From above, you can line up the perfect shot with the historic centre framed in a golden stone window.

Creative Infiorata di Noto
FESTIVAL OF FLOWERS

In the third weekend of May, the 700m stretch of Via Nicolaci turns into a tapestry of petals depicting religious or mythological designs. The artists begin their work on Friday and by Saturday the carpet of flowers is ready to be seen. The weekend program includes a historic baroque parade through the streets of the city, shows, exhibitions and tastings.

Ruins of Noto Antica
FORMER MEDIEVAL CITY

The remains of the medieval and Greek city of Noto Antica rise on Mt Alveria, surrounded by three deep gorges, 12km from Noto. Start from the Porta della Montagna in the old fortifications where you can go up the bastion and look out at the view. Continue to the Norman-Aragonese castle, which has been used as a prison – spot the prisoners' graffiti on its walls. A little further on are the remains of the 16th-century hospital and the church of Santa Maria di Loreto. Continuing on the main path, there is **Palazzo Landolina di Belludia**, one of the most sumptuous noble residences. In front of it are the remains of the Jesuit College. On the ancient Piazza Maggiore go left at the fork in the path to see the Greek city: fortifications, a gymnasium and some shrines dedicated to the cult of the dead.

GETTING AROUND

Noto is best experienced on foot as all the attractions are a short distance apart. You will need a car to reach Noto Antica – the site is not connected by public transport and is 12km from the centre.

Noto bus station is close to the historic centre, southeast of Porta Reale. If you are travelling by car, a convenient car park is available next to Porta Reale. SS115 connects Noto to Syracuse, a 45-minute drive.

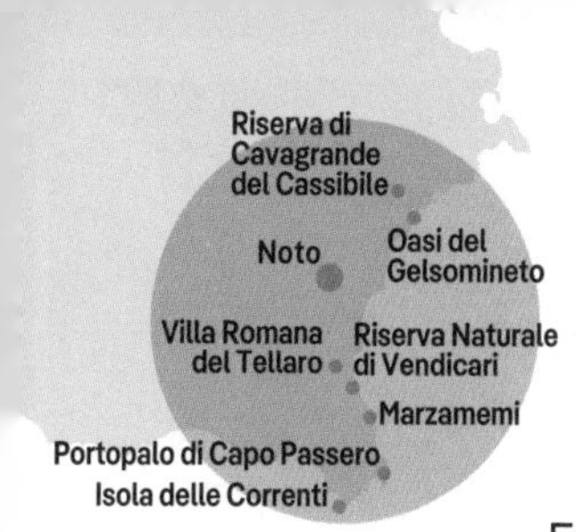
Riserva di Cavagrande del Cassibile
Noto
Oasi del Gelsomineto
Villa Romana del Tellaro
Riserva Naturale di Vendicari
Marzamemi
Portopalo di Capo Passero
Isola delle Correnti

Beyond Noto

Enjoy a relaxing day trip from Noto exploring wineries, an ancient villa with mosaics, a fishing village or a nature reserve.

TOP TIP

Don't miss a glass of fragrant Moscato di Noto or sweet flowery Passito, produced from excellent grape varieties grown around Noto. To learn more, join a wine-tasting tour or visit wineries independently along the Strado del Val di Noto (www.stradadelval dinoto.it).

Sicily's southeastern tip hides wonders around Noto. Take an unforgettable wine-tasting tour to experience the excellent wines produced in these vineyards. The small emerald lakes in Cavagrande del Cassabile will bewitch you, and the white beaches along the coast are surrounded by woods, jasmine and rocky ridges. Enjoy a lazy afternoon sunbathing and close the day visiting the Villa Romana del Tellaro and its mosaics before a sunset stroll in a fishing village. Dine by the sea while the sun gilds the stones on the square of Marzamemi. Drive south to Portopalo di Capo Passero, with what was once the largest *tonnara* on the island, and go further to Sicily's southernmost point to visit the tiny Isola delle Correnti (Island of Currents).

Mosaic, Villa Romana del Tellaro (p193)

BEST WINERIES AROUND NOTO

Tenuta Palmeri
Erika and Ueli from Switzerland run this 15th-century winery in Avola practicing organic viticulture.

Vini Rudini
Produces excellent wines near Pachino, combining traditional techniques and modern technologies. Try the Baroque with a distinctive scent of flowers.

Terre di Noto
Have a picnic among vines and olive trees. The basket contains a bottle of wine, sandwiches, olives, fruit and desserts.

Feudo Maccari
In the 1990s the Val di Noto enchanted Antonio Moretti Cuseri from Tuscany. He decided to stay.

Riserva di Cavagrande del Cassabile

A Wine Tasting Tour

DISCOVER LOCAL WINES

The area around Noto produces excellent grape varieties such as Nero d'Avola, Syrah and Moscato Bianco. Do not miss a glass of fragrant Moscato di Noto or a delicious Passito, which have a flowery flavour. Join a wine-tasting tour or choose some wineries to visit on your own (www.stradadelvaldinoto.it). All of them offer guided tours and degustations.

Pristine Oasi del Gelsomineto

A HEAVENLY BAY

This bay of fine white and pale gold sand is near the mouth of the Cassibile river, just a few kilometres from Noto. It's surrounded by a maritime pine forest and gets its name 'Gelsomineto' from the jasmine that grows nearby. Locals call it *a Marchisa* as the Marquise of Cassibile loved to relax here in the unspoiled oasis with crystalline blue sea.

You can easily climb the limestone cliffs found at the ends of the small gulf, or swim out to explore the stone arches and marine caves. If you love diving or underwater photography, this place is your paradise. You can also enjoy it by kayak or

 WHERE TO STAY AROUND NOTO

Iuta Glamping & Farm
Make the accommodation part of the experience at this stunning glamping spot. €€€

Relais Terre di Romanello
Relax and enjoy nature at this beautiful secluded place surrounded by olive groves. Great view over Noto. €€

Battimandorlo
A country guesthouse blending Sicilian charm with modern luxury: stylish decor, an infinity pool, great food. €

walking along the path connecting Gelsomineto and Gallina beach. Stop at **Roccia dei Teschi**, a rocky spur jutting out into the sea whose shape resembles a pile of skulls. In summer the beach can get very crowded so come early in the morning or at sunset. A path connects the car park to the beach.

Hike at Riserva di Cavagrande del Cassibile

FAIRY LAKES

Entering the reserve means being bewitched by nature. The beating heart of the area is the gorge carved by the Cassibile river creating a series of small emerald lakes. The canyon is about 10km long and surrounded by imposing rock walls up to 300m high. With its 2700 hectares this nature reserve is a paradise for trekkers. After a dramatic fire in 2014 the main path Scala Cruci is no longer viable, but you can use the Carrubbella path. To reach the entrance take the SS287 from Noto, following the signs for Cavagrande del Cassibile. At the crossroads leading to Scala Cruci, turn right and continue for about 1km. The path follows the course of the river, winding to its right and crossing enchanting landscapes. You will reach the canyon in 20 minutes. The 6km-long path continues down the limestone cliffs towards the lakes called *uruvi*. You can dive in for a refreshing soak after your walk. Wear sturdy shoes as the path is steep. There are no amenities in the area so bring enough water, food, sunscreen and a hat.

Villa Romana del Tellaro

ROMAN MOSAICS

Drive south from Noto along the SP19 and you will reach the 4th-century Villa Romana del Tellaro. It was destroyed by fire, but excavations have brought to light the rich mosaic floors depicting mythological, banquet and hunting scenes. It was once a senator's villa extending for about 5000 sq m.

Wonderful Riserva Naturale di Vendicari

NATURE & ARCHAEOLOGY

Around a 25-minute drive from Noto is the 7km-long stretch of coast that makes up the Riserva Naturale di Vendicari. There are four entrances – Eloro, Calamosche, Vendicari (main entrance), Cittadella – and three different routes that cross the reserve. The blue path starts at Eloro where you can see the ruins of the ancient Greek city

BEST BEACHES AROUND NOTO

Avola beach
A popular beach a short drive from Noto. Park for free in the back streets. Swim with a view of the ruins of an ancient *tonnara*.

Lido di Noto
Noto's well-equipped seaside resort, 8km from town. Calabernardo and Scogliera Bianca are the best spots to relax and swim in crystal waters.

Eloro beach
Turquoise waters lap this secluded sandy stretch flanked by a rocky headland 9km from Noto. Facilities include bar, showers and car park.

FOND OF MOSAICS

The Villa Romana del Casale near **Piazza Armerina** (p215) houses Unesco-listed mosaics considered the finest in the world.

WHERE TO EAT AROUND VENDICARI

Le Zagare di Vendicari
An agriturismo offering a view over vineyards and good Sicilian cuisine. Fresh products grown locally. €€

Torre Vendicari
A lovely family-run seaside farm. Genuine food served with a smile. €

Pantanelli di Vendicari
Dine on the terrace and hear crickets all around. Typical Sicilian cuisine, mostly fish based. €€

of **Helorus**. Keep following the track to Marianelli beach to see 5th-century quarries and end the route with a swim at Calamosche beach. The orange path starts from the main entrance to the reserve. Cross the wooden bridge to the bird-watching observation posts and you will see the imposing *tonnara* and the ruins of the 15th-century Swabian tower right on the beach. The green path starts from the southern entrance at **Cittadilla Maccari**, a Byzantine village next to San Lorenzo beach. Along the way you can see a *trigona* (Byzantine church) and a necropolis.

Snorkelling in Vendicari

AN UNDERWATER EDEN

BEST BEACHES IN VENDICARI

Marianelli
A secluded stretch of golden sand popular with naturists. Park at the northern entrance and follow the trail (300m).

Calamosche
Vendicari's most popular beach, with caves and a variety of marine fauna. No facilities.

Vendicari
A long golden beach a 20-minute walk from the main entrance.

Cittadella
A lovely cove at the southern entrance. No facilities but close to the car park.

San Lorenzo
At Vendicari's southern border. A long sandy beach with crystalline waters.

Snorkellers can explore the marine fauna living in Vendicari's crystalline waters, especially around the cliffs. You can also see marine caves, swaying branches of Posidonia and shiny silver fish swimming around you. The best places for snorkeling are Calamosche, the rocky stretch near the Swabian tower and the rocky spurs around Marianelli.

Spot Flamingos in Vendicari

BIRD-WATCHING PARADISE

Thousands of migrating birds come to Vendicari each year in spring and autumn. The saltwater lagoons, called *pantani,* provide an ideal stopover to birds resting on their way to and from Africa. Waders like curlews and marsh sandpipers are regular visitors as well as egrets, spoonbills, herons, terns and flamingos. Observation posts allow you to watch in relative comfort.

Lovely Marzamemi

ANCIENT FISHING VILLAGE

The fishing village of Marzamemi is 30 minutes from Noto. Its name derives from the Arabic *Marsà al-hamen,* meaning 'turtledoves' harbour', and it dates back to 1000 CE when the Arabs built a huge *tonnara* here. What you see today dates from the 17th century when the Prince of Villadorata expanded the *tonnara* and built his palace, the church of San Francesco da Paola and the fishers' houses around Piazza Margherita. A little island lies in front of the village. The whole area around the main square, the *tonnara* and the *balata* (port) is full of bars, restaurants and shops. In September the old *tonnara* hosts an interesting Frontier Film Festival. It explores geographical, cultural, language and symbolic frontiers through movies shown on the square and inside the *tonnara*.

 WHERE TO EAT IN MARZAMEMI

Liccamùciula
A funky restaurant-slash-concept store. Try the fig *granita*, the *cannolo* cheesecake and fish tapas. €€

Acquamadre
Don't miss the linguine with tuna *bottarga* (mullet roe), ginger and lemon, and the Avola almond parfait. €€

Cortile Arabo
Delicious food, great wines. The pasta with sea urchins and tomato flavoured dessert are top choices. €€€

Portopalo di Capo Passero

Sicily's Wild Southern Tip

BEACHES & FORTRESSES WHERE TWO SEAS MEET

Following the coast south along the SP84 you will reach **Portopalo di Capo Passero**, home to beautiful, wild and exotic beaches. Sicily's largest *tonnare* once stood here, now ruined. A 16th-century fortress is on the small island off the coast, and from its terrace you can look out over the whole island. Head out there on foot during low tide or take a short boat ride (€5 per person).

From Portopalo di Capo Passero, follow the SP8 leading to the extreme tip of Sicily where the tiny **Isola delle Correnti** lies. It is Sicily's southernmost point, further south than Tunis in Tunisia. Here the Ionian and the Mediterranean seas meet, creating a strong current – hence the name 'Island of Currents'. It's a popular spot for surfers and, if you're feeling adventurous, you can walk across to the small island at low tide and explore the ruins of a 16th-century fortress with a small lighthouse built on its terrace in 1871. Native wildlife includes hedgehogs, rabbits and gulls, and you may also spot albatrosses that stop there during their migration.

BEST BEACHES AROUND MARZAMEMI AND CAPO PASSERO

Spinazza
A long, sandy beach with crystal clear waters a 10-minute walk from Marzamemi.

Scalo Mandrie
Alternating sand and rocky cliffs with a shallow seabed that gently slopes towards the open sea.

Playa Carratois
Caribbean-like sea frequented mainly by Sicilians. Some clubs have paid facilities, but most of the beach is free to access.

Punta delle Formiche
Fine-sand beach, pristine waters and breathtaking scenery, especially at sunset.

GETTING AROUND

The best way to explore the region is by car. The Oasi del Gelsomineto is about a 20-minute drive from Noto. Take the SS287 to reach Cavagrande del Cassibile nature reserve in 25 minutes. Along the SP19, Villa Romana del Tellaro is a short drive from Noto.

It takes around 25 minutes to get to Vendicari from Noto. During summer, especially in July and August, the road can get very busy, but you should be able to park easily at the car park inside the reserve (head for the main entrance).

Marzamemi is 30 minutes away. There are several paid car parks a short distance from the centre but the most convenient is on Via Corrado Montoneri, 350m from Piazza Margherita. Explore the fishing village on foot. The nearest beaches are also within walking distance.

Portopalo di Capo Passero is south along the SP84 around 35 minutes from Noto. In summer three car parks guarantee quick and easy parking. From there, take the SP8 to Isola delle Correnti. The car park closest to the beach is not big but it is very convenient so try to arrive early.

...s well as two bodies. Ragusa Superiore is... ...sitting on the top of the hill while its historic centre, Ragusa Ibla, is further down, connected by a staircase. After the 1693 earthquake destroyed the Val di Noto, the new town was built on a higher plateau. However, the nobles who owned ancient palaces in Ibla were reluctant to leave them and chose to rebuild on the same spot.

The two towns were merged in 1927, but you still feel like you're in two different cities: Ragusa Superiore is a busy town with grid-pattern streets while Ibla is a tangle of nooks and lanes with stone houses and magnificent baroque buildings. Few places in Sicily have had their architectural masterpieces so heavily featured than those of Ragusa since Andrea Camilleri's book series on Inspector Montalbano was adapted for TV.

TOP TIP

While in Ragusa, enjoy a family meal in a local house thanks to the Cesarine network (www.cesarine.com), a Slow Food community that hosts small groups of tourists at lunch or dinner to let you taste home-cooked cuisine. You can also learn how to prepare Sicilian dishes.

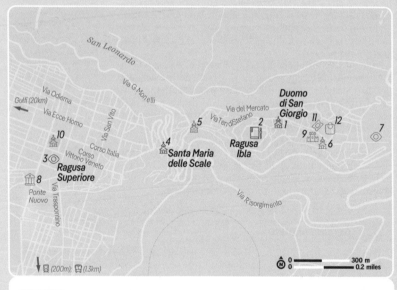

HIGHLIGHTS

1 Duomo di San Giorgio
2 Ragusa Ibla
3 Ragusa Superiore
4 Santa Maria delle Scale

SIGHTS

5 Anime del Purgatorio
6 Chiesa di San Giuseppe
7 Giardino Ibleo

8 Museo Archeologico Ibleo
9 Palazzo Arezzo di Trifiletti
10 San Giovanni Battista

ENTERTAINMENT

11 Donnafugata Theatre

SHOPPING

12 Cinabro Carrettiera

SAM TANNO/SHUTTERSTOCK ©

Ragusa Ibla

Ragusa Ibla

TANGLE OF HISTORIC LANES

From Piazza della Repubblica a flight of steps leads up to the baroque church of **Anime del Purgatorio**, which survived the earthquake. Skulls and symbols of power and wealth here warn of the transience of life. Take Via Bocchieri to reach Piazza Duomo and the **Duomo di San Giorgio**, a baroque masterpiece by Rosario Gagliardi. It stands majestically at the top of wide steps, with a convex facade and a sculpted bell tower soaring into the sky. Many scenes of the TV drama *Inspector Montalbano* were shot on this square. Opposite the church is **Palazzo Arezzo di Trifiletti**. A family member leads the tour through original hand-painted majolica floors and frescoes. Next to it are the mid-18th-centuray aristocrats' club Circolo di Conversazione and the **Donnafugata theatre**. Continue along Corso XXV Aprile to the **Chiesa di San Giuseppe** with a curved facade, columns and statues. A few steps away is **Cinabro Carrettieri**, the workshop of world-famous Sicilian cart craftsmen Castilletti and Rotella. Further downhill is the **Giardino Ibleo** with a view over the valley. It hides three churches, a Capuchin convent and the ruins of the former cathedral of San Giorgio; its Gothic portal survived the earthquake.

 WHERE TO STAY IN RAGUSA

Neropece Amazing location right behind the cathedral. Great hospitality, beautiful decor and delicious breakfast. €€	**Relais Antica Badia** In an 18th-century villa. Public rooms are frescoed, guest rooms are furnished in Sicilian and European antiques. €€	**L'Orto Sul Tetto** Not far from the Chiesa di San Giorgio. The top floor has a patio with lemon trees and vines. €

Only by getting lost will you get a real sense of Ibla and its patchwork quilt of narrow streets and winding alleys. Let your curiosity drive you. Spending some time meandering about will gift you small courtyards, picture-postcard scenes and churches unchanged by time.

WHERE TO TRY RAGUSAN SPECIALITIES

Panificio Giummarra
Serves the town's best *scaccia*, a kind of flatbread stuffed with tomato, ricotta or veggies.

Gelati DiVini
The wine-flavoured ice creams are unmissable. Try Passito, Moscato or Marsala.

Salumeria Barocco
Order a platter of charcuterie. Taste the Ragusan *caciocavallo* and the *pecorino al Nero d'Avola*, a sheep-milk cheese matured in wine.

Cantunera
Best *arancini* in the Hyblean area, freshly prepared and served hot. Big variety of local craft beers. Very good *cannoli* too.

A View Over Ragusa Ibla

CLIMB THE STAIRS

The best spot to capture Ragusa Ibla is by the bell tower of the 15th-century church **Santa Maria delle Scale**, rebuilt in the 1700s. Its name derives from the flight of 300 steps leading down from Ragusa Superiore to Ibla. While climbing, stop at Palazzo Cosentini, Palazzo Nicastro and Santa Maria dell'Itria with its blue-domed bell tower and rococo-style polychrome majolica. It stands in the old **Jewish Quarter** and was founded by the Knights of Malta in the 14th century. In October the food festival Scale del Gusto invades Ragusa Ibla's stairs, squares and streets.

Stroll Around Ragusa Superiore

CATHEDRAL, PALACES & A MUSEUM

The less attractive half of the city houses the enormous cathedral of **San Giovanni Battista** by the baroque architect Rosario Gagliardi. The sculpted facade was completed in 1778 and is set off by Mario Spada's bell tower. Climb the 129 steps to the top. As you stroll around outside the cathedral you will stumble upon noble palaces such as Palazzo Schininà di Sant'Elia on Via Roma, Palazzo Bertini on Corso Italia and the magnificent Palazzo Zacco nearby. Just below Ponte Nuovo is the **Museo Archeologico Ibleo** displaying notable prehistoric finds.

FestiWall: A City of Murals

DISCOVER STREET ART

Ragusa Superiore is awash with murals, the result of five editions of FestiWall, an international art festival held in Ragusa from 2015 to 2019. The urban regeneration project led to the creation of 30 artworks as murals and installations. The recovery of disused municipal assets gave a new identity to anonymous spaces. Find a map on www.festiwall.it.

GETTING AROUND

Ragusa Ibla is closed to non-residential traffic. The best way to get there is to catch the hourly bus connecting via Zama (Ragusa Superiore) to the Giardino Ibleo (AST lines 11 and 33, Monday to Saturday, line 1 on Sundays).

Park at Piazza della Repubblica. A flight of steps leads up to the centre; the labyrinth of narrow streets is best enjoyed on foot.

If you feel fit enough take the stairs connecting Ragusa Superiore to Ragusa Ibla. You will be gifted stunning views over the old city. Ragusa Superiore is easier to explore by car. Parking there is not difficult with on-street free parking and an underground car park near the cathedral of San Giovanni.

Beyond Ragusa

Follow in the footsteps of Inspector Montalbano and be amazed by the surroundings of Ragusa, rich in history and architecture.

TOP TIP

In summer you can count on a special train service (Barocco Line) connecting the Ragusan baroque sites, including the Donnafugata castle.

Made famous by the internationally successful TV drama *Inspector Montalbano* based on the books of Andrea Camilleri, the Ragusa area is known for its magnificent baroque architecture and the white dry-stone walls surrounding the olive and carob groves. Modica's alleys climbing towards the church of San Giorgio, the airy squares of Comiso, the adorned churches of Scicli, the astonishing terrace of the Donnafugata castle: in the TV series all of them represent the imaginary city of Vigàta. Now you can visit the real places, as well as the daring gorge of Cava d'Ispica with prehistoric caves, the golden beaches along the coast and the sleepy atmosphere of the country village Chiaramonte Gulfi.

Donnafugata Castle (p200)

LANDSCAPE STOCK PHOTOS/SHUTTERSTOCK ©

BEST BEACHES AROUND ISPICA

Ciriga
Easy-access sandy beach, white cliffs and rock formations in the sea.

Santa Maria del Focallo
A long paradisiacal beach caressed by a transparent sea, lined by dunes and pine trees. No facilities.

Marina di Modica
A small and comfortable sandy bay lined with bars and beach clubs. In July and August it is popular with families. You can also surf and windsurf.

Sampieri
A world away from the busy beach clubs packed with tourists, near the homonymous fishing village. Golden sand and crystalline waters.

Vast Cava d'Ispica

PREHISTORIC CAVES

This extensive cave system 24km from Ragusa was inhabited from 2000 BCE, then used as early Christian tombs and medieval dwellings. Explore the 13km-long gorge following a path along the verdant valley. Do not miss the 18th-century watermill hosting the Museo Cavallo d'Ispica about ancient rural life.

Stylish Ispica

CITY REBUILT BY A PRINCE

Ispica is on a hill 33km from Ragusa. Start your visit at the church of **Santa Maria Maggiore**, rebuilt after the 1704 earthquake with the financial support of Prince Francesco V Statella to whom Ispica owes its reconstruction. The **Mother Church of San Bartolomeo** was built by the Normans and rebuilt after the earthquake in late-baroque and neoclassical styles. Palaces worth mentioning are **Palazzo Gambuzza**, a noble residence from the early 1700s with an arched courtyard, and **Palazzo Bruno**, an impressive art nouveau building by the architect Ernesto Basile.

Donnafugata Castle

A FASCINATING LEGEND

The name of this castle 15km from Ragusa means 'the woman who fled'. A legend says that Queen Blanche of Navarre, King Martino's widow, was imprisoned here by Bernat de Cabrera, a Spanish warlord who wanted to steal Martino's throne, but the Queen managed to escape. In reality the castle's name is a corruption of the Arab name Ayn al-Sihhat (Source of Health) that over time became Ronnafuata in the Sicilian dialect, and was later Italianised to Donnafugata.

A white stone facade, two circular towers and a loggia with pointed arches welcome you. Baron Corrado Arezzo De Spuches rebuilt the castle in the 19th century blending a variety of styles. Visiting means taking a leap into Sicilian aristocracy. Scenes of *Il Gattopardo (The Leopard,* 1963) by Visconti and *Inspector Montalbano* were shot here. The pleasant park hides some jokes to entertain the Baron's guests, including a labyrinth.

Lost in Modica

A CITY SPLIT IN TWO

Clinging to a steep gorge 20 minutes from Ragusa is the city of Modica. Its architectural landscape changed following

WHERE TO STAY IN MODICA

Palazzo Failla
An 18th-century palace with the atmosphere of an authentic Sicilian noble palace. €€

Edel Modica
A stunning boutique mixing luxury and tradition. Large rooms and terraces with a view. €€

L'Orangerie B&B
Housed in a 19th-century building. Quirky with a great view from the terrace. €

DALIU/SHUTTERSTOCK ©

Modica

BEST RESTAURANTS IN MODICA

Cappero Bistrot
Classic Sicilian dishes. Try the homemade pasta with ancient grains and the spaghetti with truffles.

Osteria dei Sapori Perduti
Ancient Sicilian culinary tradition and typical Modican cuisine served by the Muriana family.

Accursio
Creative Michelin-starred dishes. Affordable sister restaurant Accursio Radici is nearby.

Enoteca Rappa
Good wines with delicious platters. Try the *tumazzo modicano,* an ancient blue cheese produced in caves.

the 1693 earthquake when the medieval town carved into stone was replaced by stunning baroque buildings. It can take a little while to orientate yourself as the town is split into Modica Alta and Modica Bassa, connected by a maze of stairways and winding streets. Accept that you may well take a wrong turning, but you will be rewarded with unexpected views.

Start from the **Duomo di San Giorgio**, one of Sicily's most impressive baroque churches by Rosario Gagliardi, which towers over the medieval alleyways. Although San Giorgio obscures all the other churches, the **Duomo di San Pietro** and **Chiesa di San Giovanni Evangelista** are also worth a visit. The Duomo is a baroque church with a monumental staircase adorned with the statues of the 12 apostles. San Giovanni Evangelista has a magnificent neoclassical facade and a belvedere.

Do not miss **San Nicolò Inferiore**, a 12th-century church carved into rock, discovered by accident in 1987. Along your way up, pay a visit to the **Casa Natale Salvatore Quasimodo**, home to the Nobel-prize-winning poet. End your tour at the 13th-century **Castello dei Conti** on a rocky outcrop high above the town.

WHERE TO EAT IN SCICLI

Baqqala
Boho eatery serving such Sicilian classics as anchovy *parmigiana.* Book to sit in front of Palazzo Beneventano. €€

My Name is Tanino
Small restaurant serving Sicilian tapas. Try the *vastidduzza,* a fried dough with sugar or oregano. €€

La Grotta
Scicli's most atmospheric place to eat. A restaurant in a cave serving good Sicilian food. €€

Costa di Carro
A golden-sand beach next to the fascinating Scogliera di Venere (Venus' Cliff).

Cava d'Aliga
Glimpse snorkellers from the cliff around the Grotta dei Contrabbandieri (Smugglers' Cave).

Donnalucata
This long beach often appeared in the TV drama *Inspector Montalbano.* Daily fish market.

Playa Grande
Fine golden sand washed by a cobalt blue sea, on the edge of the Irminio river nature reserve.

Punta Secca
Drive to Punta Secca to swim in front of Inspector Montalbano's home.

Enjoy a Chocolate Experience

AZTEC CHOCOLATE IN SICILY

As part of the Spanish Kingdom, Sicily learned the Aztec method of chocolate making that was brought to Europe from Latin America. Four centuries later, Modica continues to produce chocolate through a cold-working process, shown at the **Museo del Cioccolato**. The result is a chocolate that crumbles instead of melts, often flavoured with chilli, cinnamon and even wine. Try it at **Antica Dolceria Bonajuto**, the oldest factory. Savour also the *mpanatigghi,* traditional Modican biscuits filled with meat and chocolate.

Scenic Scicli

ATTRACTIVE BAROQUE

In a scenic location between ridges, the Unesco-listed baroque city kept its medieval layout. The most attractive buildings are along Via Penna. Visit the 17th-century **Palazzo Spadaro** and the 19th-century **Palazzo Bonelli Patanè**. Along the same street is the **Museo del Costume** in a former monastery. An old canal built by the Spaniards is a few steps away on Via Aleardi. The town hall is the filming location for Vigàta police station in the *Inspector Montalbano* TV series. Right behind it, **Palazzo Beneventano** stands out for its balconies with bizarre grotesque creatures. Nearby is the **Antica Farmacia** dating from 1902, another Montalbano filming set.

From the city centre, it's a 20-minute walk to the church of **Santa Maria della Croce** on a hill overlooking the city. You're not here for the church, which is no longer in operation; you're in this special place for the view over Scicli from above. Come at sunset.

Caves of Chiafura

A QUARTER DUG IN STONE

From Scicli's Antica Farmacia walk 10 minutes to reach the abandoned church of San Matteo and take in the incomparable view of the city. Continue to the ruins of the 13th-century **Castellaccio**. Under the castle is **Chiafura**, a series of clustered cave dwellings. They were built with a defensive position on the slopes of the hill and were inhabited up until the 1950s. One of the caves, **A rutta di Don Carmelu**, can be visited to see what life was like for people that lived in cave houses. Under the cliff is the 15th-century church of **San Bartolomeo**.

 WHERE TO EAT IN COMISO

Disio
Food is genuine, tasty and generous at a very affordable price. Extremely friendly owners. €

Borgo Nove
Good beer, great wine, well-cooked food and a welcoming atmosphere. Pizza is also excellent. €€

Mannarino Osteria Contemporanea
Traditional Sicilian with a twist. Try the *cavati al carrubo,* a fresh pasta with carob. €€€

Festa della Madonna delle Milizie

A WARRIOR MADONNA

At the end of May, Scicli celebrates the Madonna delle Milizie, the only warrior Madonna of Christianity. A re-enactment with people in period dress recalls the legendary battle between the Normans and the Arabs (then called Turks) on the shores south of Scicli. The Virgin intervened on horseback to save Sicily from invasion. The legend also inspired a dessert called Turk's head, a turban-shaped cream puff.

Comiso

A CITY-THEATRE

Due to the layout of the town, native writer Gesualdo Bufalino called Comiso 'a city-theatre', a performing space ready-made for a show. Start from **Piazza Fonte Diana** with the 18th-century town hall, built on a Roman bath, and Palazzo Iacono-Ciarcià, which survived the earthquake. A few steps away is the church of **San Biagio** and the **Castello dei Naselli**, a 15th-century fortified palace. Admire the nearby church of **Santa Maria delle Stelle** dating back to the 12th century but reworked several times. Continue to **Piazza delle Erbe**'s beautiful old market surrounded by a loggia. With a short detour reach the 14th-century church of **San Francesco all'Immacolata** housing the mausoleum of the Naselli family, an ancient family from Lombardy who settled in Sicily in the 13th century and reigned over Comiso as counts. A splendid sarcophagus is kept in the church.

Chiaramonte Gulfi

A MEDIEVAL HILLTOP TOWN

From Ragusa, drive the scenic SP10 to Chiaramonte Gulfi. The view stretches from Gela to Mt Etna. Despite the 1693 earthquake, its medieval centre is well preserved. Enjoy a stroll around the old town full of interesting churches, such as the cathedral of **Santa Maria La Nova**, built in the Gothic style and rebuilt in the baroque, or the church of **San Giovanni Battista** and its stuccowork. End by visiting the Franciscan convent of **Santa Maria del Gesù** dating from 1200. It contains stuccoes by sculptor Giacomo Serpotta and a painting by Mattia Preti. Chiaramonte is famous for its olive oil and its pork meat. Among the town's several museums, stop by the Museo dell'Olio to learn more about local farming history and rural life.

DELIGHTS TO TASTE IN CHIARAMONTE GULFI

Supprissata
A traditional salami prepared with pork meat cut by hand, dried for 60 days and stuffed into a natural casing.

Donkey mortadella
Produced with donkey meat and pistachio, it has a delicate and unique flavour. Buy it at the butcher's shop, Il Chiaramontano.

Olive oil
Chiaramonte Gulfi has become world-famous for the quality of its olive oil. At Tenuta Chiaramonte you can adopt an olive tree and receive its oil every year.

Chiaramonte Gulfi

GETTING AROUND

Exploring around Ragusa is far easier by car. In summer there's a special train service called the Barocco Line connecting all the Ragusan baroque sites, including Donnafugata castle.

Cava d'Ispica can only be reached by car on the SS115 (about 30 minutes). Modica is 20 minutes from Ragusa. Leave your car in Modica Bassa, then tackle the stairways and streets of the historic centre on foot.

Parking in Scicli, about 35 minutes from Ragusa, is not difficult. Try the main square, Piazza Italia, or the nearby Via San Giuseppe.

Comiso is served by a small airport but there is no public transport, so you will need to rent a car. Look for spaces in the back streets rather than the historic centre. The car will also be useful to get to Chiaramonte Gulfi via the SP10 (20 minutes from Ragusa).

CENTRAL SICILY

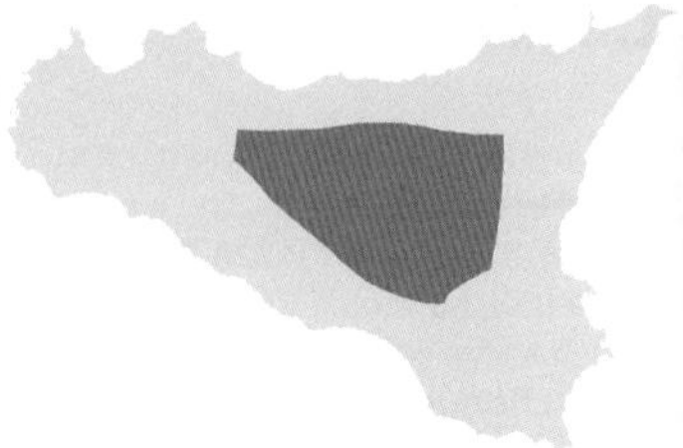

SILENT LANDSCAPE & TRADITIONS

Driving through immense wheat fields and rolling hills to discover the many cultures that have inhabited the sleepy heart of Sicily.

It's a shame most visitors don't venture far beyond the coast because Sicily's inland has much to offer. Towns and villages with over 2500 years of history, beautiful Greek and Roman remains, Norman treasures, noble palaces, traditions worth discovering and a surprising landscape dominated by silence. Driving among the rolling hills, through glorious golden wheat fields swaying in the wind, is an experience in itself.

The trip to the provincial capital of Enna, perched on a 970m-high rock, will make you skip a heartbeat; from above you will see the shimmering Lago di Pergusa in the distance. Walking through sleepy villages that seem to still live in the past, you will discover the many cultures that have inhabited the heart of Sicily – from ancient necropolises to Norman churches and beyond.

The Villa Romana del Casale houses the best preserved mosaics in the world but it is also worth dedicating a day to the nearby town of Piazza Armerina, whose noble palaces are built in golden stone.

Another superstar location of the area is Caltagirone, with its handcrafted ceramics and famous staircase that seems to climb the sky. And yet it still has other secrets to reveal, such as its art nouveau buildings and nearby some villages worth exploring in a literary-themed road trip.

RESTUCCIA GIANCARLO/SHUTTERSTOCK ©

THE MAIN AREAS

ENNA
The navel of
Sicily p210

CALTAGIRONE
City of renowned
handcrafted ceramics
p217

Calascibetta (p214). Left: Majolica mosaic, Caltagirone (p217)

Find Your Way

Enna is the Italy's highest provincial capital, and it's a very dramatic sight standing as it does atop a mountain. Its surroundings also offer breathtaking views. Prepare to be surprised.

Sant'Ambrog

Castelbuo

Monti Madoni

Piano Pomieri

Geraci Siculo

Vicari

Caltavuturo

Parco Naturale Regionale delle Madonie

Polizzi Generosa

Petralia Sottana

Alia

Castellana Sicula

Petralia Soprana

Lercara Friddi

Riserva Naturale Orientata Monte Carcaci

Vallelunga Pratameno

Lago Fanaco

Villalba

Santa Caterina Villarmosa

CAR

Enna is in the centre of Sicily, on the A19 between Catania and Palermo. Caltagirone is just a one-hour drive away from Catania. It is easy to park almost everywhere, and by car you'll be able to reach areas that aren't connected by public transport.

Mussomeli

Bosco Gabbara

San Cataldo

Caltanissetta

Bompensiere

Montedoro

Pietraperzia

BUS

Don't have a car? The best way to get to Enna is by SAIS bus. Get off at Enna Alta where all the attractions are. The lower part of the city is 3km downhill, so avoid getting off here. Caltagirone is one hour away from Enna.

TRAIN

Taking the train to reach Enna is not recommended: the railway station is far from the town and is connected only by expensive private taxi on request. Caltagirone likewise is not well connected by train.

Sommatino

Riesi

Ravanusa

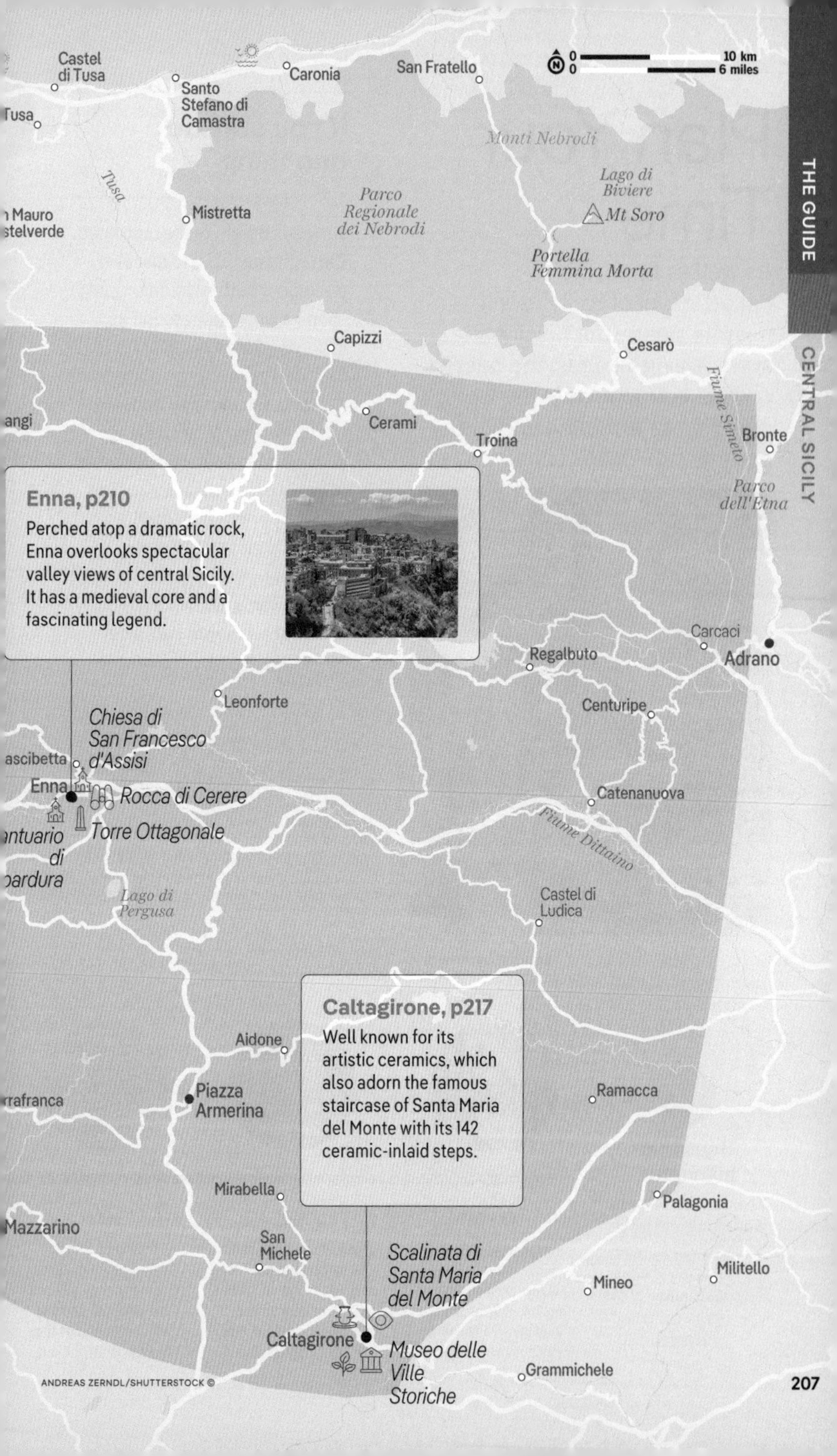

Castel
di Tusa

Tusa

Santo
Stefano di
Camastra

Caronia

San Fratello

n Mauro
stelverde

Mistretta

Tusa

Monti Nebrodi

*Parco
Regionale
dei Nebrodi*

*Lago di
Biviere*

△ Mt Soro

*Portella
Femmina Morta*

Capizzi

Cesarò

Fiume Simeto

angi

Cerami

Troina

Bronte

*Parco
dell'Etna*

Enna, p210

Perched atop a dramatic rock,
Enna overlooks spectacular
valley views of central Sicily.
It has a medieval core and a
fascinating legend.

Carcaci

Regalbuto

Adrano

Leonforte

Centuripe

*Chiesa di
San Francesco
d'Assisi*

ascibetta

Enna 🏛 🏛 *Rocca di Cerere*

Catenanuova

🏛 *Torre Ottagonale*

antuario
di
pardura

Fiume Dittaino

*Lago di
Pergusa*

Castel di
Ludica

Caltagirone, p217

Well known for its
artistic ceramics, which
also adorn the famous
staircase of Santa Maria
del Monte with its 142
ceramic-inlaid steps.

Aidone

Ramacca

rafranca

Piazza
Armerina

Mirabella

Palagonia

Mazzarino

San
Michele

*Scalinata di
Santa Maria
del Monte*

Mineo

Militello

Caltagirone 🌿 🏛 *Museo delle
Ville
Storiche*

Grammichele

N

0
0

10 km
6 miles

Plan Your Time

As well as Enna, the so-called 'navel of Sicily', don't miss its sleepy but fascinating surrounding villages, the best preserved mosaics in the world near Piazza Armerina and the ceramics of Caltagirone.

Sicilian ceramics

If you only do one thing

● Head straight to the renowned **Caltagirone** (p217) to discover an ancient pottery tradition and spend a whole day around its fascinating streets decorated with coloured majolica and dotted with amazing **art nouveau buildings** (p218). Here you can challenge yourself with a ceramic workshop or browse the artisans' shops to find the perfect Testa di Moro (Moor's Head) to take home.

● Afterwards climb the famous **Scalinata di Santa Maria del Monte** (p218), then explore the street art in the **Sant'Agostino district** (p218). It is worth stopping until evening falls to enjoy the illuminated staircase and take in its fairytale atmosphere.

Seasonal highlights

Thanks to its altitude, Enna is a great place to escape in summer while the sun bakes the coast. Inland areas have a more continental climate.

MARCH

Also held in April, Holy Week in Enna is the most stunning legacy of Spanish rule and involves several religious brotherhoods.

APRIL

Held the last weekend of April is the ricotta cheese festival in Vizzini with a programme filled with gastronomy, folklore and shows.

MAY

On May 3 Piazza Armerina celebrates the Madonna di Zazza Vecchia, the saint to which the end of the plague is attributed.

FRANCESCO LORENZETTI/SHUTTERSTOCK ©, JANNHUIZENGA/GETTY IMAGES ©, DALIU/SHUTTERSTOCK ©

Enna to Piazza Armerina in two days

● **Enna** (p210) deserves at least half a day to explore the historical and architectural beauties it offers. In the afternoon go sunbathing on the shore of **Lago di Pergusa** (p214), linked to the mythical Rape of Persephone, or visit the ancient necropolis of **Realmese** (p214) near the lovely town of Calascibetta.

● The next day head to **Villa Romana del Casale** (p216) and be amazed by the best-preserved mosaics in the world. In the afternoon stroll the nearby **Piazza Armerina** (p215) enjoying its golden streets lined by noble palaces and majestic churches.

If you have more time

● Start in Caltagirone and stay overnight to see the famous **Scalinata di Santa Maria del Monte** (p218) at night. The next day drive to to **Aidone** (p216) to meet the stunning Dea di Morgantina at the small but fascinating museum and discover a village lost in time. The nearby archaeological site of **Morgantina** (p216) also deserves a visit.

● Have lunch in the countryside before heading to **Piazza Armerina** (p215) to enjoy a stroll among its palaces and churches, then visit nearby **Villa Romana del Casale** (p216) with its astonishing mosaics. End your trip in Enna, arriving via scenic wheat fields.

JULY	AUGUST	SEPTEMBER	DECEMBER
From 24–25 July the steps of Santa Maria del Monte in Caltagirone are lit up at night with 5000 lamps.	The Palio dei Normanni in Piazza Amerina is the most important medieval reenactment in southern Italy, with over 600 characters.	The Palio dei Berberi is a horse race in Calascibetta that evokes the moment the Arabs tried to conquer Enna in 800 CE.	Christmas is the best time to discover the ancient tradition of Caltagirone's handmade *presepi* (nativities).

ENNA

Palermo

Enna

Italy's highest provincial capital, Enna is built upon an ancient acropolis that's topped by the formidable Castello di Lombardia (970m). Due to this dominant position overlooking the surrounding territory, the Romans called it 'Urbs Inexpugnabilis' (impregnable city) for its strength to withstand attack thanks to its location and mighty fortifications. It is also known as the 'navel of Sicily' for its geographical position in the centre of the island.

For centuries Enna has been a crossroads of cultures. Today it bears the signs of all the peoples who have inhabited here: Sicani, Greeks, Romans, Byzantines, Arabs, Normans, Swabians and Aragonese have all contended for it.

Although it is among the least visited cities in Sicily, it has one of the richest historical and artistic heritages, especially along Via Roma, which runs through the centre reaching the castle on a rock.

TOP TIP

Enna is split in two: Enna Bassa, below, is the modern town, while Enna Alta is up top, built on a rocky spur. Everything of interest is up in Enna Alta. Parking your car is easy but it is better to walk around so you don't miss anything.

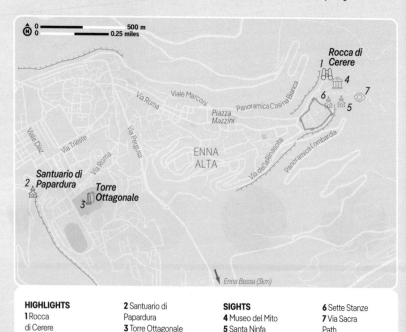

HIGHLIGHTS
1 Rocca
di Cerere

2 Santuario di
Papardura
3 Torre Ottagonale

SIGHTS
4 Museo del Mito
5 Santa Ninfa

6 Sette Stanze
7 Via Sacra
Path

Torre Ottagonale

HOLY WEEK IN ENNA

The week preceding Easter is renowned throughout Sicily for its pathos and magnificence, culminating with the Good Friday procession. Almost 2500 hooded devotees from 16 religious brotherhoods parade along the streets accompanied by a band, a legacy of the Spanish occupation. The city lights are replaced by flame torches and the surreal silence creates an electrifying atmosphere of religious revelry.

On Top of Torre Ottagonale

THE TOWER OF FREDERICK II

Once part of the defence system, Torre Ottagonale now stands 27m high inside the city's public garden. It dates back to the Middle Ages and has an octagonal shape with vaulted ceilings and pointed windows that recall Norman-era architecture. A spiral staircase reaches the top from where you'll have the whole city at your feet.

Walk the Ancient Via Roma

ENJOY A WALKING TOUR

Walking is the best way to discover Enna. Start from **Piazza Crispi**, a terrace that overlooks the valley and the town of Calascibetta. A fountain here commemorates Enna's best-known legend, the Rape of Persephone. Following Via Roma you will pass the baroque church of **San Giuseppe**, built in 1390, and the stunning **Palazzo Pollicarini**, a 16th-century fortified residence built in Catalan–Gothic style. On the same street is the Gothic-style **Maria Santissima della**

HOLY WEEK IN TRAPANI

A truly spectacular Holy Week takes place in Trapani in the week preceding Easter with the procession of the so-called **Misteri** (p90), 20 sculptures portraying the main events of Christ's passion that parade through the streets of the city.

WHERE TO STAY IN ENNA

B&B WelcHome
Spacious and modern rooms with mini fridge and spectacular mountain views. Good breakfast included. €

Locanda Susuiusu
A gem with beautifully decorated rooms and the best breakfast you could wish for. €€

Baglio Pollicarini
A 17th-century convent near the Lago di Pergusa where the monks' cells have been converted into guest rooms. €

Visitazione cathedral, which burned down in 1446 and has since been rebuilt several times. The bell tower dates back to the 17th century, while the portal is from 16th century and features a coffered wood ceiling, grey basalt columns and a beautiful altar. Not far from the cathedral is **Museo Archeologico di Palazzo Varisano**. The museum here feels a bit dated but it's still worth a visit, at least to see the 5th-century-BCE Attic-style krater. The tour ends with a visit to **Castello di Lombardia** on Enna's highest point. Originally built by the Arabs on the ancient acropolis, it was subsequently fortified by the Normans. Only six of the original 20 towers remain, the tallest of which is Torre Pisana.

Rocca di Cerere

HOUSE OF DEMETER

This huge rock was once home to the temple of Demeter, goddess of the harvest, built in 480 BCE and destroyed by the Romans in 173 BCE. Two large hollows in the rock show where two colossal statues were located: Demeter and Triptolemus, to which the goddess taught the art of agriculture so that he could pass on the knowledge to others. Stop at the nearby **Museo del Mito**, an interactive space covering the myth of Persephone.

Area Archeologica di Santa Ninfa

STROLL ALONG THE ANCIENT VIA SACRA

Take a dip in the past to explore the sanctuary (ancient place of worship) of Santa Ninfa and the Sette Stanze (seven rooms) dug into the rock below Castello di Lombardia. Here the Via Sacra starts; an ancient path, short but steep, connecting the valley to the temple of Demeter. Follow it to the **Grotta dei Santi**, a cave with Byzantine frescoes.

Santuario di Papardura

A SANCTUARY DUG INTO STONE

Standing on a slope southeast of Enna Alta, Santuario di Papardura is named after the Arabic word meaning 'rock of flowing water' due to a nearby spring. Legend has it that here in 1659 some pious women dreamed of a crucifixion scene painted on a stone slab, which was actually found. The sanctuary was built to protect the relic.

GETTING AROUND

There is handy free parking on Piazza Rosso right beside Castello di Lombardia. You can also park on Piazza Europa near the Torre Ottagonale.

To ensure you don't miss anything, Enna is best explored on foot; however be prepared to climb some stairs. Rocca di Cerere, near Castello di Lombardia, can be reached only on foot. Taking the Via Sacra that starts nearby, be aware the path can be overgrown so wear sturdy shoes and long trousers. Also in winter it can be snowy and slippery, so be careful while walking along cobblestone streets.

To reach Lago di Pergusa by public transport take bus 5.

Sperlinga Nicosia

Calascibetta
Enna

Piazza
Armerina
Villa Romana
del Casale   Caltagirone

Beyond Enna

Although the surroundings of Enna are less
visited than other areas of Sicily, it's a region
that'll surprise you with well-hidden wonders.

The layers of history around Enna span from prehistory to
contemporary Sicilian culture. Cross the countryside carpeted
with wildflowers and golden wheat fields to reach mountain-
top villages and castles dug into the stone such as Sperlinga.
Explore Calascibetta's maze of narrow streets and its ancient
necropolis. Discover the myth of Persephone while sunbathing on Lago di Pergusa's shore and enjoy a road trip through
sleepy inland villages full of Norman, baroque and modern-day
treasures. In Piazza Armerina you will discover a surprising
town full of artistic jewels such as its golden stone buildings,
before moving on to admire the magnificent mosaics of Villa
Romana del Casale. Finally, let yourself be enchanted by the
colours of Caltagirone's ceramics.

TOP TIP

Without a car it's difficult,
if not impossible, to
explore the area around
Piazza Armerina and the
villages near Enna.

Ceramics, Caltagirone (p217)

MARCO OSSINO/SHUTTERSTOCK ©

LOCAL PASTRIES TO GO CRAZY FOR

Cuffitteddi di Calascibetta
Traditionally prepared during Christmas, today you can find these biscuits filled with almonds and dried figs in Calascibetta's bakeries year round.

Nocattoli di Nicosia
These crumbly biscuits with an almond-based topping are among the many sweets the Arabs imported to this area during their occupation.

Cassatelle di Agira
These crescent-shaped shortcrust pastries are filled with cocoa, ground almonds, dried lemon peel and cinnamon.

VVOE/SHUTTERSTOCK ©

Piazza Garibaldi, Piazza Armerina

Calascibetta

A LABYRINTH OF NARROW STREETS

Set above a precipice 6km north of Enna, Calascibetta – translating to 'Castle on Mount Xibet' – was built by the Arabs in 851 CE. In September it hosts the **Palio dei Berberi**, a horse race evoking the Arabs' attempts to conquer Enna. Its 14th-century **Chiesa Madre** was built on the ruins of a castle with an early Christian church inside, still visible through a window on the floor. Located 2km north is the **Necropoli of Realmese** with 288 rock tombs dating from 850 BCE.

Nicosia & Sperlinga

CLIFFS & CASTLES DUG INTO STONE

Set on four hills, the ancient town of **Nicosia** is overlooked by the ruins of its medieval castle and was allegedly founded in the Byzantine age around the 7th century. The Cattedrale di San Nicolò is in Gothic-Norman style, while the 13th-century Basilica di Santa Maria Maggiore has a Baroque entrance and Renaissance interior. **Sperlinga** is 8km from Nicosia and features the stunning Castello di Sperlinga that's partly dug into stone.

Lago di Pergusa

THE MYTH OF PERSEPHONE

Located 9km south of Enna, Lago di Pergusa is linked to the myth of Persephone, who was abducted by Hades, god of the

 WHERE TO STAY AROUND ENNA

Villa Pastorelli
A peaceful oasis surrounded by greenery near the Lago di Pergusa. Warm welcome by Armando. €€

Baglio San Pietro
An *agriturismo* (farm stay) near Nicosia with rustic-style rooms and a restaurant offering good regional cuisine. €€

Borgo Ginuga
An old farmhouse near Centuripe, completely renovated to preserve its original structure. €€€

underworld, while she was gathering flowers on the shore. Due to her grief at losing her daughter, Demeter, the goddess of agriculture, made the land parched. Eventually Zeus ordered Hades to release Persephone for half of each year. Sunbathe on the lake's shore (no facilities available) surrounded by a former race track. A street (SP3) runs along the lake just above the track. You can follow it by car or on foot (4.5km) to enjoy the view. You can also have lunch among the trees in the picnic area Selva Pergusina.

Road Trip to the Villages

A MORE RELAXED PACE

From Enna drive 30 minutes to reach the baroque town of **Leonforte** and its Granfonte fountain with 24 jets. **Agira** is a 20-minute drive from Leonforte and is crowned by a medieval castle. Continue driving along SS121 to **Centuripe** for 45 minutes, known as 'Sicily's Balcony' due to its majestic views. A few kilometres away is **Carcaci**, an abandoned village dating back to 1700 and inhabited by peacocks. Follow the SS575 for 45 minutes towards **Troina** to visit the Norman castle built by Count Roger with its central tower called Torre Capitania, the Norman cathedral of Maria Santissima Assunta and the Oratorio dei Bianchi, a crypt under the cathedral. While you're here, don't miss Robert Capa's Photography Museum.

Piazza Armerina

THE NOBLE CITY

Built on three hills, Iblatash was founded by the Arabs in the 10th century on the slope of Colle Armerino. It then expanded in the 15th century to change its name to Platea, hence Piazza. It retains its Norman-style fishbone urban layout and is filled with beautiful 16th- and 17th-century noble palaces. Start from **Piazza Duomo**, where in mid-August the famous Palio dei Normanni is held to re-enact Count Roger's reconquest of the city in 1087. Visit the huge cathedral dating to the 18th century (except for its 14th-century, 44m-high bell tower), and you can enjoy its blue-and-white interior. Behind the altar is the painting of *Madonna delle Vittorie* (Virgin of the Victories), celebrated with a great feast in May. The recently restored baronial Palazzo Trigona is located next to the church. A few steps away along the 13th-century Via Monte is the **Pinacoteca Comunale**, housing artwork from the 15th to 19th centuries. Then take Via Floresta to reach the 14th-century **Castello Aragonese**. Stop at **Collegio dei Gesuiti** to see the beautiful Oratorio, now a public library, with frescoes and stuccoes. Head to **Piazza Garibaldi** to see the late-baroque town hall and the magnificent Chiesa

I LIVE HERE: BEST PLACES TO EAT IN PIAZZA ARMERINA

Salvatore Ficarra, Piazza Armerina–born travel guide and member of the Associazione Regionale Guide Sicilia.

Trattoria Al Goloso
Local delicious food and great hospitality in this family-run restaurant next to Piazza Garibaldi.

Trattoria da Gianna
Hearty kitchen with fresh ingredients Gianna sources and cooks while her husband warmly welcomes you.

La Locanda
Traditional flavours with a twist. Try the pasta with sardines and wild fennel.

Zingale
Not to be missed are their *frittelle* (fried doughnuts) filled with ricotta or chocolate, prepared only on Sunday mornings.

Disiu
Best gelato in town. Ask for the pistachio cream on top. Vegan options too.

 WHERE TO EAT AROUND PIAZZA ARMERINA

Al Fogher
Among central Sicily's best restaurants, with modern cuisine and a 400-label wine list. €€€

Trattoria La Ruota
Good lunch after visiting Villa Romana del Casale. Try rabbit *alla stemperata* (with veggies in sweet and sour sauce). €€

Vecchia Aidone
Warm service and outstanding Sicilian food, especially the antipasti; great in quality and quantity. €€

Sara Mostaccio
@fritha

This country villa that belonged to a rich family of the late-imperial period (284-476 CE) is a marvel housing stunning mosaics from the 4th century CE. Walking through its rooms is a dip into the ancient world and its size leaves me speechless every time I return. My favourite mosaic is the one depicting children while they're playing with farm animals. It sits to the right of the basilica and it vividly shows children's daily life from such a distant past.

MORE MOSAICS

The **Villa Romana del Tellaro** (p193) is near Noto while the **Villa Romana di Durrueli** (p234) is a few kilometres from Agrigento. They are much smaller than Villa Romana del Casale, but worth a visit.

di San Rocco, also called Fundrò. From here take Via Umberto I to reach **Chiesa di San Giovanni Evangelista**, known as Sicily's Sistine Chapel due to Dutch painter Guglielmo Borremans' frescoes. The austere but fascinating church **Commenda dei Cavalieri di Malta** is nearby.

Villa Romana del Casale

BEST-PRESERVED MOSAICS IN EXISTENCE

Villa Romana del Casale, 5km southwest of Piazza Armerina, is famed for its Unesco-listed Roman mosaics, considered the finest in the world. Its size is astounding, with 3535 sq metres of floor mosaics. It is thought to have been the country retreat of Marcus Aurelius Maximianus, Rome's co-emperor during the reign of Diocletian in the 3rd century. In the 12th century it was covered 10m deep in mud due to a landslide and was recovered in the 1950s. Today a wooden roof protects the mosaics and an elevated walkway allows visitors to see them from above. Don't miss the triumphal entrance, the baths, the vast basilica and, of course, the stars of the complex: the 'bikini girls' mosaic, along with hunting scenes in the huge *Grande Caccia* and depiction of Hercules in the *triclinium* (banquet room).

Aidone & Morgantina

HOUSE OF THE GODDESS

Situated 10km from Piazza Amerina lies **Aidone**, a hilltop village with an interesting archaeological museum. Here you can view the long-lost Dea di Morgantina, a 5th-century statue representing Demeter from a clandestine excavation, returned to Sicily in 2011 by the Getty Museum in Los Angeles. Do not miss the church of San Domenico with its diamond-point facade, a rare feature for a religious building. The ruins of **Morgantina**, an early Sicilian settlement then a Greek trading post, are a short drive away. Here you'll encounter remnants of two *agora* (marketplaces), a trapezoidal stairway, a theatre, a public bath and residential quarters with wall decorations and mosaics.

Parco Minerario Floristella-Grottacalda

INDUSTRIAL ARCHAEOLOGY SETTLEMENT

About 15km north of Piazza Armerina are the historic remains of the region's mid-20th-century sulphur mining days, among the most significant industrial archeology settlements in southern Italy. A museum recalls the harshness of the miners' lives, including children forced to work.

GETTING AROUND

Calascibetta is connected to Enna by bus (20 minutes). If you drive, parking here is easy. Other villages and towns can be reached by car.
   There is a large car park on Piazza Europa at the northeastern edge of Piazza Armerina's old city, although parking is not difficult. From there

you can follow signs to the Villa Romana del Casale or go by bus (summer only) departing from Piazza Senatore Marescalchi. Walking takes one hour but it is not recommended in summer and the walk back is very steep. A pre-booked taxi will cost €25 return.

CALTAGIRONE

Palermo

Caltagirone

Renowned for the high quality of clay found in the area Caltagirone is a destination best known for its ceramics. An industry that dates back more than 1000 years, the earliest settlers worked with terracotta but it was the Arabs in the 10th century who introduced glazed polychromatic colours. Since then, Caltagirone's ceramics have become recognisable for the quality of their workmanship and their distinctive colours, especially blue and yellow.

But Caltagirone has much more to offer beyond ceramics. Despite its name deriving from Arabic words *qalat* and *gerun* – 'castle' and 'cave' – its history dates back to pre-Greek times. In 1693 an earthquake destroyed the city (as it did most of eastern Sicily), and Caltagirone was rebuilt in the typical Sicilian Baroque style. Most of the city's attractions, especially its churches, date to this period, but the town also reserves an unexpected surprise: its historic centre, dotted with art nouveau buildings.

TOP TIP

Car is the best way to get to Caltagirone. Park on Viale Regina Elena to walk around by foot – which is especially useful in reaching the villas downhill. You can also get to Caltagirone by bus.

Scalinata di Santa Maria del Monte

Chiesa di San Francesco d'Assisi

Viale Cristoforo Colombo

Via Circonvallazione

Giardino Pubblico

Museo delle Ville Storiche (1.3km)

HIGHLIGHTS
1 Chiesa di San Francesco d'Assisi
2 Scalinata di Santa Maria del Monte

SIGHTS
3 Carcere Borbonico
4 Cattedrale di San Giuliano
5 Centrale Elettrica
6 Giardino Pubblico
7 Ponte San Francesco

ACTIVITIES, COURSES & TOURS
8 Filippo Vento Ceramic Workshop
9 Giacomo Alessi Ceramic Workshop

217

FOR CERAMICS LOVERS

Handmade pottery in **Sciacca** (p236), on the Mediterranean coast of Sicily, is appreciated all over the world. The art of ceramics there dates back to the 4th century.

Churches, Palaces & Backstreets
A STROLL IN CALTAGIRONE

Start from **Chiesa di San Francesco d'Assisi**, a 13th-century baroque church with an interesting museum. Admire the gothic facade of **San Pietro**, then head to the 18th-century exedra **Tondo Vecchio** and cross ceramic-clad Ponte San Francesco. After passing Carcere Borbonico, a former Bourbon prison and now museum, you'll find yourself in front of the **Cattedrale di San Giuliano**. Immediately beyond is Piazza Municipio lined by the **Corte Capitaniale** (dating to 1061) and the **Palazzo Senatorio**, where the town senate once sat.

Scalinata di Santa Maria del Monte
THE CERAMIC-INLAID STAIRCASE

Caltagirone's most famous sight is the impressive 142-step staircase that rises from Piazza Municipio up to Scalinata di Santa Maria del Monte. It was built in 1606, then remodelled in 1844, to link the old hilltop centre to a new neighbourhood. The majolica tiles, added in 1954, reproduce traditional decorative styles from the 10th to the 20th century. During celebrations in honour of San Giacomo on 24 to 25 July it is lit by 5000 *coppi* (oil lamps) drawing a motif linked to the saint. The show is repeated on 14 and 15 August.

A Pottery Workshop
LEARN TO WORK WITH CERAMICS

Don't miss the opportunity to take part in a workshop to learn how Caltagirone's ceramics are made. Here you'll learn techniques such as shaping, enamelling and decoration directly from the artisans and you can take your creation home or have it shipped to you. Giacomo Alessi and Filippo Vento offer half-day or one-day workshops.

Street Art in Borgo Sant'Agostino
AN URBAN CANVAS

In in an effort to revive Caltagirone's oldest neighbourhood, back in 2014 street artists were commissioned to decorate many of the buildings in Borgo Sant'Agostino with murals. The area has become an urban canvas with a mix of works by renowned and emerging artists so don't miss a walk through these alleys to fall in love with where the past and present meet.

 WHERE TO EAT IN CALTAGIRONE

Coria
Michelin-starred restaurant to taste excellent traditional food with an innovative twist. Reservation required. €€€

A Cumacca
Friendly place with high-quality food and bargain prices. Ask for *maccu verde,* a traditional broad bean soup. €€

Il Locandiere
Good wine list and excellent seafood. Try the fish couscous and the *cannolo scomposto* (in a cup) with fig cream. €€

Giardino Pubblico & Museo della Ceramica

A MAJOLICA-THEMED STROLL

A lovely place for a stroll, here in **Giardino Pubblico** you'll find yourself among trees, balconies and lampposts decorated with ceramics and a majolica-covered pavilion. Also don't miss a visit to the adjacent **Museo della Ceramica** showing the art of ceramics from prehistoric times to the 19th century. There is also a section dedicated to the *presepi* (nativities).

Art Nouveau Buildings

UNEXPECTED CALTAGIRONE

Art nouveau buildings in the heart of a baroque city? Who would've thought, but that's what you'll find in Caltagirone. Start along Corso Vittorio Emanuele to see the **pharmacy** at number 16, **Casa Polizzi** and **Palazzo delle Poste**. Along **Via San Giovanni Bosco** at number 8 is the former power station **Centrale Elettrica**. Turn left on Via Palazzo di Giustizia and immediately right on Via Luigi Sturzo to admire **Palazzo Salieri**, also known as Palazzo della Magnolia. Other art nouveau buildings located just outside the historic centre include the **Politeama Ingrassia** theatre near the Giardino Pubblico, **Casa Sinatra** on Via Roma 309 and the **Monumental Cemetery**, a five-minute drive from town. The 170 arcades lining the four main avenues are in art nouveau–style inspired by Sicilian Gothic. Many tombs also feature art nouveau touches.

Villa Patti

HISTORIC NOBLE VILLAS

A five-minute drive from the centre is the noble country house of Villa Patti, built in neo-Gothic style in the 19th century by the Patti aristocrat family. It houses the Museo delle Ville Storiche, where you'll learn about other villas in the surrounding area. Sometimes you can visit them with a guided tour on summer weekends (www.villestorichedicaltagirone.it).

A SWEET BREAKFAST IN CALTAGIRONE

Bar Forte
Mandatory stop for a sweet unforgettable breakfast including *fagottino al pistacchio* (sweet dough filled with pistachio cream), *cannoli,* and mini *cassata.*

Bar Judica
What's a typical Sicilian breakfast? *Granita* and brioche, and here they are both very good. They also do delicious pizzas by the slice, *calzoni* and *arancini.*

Panificio Grazioso
Bakery doing biscuits and Sicilian specialities, including *cubbaita,* a dessert of Arab origin similar to a nougat. Here in Caltagirone it's made with chickpeas.

Pasticceria Scivoli
Just outside the historic centre is this worthwhile stop to try the pistachio cannoli, huge croissants and their renowned *cassatina* (mini *cassata*).

 GETTING AROUND

You can tackle Caltagirone on foot but be aware that there are many hilly ups and downs, especially along the upper town streets. If travelling by car and staying in the upper town, you'll find useful parking on Viale Regina Elena.

A car is required to reach the villas located downhill but you can also get to Villa Patti on foot in 20 minutes and then join a walking tour to visit the other villas nearby. Walking back is not too steep.

If the 142 steps of Scalinata di Santa Maria del Monte frighten you, take the top of the staircase through the less steep backstreets of Borgo Sant'Agostino and then follow the stairs downhill, enjoying it without being out of breath.

Caltagirone Mineo

Grammichele Vizzini

Cunziria

Beyond Caltagirone

It is worth exploring the area around the renowned Caltagirone to discover off-the-radar villages full of history and beauty.

The region surrounding Caltagirone is less travelled, but it's well worth dedicating at least one day for a road trip through the villages not far from the city. Highlights include the surprising Grammichele with its hexagonal urban layout and the not-to-be-missed ancient Mineo, home of the writer Luigi Capuana, from which views sweep 360 degrees across the distant mountains. And what about the noble Vizzini that gave birth to the writer Giovanni Verga? They are all a short distance from each other and offer beautiful photo opportunities, a slower-paced life, enchanting architectural beauties and a very long history with roots set in the mists of time.

TOP TIP

It's not easy exploring this part of the island without a car. Only Caltagirone is connected by bus to the main cities.

Grammichele

MICHELE RINALDI/SHUTTERSTOCK ©

Castello di Mongialino, Mineo

Grammichele, Mineo & Vizzini

A ROAD TRIP NEAR CALTAGIRONE

A 20-minute drive from Caltagirone, **Grammichele** was built after the medieval city called Occhiolà was razed to the ground by the 1693 earthquake. Only the sanctuary of Madonna del Piano remains from the medieval village. At its hexagonal historic centre you'll find a large sundial and a beautiful baroque Mother Church that sit on the central square. The Renaissance town hall is also worth a visit.

Mineo is 25 minutes away from Grammichele and features mountain views over Etna, Iblei, Nebrodi and the Erei. Here you can visit the 17th-century Jesuit college, now the town hall, and the church of Santa Maria Maggiore, formerly a pagan temple, near the ruins of Castello di Ducezio. Don't miss Casa Museo Luigi Capuana, once home to the Sicilian writer. Also nearby is the 13th-century Castello di Mongialino located on a hill inhabited since the Bronze Age.

Complete your trip in **Vizzini**, home to the writer Giovanni Verga whose family palace sits on Piazza Umberto I. Next to it is Salita Marineo, a majolica-decorated staircase. Other sights include the Mother Church's Norman-Gothic portal, which survived the earthquake, and the nearby Basilica di San Vito thats built in late-Baroque style. Not far from the centre is the now abandoned 16th-century village Cunziria (tannery) where Verga set one of his stories. Come in spring to enjoy the Sagra della Ricotta, held at the end of April, a ricotta cheese festival with a programme full of gastronomy, folklore and shows.

BEST RESTAURANTS

Piaciri
Try the famous Grammichele sausage: the meat is not minced but cut by hand *(al ceppo)* and served with sautéed chicory.

Borgo Antico
An *agriturismo* 10km away from Mineo. Try the *pasta al ragù* with Nebrodi pork followed by a lemon cake.

Ristorante del Campanile
Right in the centre of Vizzini is this charming restaurant in a rustic courtyard. Traditional Sicilian food and excellent pizzas.

La Giara
Family run trattoria in Vizzini featuring antipasto from locally grown veggies.

GETTING AROUND

Although Caltagirone is connected by bus to the main cities, it would be very time consuming trying to reach the nearby towns by public transport. Hence a car is the way to go and a road trip allows you to see them all in one day. Follow the SS124 to Grammichele, the SP33 and SS385 to reach Mineo, then continue to Vizzini along the SP86. You will find free parking everywhere.

Scala dei Turchi (p234). Right: Tempio della Concordia, Valley of the Temples (p230)

MEDITERRANEAN COAST

SEA & TEMPLES

Amazing ancient temples and contemporary
art among a wild natural landscape and kilometres of
spectacular beaches and dazzling cliffs.

No doubt the main attraction of the Mediterranean coast is the magnificent Valley of the Temples, one of the great ancient Greek wonders outside of Greece. Agrigento itself also reserves some surprises with its historic centre made of long and narrow stairs branching off from the central Via Atenea. It also reveals a bustling and unexpected nightlife. Not far away is Farm Cultural Park, an innovative centre of contemporary art occupying a revived old neighbourhood in the town of Favara.

Explore the coast leading to the spa town of Sciacca. Along the way, discover the Scala dei Turchi, a magnificent white cliff diving into the bluest sea, as well as the wild nature of the Riserva Naturale di Torre Salsa and the ancient city of Eraclea Minoa. Sciacca is worth stopping a few days both to explore its artistic offerings and culinary treasures without neglecting a trip to the inland villages of Caltabellotta and Sambuca di Sicilia.

Finally, go back to Porto Empedocle and jump on a ferry to reach the paradisiacal beaches of the remote island of Lampedusa, 200km offshore. If you are not yet satisfied with history, traditions and sunbathing, embark on a road trip along the coast east of Agrigento to discover the archaeological treasures of Gela, ancient noble castles and dream beaches.

THE MAIN AREA

AGRIGENTO
Home to the
Valley of the
Temples **p228**

223

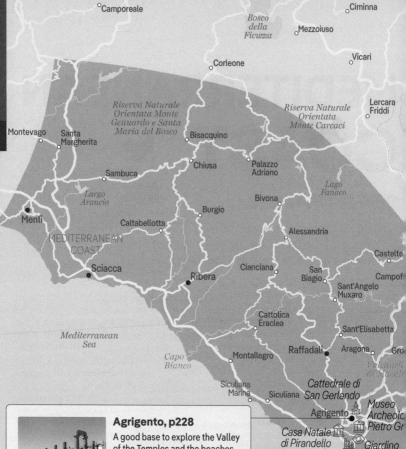

Camporeale

Bosco della Ficuzza

Ciminna

Mezzoiuso

Vicari

Corleone

Lercara Friddi

Riserva Naturale Orientata Monte Genuardo e Santa Maria del Bosco

Riserva Naturale Orientata Monte Carcaci

Montevago

Santa Margherita

Bisacquino

Sambuca

Chiusa

Palazzo Adriano

Largo Arancio

Burgio

Bivona

Lago Fanaco

Menfi

Caltabellotta

MEDITERRANEAN COAST

Alessandria

Castelte

Sciacca

Ribera

Cianciana

San Biagio

Campof

Sant'Angelo Muxaro

Mediterranean Sea

Cattolica Eraclea

Sant'Elisabetta

Capo Bianco

Montallegro

Raffadali

Aragona

Gro

Vulcanelli di Macale

Siculiana Marina

Siculiana

Cattedrale di San Gerlando

Agrigento

Museo Archeolc Pietro Gr

Casa Natale di Pirandello

Valley of the Temples

Giardino della Kolymbet

Agrigento, p228

A good base to explore the Valley of the Temples and the beaches along the coast, but it also hides an interesting historic centre and lively nightlife.

CAR

Even though a car in Agrigento will give you the freedom to go around every village in the area, parking here can be a nightmare. Metered parking is available on Piazza Vittorio Emanuele or ask your host; some hotels have stalls reserved for customers.

BUS

Bus is the easiest way to get to Agrigento. The bus station is on Piazza Rosselli, just off Piazza Vittorio Emanuele. From here local buses (TUA) depart from Agrigento to the Valley of the Temples (lines: 1, 2, 3) and the nearby towns.

TRAIN

Trains run regularly to/from Palermo. However if you arrive from Catania a bus is a far better option as there are no direct trains and the journey would become long and unnerving with too many changes.

Find Your Way

Whether you are travelling along the coast or exploring one of the hillside villages, the dazzling Mediterranean sea caressing the south of Sicily will always be in sight, inviting you to immerse yourself in its waters.

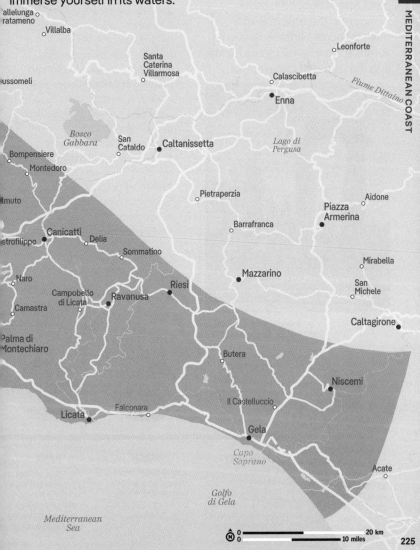

Cerda
ntemaggiore
allelunga
ratameno
Villalba
Leonforte
ussomeli
Santa Caterina Villarmosa
Calascibetta
Fiume Dittaino
Enna
Bosco Gabbara
San Cataldo
Caltanissetta
Lago di Pergusa
Bompensiere
Montedoro
muto
Pietraperzia
Aidone
Piazza Armerina
strofilippo
Canicattì
Delia
Barrafranca
Sommatino
Mirabella
Naro
Riesi
Mazzarino
San Michele
Campobello di Licata
Ravanusa
Camastra
Caltagirone
Palma di Montechiaro
Butera
Niscemi
Licata
Falconara
Il Castelluccio
Gela
Capo Soprano
Acate
Golfo di Gela
Mediterranean Sea

N
0   20 km
0   10 miles

Plan Your Time

The Valley of the Temples captures all the attention but don't forget about the other wonders in the area: the spa town Sciacca; cliffside Scala dei Turchi; the ancient Eraclea Minoa; and the island of Lampedusa.

APOSTOLIS GIONTZIS/SHUTTERSTOCK ©

Tempio di Hera Lacinia, Valley of the Temples (p230)

If you only do one thing

● Go straight to the Unesco-listed **Valley of the Temples** (p230) where lie the vestiges of an ancient and powerful city and the best-preserved Doric temples in the entire Mediterranean. Strolling the pathway to the temples along the ridge will take a whole morning (around 5km). Do not miss **Giardino della Kolymbetra** (p231), a beautiful garden in the western zone of the valley where you can pack along a picnic.

● Just north of the temples, spend an hour visiting the **Museo Archeologico** (p229), one of Sicily's most prominent. Then head to **Agrigento** (p228) to stroll along Via Atenea and enjoy an *aperitivo*.

Seasonal highlights

Thanks to the agreeable Mediterranean climate you can visit this area year-round. In winter it's less crowded and in summer the Valley of the Temples is open until midnight.

FEBRUARY

Held between February and March, Sciaccia's SciacCarnevale is opened by carnival king Peppe Nappa receiving the keys to the city.

MARCH

Late February to early March in Agrigento is the Sagra del Mandorlo in Fiore celebrating folk traditions.

APRIL

Favara celebrates Easter by preparing a traditional marzipan sheep called *agnello pasquale*, symbolising purity and sacrifice.

TERJE LILLEHAUG/ALAMY STOCK PHOTO ©, REDA &CO SRL/ALAMY STOCK PHOTO ©, GANDOLFO CANNATELLA/SHUTTERSTOCK ©

Three days to travel around

● After spending a day between the Valley of the Temples and Agrigento, move along the coast to discover spectacular white cliffs at **Scala dei Turchi** (p234) and swim in its amazing sea. In the afternoon visit **Villa Romana di Durrueli** (p234) right on the beach, and then enjoy a sunset from the ruins of **Eraclea Minoa** (p235).

● Spend a day in **Sciacca** (p237) strolling among its streets full of churches and noble palaces. Browse **artisan shops** (p236) admiring renowned ceramics and Sciacca coral jewellery.

● End your tour in **Caltabellotta** (p236) by visiting a fascinating hillside village where time seems to have stopped, then enjoy dinner with a view.

If you have more time

● Start from **Gela** (p239) to enjoy its well-preserved Greek fortifications before continuing along the coast to discover old castles, stunning beaches and the buzzing daily life in **Licata** (p239).

● After visiting the Valley of the Temples, head to **Porto Empedocle** (p233) and take a boat to the enchanting island of **Lampedusa** (p239). Here you can spend two or three days exploring its renowned beaches while swimming, snorkelling, diving and enjoying local seafood.

● From there catch a ferry to **Linosa** (p2451), another of the Pelagie islands with a very different attitude: it is less touristy and due to its volcanic origin its beaches have black sand and richer vegetation.

MAY	JULY	AUGUST	SEPTEMBER
The Sagra delle Minni di Virgini held in Sambuca di Sicilia celebrates a dessert evoking the shape of the Virgin's breast.	The Festa di San Calògero in Agrigento lasts eight days, from the first Sunday of July. Devotees go to the sanctuary barefoot.	On the last Sunday of August, a fun photographic treasure hunt is held along the old streets of Sciacca.	Turtle eggs hatch in Lampedusa and the newborns run towards the sea.

GENTO

Palermo

Agrigento

...ms Agrigento was founded by Cre-... ...t Daedalus and his son Icarus. His-... ...date the ancient city-state of Akragas to 580 ... ...Greek poet Pindar once described Akragas as the most beautiful city ever built by mortals, while Agrigentine philosopher Empedocles famously said that its inhabitants 'feast as if they will die tomorrow and build as if they will live for ever'.

Situated about 3km below the modern city of Agrigento, the Unesco-listed Valley of the Temples is one of the most mesmerising sites in the Mediterranean, boasting the best-preserved Doric temples outside Greece. On the travel radar since Goethe sang their praises in the 18th century, the temples now constitute Sicily's single biggest tourist site, with more than 600,000 visitors a year – to dodge crowds and summer heat, visit early morning or at sunset (open until midnight in summer). As impressive as the temples are, what you see today are mere vestiges of the ancient city of Akragas, which was once the fourth-largest city in the known world.

TOP TIP

Before heading to the Valley of the Temples download the official app, with audioguide and itineraries, and visit the town's Museo Archeologico housing stunning artefacts from the site (including the telamon, a colossal 8m-high statue that once supported the now ruined Temple of Zeus).

BEST RESTAURANTS

La Scala
Fabulous restaurant in a historic building on Via Atenea. Excellent food based on local seafood and produce.

Il Re di Girgenti
Fine-dining experience with the temples in the distance. Book ahead to sit outdoors.

Aguglia Persa
Specialises in seafood. Must try: linguine with shrimps and black garlic.

Kalòs
Just outside the historic centre, Kalòs has a great *pasta all'agrigentina* (tomatoes, basil and almonds).

A' Putia Bottega Siciliana
For a more informal dinner, try platters of local cheese, focaccia, grilled veggies and craft beers here.

The Old Town of Agrigento

NOBLE PALACES & HIDDEN CHURCHES

Sitting at the medieval core of Agrigeno is pedestrianised main street **Via Atenea**, lined with shops, restaurants and bars. Narrow alleys and stairways wind upwards and downwards off the main street, past noble palaces and historic churches. Start inside 11th-century **Cattedrale di San Gerlando**, altered over the centuries, with a facade reached by a wide stairway flanked by an unfinished 15th-century bell tower. Among the treasures it safeguards is a Norman painted wooden ceiling and an outstanding Roman sarcophagus. No one has ever been able to decipher the enigmatic 'letter of the devil', a 17th-century manuscript addressed to a nun in cryptic characters.

From Via Duomo, walk five minutes southeast along Via de Castro and Via Garufo to **Chiesa di Santa Maria dei Greci**. Inside the enchanting compact church, look up to admire the Norman ceiling, Byzantine frescoes and traces of the original Doric columns of the 5th-century temple on which the church was built. Another 10-minute wiggle east along old-town streets brings you to **Monastero di Santo Spirito**, a Cistercian convent founded in 1290 with magnificent stuccowork by late baroque and rococo genius Giacomo Serpotta (1656–1732). Nuns in residence here bake delicious sweets, including *cuscusu* (sweet couscous made with local pistachios); press the doorbell to enter and buy.

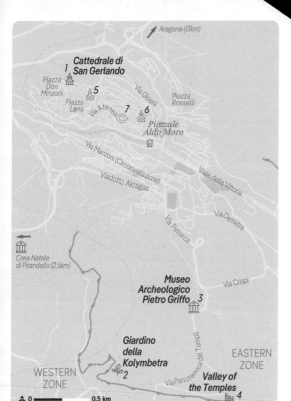

HIGH...
1 Cattedrale...
Gerlando
2 Giardino della
Kolymbetra
3 Museo Archeologico
Pietro Griffo
4 Valley of the Temples

SIGHTS
5 Chiesa di Santa Maria
dei Greci
6 Monastero di Santo
Spirito
7 Via Atenea

Casa Natale di Pirandello

NOBEL-WINNING WRITER'S HOUSE

Visit the family villa where the writer Luigi Pirandello (1867–1936) was born, 5km southwest of Agrigento. Inside the museum you can see photographs, memorabilia and first editions of his works such as *The Late Mattia Pascal* (1904), *The Old and the Young* (1913) and *One, None and a Hundred Thousand* (1926). Pirandello's ashes are buried at the foot of a pine tree in the garden.

Museo Archeologico Pietro Griffo

ARTEFACTS FROM THE ANCIENT PAST

North of the temples lies Museo Archeologico, one of Sicily's most important museums, which houses a stunning collection of artefacts from the Valley of Temples site.

 WHERE TO STAY IN AGRIGENTO

Cortile Baronello
A stylish place to stay in a renovated old house right in the city centre. Very friendly hosts. €

Camere a Sud
A B&B located in the heart of the historical centre. Modern design and traditional Sicilian touches throughout. €

Terrazze di Montelusa
In an atmospheric old *palazzo* with original furniture along with lovely, leafy panoramic terraces. €

...modern of Agri-... Temples boasts ...ic temples outside ...ee are mere vestig-... ...ity of Akragas, the ...n the ancient world. Sta... ...ion from the ticket office. A sho... ...eads to the 5th-century-BCE **1 Tempio di Hera Lacinia** (also called Tempio di Giunone), perched on the ridge top. The colonnade and sacrificial altar remain largely intact. Red traces are the result of fire damage likely dating to the Carthaginian invasion of 406 BCE. Descend past a 500-year-old olive tree and Byzantine tombs to **2 Tempio della Concordia**. This remarkable edifice, the model for Unesco's logo, has survived almost entirely intact since its construction in 430 BCE, partly due to its conversion into a Christian basilica in the 6th century,

and partly thanks to the shock-absorbing, earthquake-dampening qualities of the soft clay underlying its hard rock foundation. Further downhill, **3 Tempio di Ercole** is Agrigento's oldest, dating from the end of the 6th century BC. Down from the main temples, miniature **4 Tomba di Terone** dates to 75 BCE.

Cross the pedestrian bridge into the western zone, stopping at **5 Tempio di Giove**. This would have been the world's largest Doric temple had its construction not been interrupted by the Carthaginian sacking of Akragas. Take a brief look at the ruined 5th-century BCE **6 Tempio dei Dioscuri** and the 6th-century BCE complex of altars and small buildings known as the **7 Santuario delle Divine Chtoniche**, before ending your visit in the Giardino della Kolymbetra and enjoying live music in the citrus grove.

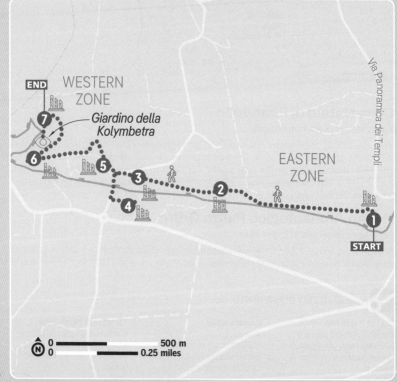

DALUU/SHUTTERSTOCK ©

Tempio dei Dioscuri, Valley of the Temples

For a better understanding of how the temples originally appeared try to visit here before heading to the Valley. Highlights include painted ceramics and the *telamon,* a colossal statue which used to support the now ruined Temple of Zeus in the Valley.

Giardino della Kolymbetra

SLICE OF PARADISE ON EARTH

According to the ancient Greek historian Diodorus Siculus, the valley had been dug by Carthaginian slaves in 480 BCE. to make it a water-supplying pool and a fish nursery. Then during the Middle Ages it was transformed into a lush garden thanks to the irrigation system built in ancient times and still in use. Giardino della Kolymbetra hosts more than 300 species of plants, including citrus varieties no longer cultivated elsewhere. The climb down may be steep, but it's short and easy. It lies at the western end of the Valley of the Temples, you can spot ancient columns among the trees and you can also visit a hypogeum. Tables and benches are available if you want to pack a picnic, and on summer evenings you can sip an aperitif in the citrus grove listening to live music.

I LIVE HERE: BEST NIGHTLIFE IN AGRIGENTO

Erika Cancialosi,
content creator and admin of *@ig_agrigento*

Cantina Granet Enobistrot
In the *dammuso* (vaulted stone room) of a historic building on Via Atenea, it is the perfect spot to taste very good wines accompanied by great food. In summer you can also sit outdoors.

Café Girasole
A trendy hangout with DJ set and outdoor seating. Stop by to have an *aperitivo* or a cocktail.

'Nzolia
A wide selection of wines in a very nice atmosphere. You can also eat amazing finger food.

Caffè San Pietro
Adjacent to the 18th-century church of San Pietro, now used as a cultural venue, this hip cafe serves wines and *aperitivi.*

 GETTING AROUND

The historic centre is best explored on foot. To get to the Valley of the Temples, hop on city bus 1 which runs half-hourly from Agrigento's bus station on Piazzale Rosselli and train station to the archaeological museum (10 minutes) and valley's Porta V entrance (20 minutes) on Via Caduti di Marzabotto.

Buses 2 and 2/ both use the Tempio di Giunone stop on Via Panoramica dei Templi by the eastern entrance to the

temples; 2/ is the quicker route, taking just 10 minutes. Find schedules online (www.trasportiurbaniagrigento.it) and at bus stops; drivers sell tickets or buy in advance at tobacconists.

Alternatively, Agrigento's Temple Tour Bus (www.templetourbusagrigento.com) includes the Valley of the Temples on its hop-on-hop-off tourist circuit. Motorists can use official car parks at both entrances.

Beyond Agrigento

Plenty of hidden gems wait to be discovered around Agrigento along the extensive and unspoiled Mediterranean coast.

Sambuca di Sicilia
Caltabellotta
Sciacca
Riserva Naturale   Agrigento
di Torre Salsa
Favara
Porto
Empedocle   Palma di
Montechiaro

Whether you love wandering through ancient ruins or discovering hillside villages, tasting local delicacies or simply lazing about sunbathing, this region hides many treasures waiting to be explored. An extraordinary contemporary art gallery, a wild coastline dotted with fortifications and fascinating cities overlooking the shining Mediterranean Sea are just a taste of what's on offer. Cross the Mediterranean to reach the island of Lampedusa surrounded by aquamarine waters. Due to its position in the Sicilian Channel, Lampedusa has often been a landing place for people in search of a new horizon. If for those who arrive here on vacation its small port is the first step towards a heavenly experience, for refugees it represents the end of a life-threatening journey and the hope of a safer life.

TOP TIP

Moving around by public transport along the Mediterranean coast is almost impossible; only larger towns are connected. Better to use the car.

Torre Salsa (p234)

POLUDZIBER/SHUTTERSTOCK ©

Farm Cultural Park

AN UNEXPECTED ART GALLERY

Located in Favara, 15 minutes away from Agrigento, the art gallery at Farm Cultural Park is one of a kind. Bringing some new vibrancy into the local community, the founders Andrea Bartoli and Florinda Saieva took over a nearly abandoned quarter in the unoccupied buildings of the old town centre to create a contemporary art gallery with spaces for international exhibitions and artist residencies.

Here innovation and tradition blend, using contemporary art to enhance the past and present of the village – opening up to the whole world while also involving locals, including some elderly women who still live in the neighbourhood. Over time the Farm has grown as it incorporates more of the town's dilapidated houses. Building walls bear giant murals, courtyards are full of sculptures and installations. Walking through its streets you can discover international art, buy local craftworks, watch a movie, join a talk or a workshop, have a coffee and discuss politics.

Discover Favara

A CASTLE & AN ALMOND MUSEUM

Focused around Piazza Cavour, Favara's town centre is also worth a visit. Start from the **Castello di Chiaramonte**, then head next door to the beautiful **Chiesa SS Rosario** with stunning stuccoworks inside. Nearby is the **Biblioteca Barone Mendola**, a little gem not to be missed. The first floor hosts the Baron's books, including precious volumes dating back to 1500. End your tour at **Marzipan**, a museum devoted entirely to local almond. The exhibition unfolds the history of the nut, how it is produced in Sicily and its many uses in both sweet and savoury traditional dishes. Its shop sells gourmet products too.

Porto Empedocle

ANDREA CAMILLERI'S HOME

In ancient Akragas sulphur and rock salt were shipped from Porto Empedocle, 10km southwest of the Valley of the Temples on the coast. Originally called Marina di Girgenti, the port changed its name in 1863 to commemorate Greek philosopher Empedocle, who was born here. The town's best-known modern son is novelist Andrea Camilleri (1925–2019), whose wildly popular detective novels starring Inspector Montalbano are set in the fictional city of Vigàta – Porto Empedocle in disguise. Find a street mural dedicated to the writer on Via Salita Chiesa.

AGNELLO PASQUALE DI FAVARA

This traditional local sweet is a beautifully decorated marzipan in the shape of a *pecura* (sheep) that's made with *pasta reale* (almond paste) and stuffed with pistachio paste. The lamb is the most prominent symbol of Easter and in Christianity it symbolises purity and sacrifice in its association with Jesus Christ. The basic form of the lamb is created using a mould, and is then decorated by hand. According to legend, this dessert was originally prepared by the nuns of the Collegio di Maria and the recipe was handed down through the generations by spoken word. The oldest written recipe goes back to 1898 and belonged to a rich family as it was prepared mainly at home. Today you can buy it in every pastry shop in town. The best place to grab one is Cosi Dunci.

 WHERE TO EAT IN FAVARA

Ostrea Aperitif Fish
No matter what you order, the seafood here is always fresh, delicious and paired with good Sicilian wines. €€

U Maccicuni
A picturesque location overlooking the square with good food, a friendly owner and complimentary *amaro*. €€

Garde Manger
A tasty, informal lunch of mainly local fish dishes. Try aubergine-stuffed *piadina* (flatbread) or couscous *arancini*. €

**WHY I LOVE
SCALA DEI
TURCHI**

Sara Mostaccio,
@fritha

I used to climb on this cliff as a teenager during my summer holidays with friends. Until a few years ago you could still climb on it and walking barefoot on the chalky marl made your feet turn white. Looking towards the horizon from above you had the impression of being immersed in the indigo blue sea water lapping the cliff. Today it's no longer allowed to climb upon for both safety reasons and to safeguard the natural site – a choice that I approve of. We can still enjoy the beauty of this place from the nearby beach or while sailing on a boat, feeling like old navigators who, passing through here, remained open-mouthed with astonishment.

Scala dei Turchi

SPECTACULAR CHALKY CLIFF

This blinding-white cliff, 15km west of Agrigento, is shaped like a giant staircase and named Scala dei Turchi (Turkish Stairs) after the Arab pirates who used to seek safety from stormy weather beneath it. The passing of time has transformed this rocky outcrop into a spectacular sight. It's a very popular spot, so unless you arrive early, finding a parking space will be difficult. On the drive here you'll be treated to panoramic viewpoints along the way. You can only reach the beach (five to 10 minutes walking) as climbing the cliff is no longer allowed. The Scala is clearly visible on the right side from the main beach, a sandy stretch perfect to sunbathe and go for a swim.

Villa Romana di Durrueli

MOSAICS & SPA BY THE SEA

Situated 12 km from Agrigento, Villa Romana di Durrueli in Realmonte is a small treasure preserved over time. It was the seaside residence of Publius Annus, a rich sulphur businessman from the 1st century CE, and was rediscovered in 1907 during excavations for a railway. Its rooms are decorated with marble slabs and mosaics, reflecting the wealth of the family who lived there. In a second wing of the villa there's a spa area, probably built at a later time.

Riserva Naturale di Torre Salsa

SICILY'S WILDEST BEACH

Seeking some solitude and wanting to escaping the crowds? Then come by to explore the rugged beauty of Riserva Naturale Torre Salsa, a nature reserve covering more than 760 hectares and managed by the WWF. It lies 30km from Agrigento and offers a unique combination of sandy beaches, turquoise blue waters, dunes, chalk cliffs (including a smaller Scala dei Turchi called Dama Bianca) and wetlands providing a perfect habitat for several species of wildlife, including Caretta Caretta turtles.

There are plenty of hiking options for those who prefer to keep active. Otherwise if you want to get underwater this is an incredible place to snorkel with some wonderful marine life. You can see Posidonia meadows swaying in the water, red anemones and schools of silver fish swimming around you.

During summer things can get surprisingly quiet, so if you're planning on spending a few hours here come prepared as there are no facilities. There are four main entrances: Pantano,

 WHERE TO EAT ALONG THE COAST

**Nodo Ammare,
Realmonte**
Refined gourmet cuisine with a view over the Scala dei Turchi. €€

**Pizzeria Sitári,
Villaggio Mosé**
This award-winning pizzeria is 7km from Agrigento. Best pizza ever! €€

**Gelateria Le Cuspidi,
San Leone**
End your meal with an excellent ice cream. The bestseller is the Raffadali pistachio flavour. €

Scala dei Turchi

Eremita, Cannicella and Omomorto. The most recommended is Pantano from where the parking lot is a short stroll to the beach.

Eraclea Minoa

ANCIENT GREEK SETTLEMENT

Here you can dip your toes into both the sea and history at the same time. Today its greatest attraction is the strip of golden sand backed by trees and cliffs, but Eraclea Minoa is also a significant historical site and important Greek settlement. According to legend it was founded by the Cretan King Minos during his seach for Daedalus after his escape, but in actuality it was founded by Greek colonists in the 6th century BCE. Explore the archaeological park that sits on a promontory jutting out towards a stunning seascape. The view from the remains of the Greek theatre, dating back to the 5th century BCE, is incomparable. The theatre itself is interesting because of the construction material, the same rock as the Scala dei Turchi. There are also some well-preserved dwellings made of rough bricks and an antiquarium displaying a collection of objects found on site.

BEST BEACHES NEAR TORRE SALSA & ERACLEA MINOA

Siciulana Marina
A stretch of fine golden-sand beach backed by a hill on which the old town of Siciulana stands.

Torre Salsa
A 6km-long coastline inside the WWF-protected nature reserve. Surprisingly quiet. Offers respite from the busy beaches along the coast.

Bovo Marina
A stretch of golden sand contrasted by a blue sea and the milky Capo Bianco at sunset. Magical at sunset.

Eraclea Beach
Between the Platani river and the Capo Bianco promontory, this white beach and transparent sea is surrounded by a pine forest.

Capo Bianco
This beach is right below a high white cliff lapped by a turquoise sea. Near the Platani River nature reserve, it's reached by a short walk through the woods.

 WHERE TO EAT IN SICULIANA MARINA

Lustru di Luna
If you're a seafood lover you won't be disappointed. Great location to witness a stunning sunset. €€

Maioliche Bistrot
Try their *pasta al ragù di crasto*, in a slow cooked lamb meat sauce, or choose a gourmet burger. €

La Scogliera
Locally sourced food, seafront location, friendly staff. Don't miss the spaghetti with sea urchins. €€

SCIACCA CORAL

This unique coral is closely tied to the submerged Ferdinanea island right in front of Sciacca. Its most recent appearance was in 1831 before a year later it sank again back beneath the waters. Thanks to the exceptional microclimate determined by volcanic phenomena, huge coral reefs developed. It is said that in 1875 the captain Bettu Ammareddu was out fishing with his friends when he lost his necklace, a love token from his beloved Tina. He dived to retrieve it and discovered fields of coral. Due to its peculiarities, Sciacca coral is eco-sustainable as it is fossilised and already detached from the reef. You can buy amazing coral jewels at Sabrina Orafa's boutique.

Sciacca coral

Castello Incantato

THOUSANDS OF SCULPTED HEADS

About 2km east of Sciacca is this so-called 'enchanted castle', actually a large open-air museum filled with thousands of sculpted heads made by the local artist Filippo Bentivegna (1888–1967). He was considered mad when he started to carve heads in rock and wood in his piece of land at the foot of Monte Kronio. He considered himself a sovereign of sorts while the heads were his subjects.

Shopping for Ceramics in Sciacca

HANDMADE POTTERY

The art of ceramics has deep roots in the town's history with the first furnaces appearing in the area in the 4th century. Today Sciacca's handmade pottery is appreciated around the world. If you're after colourful local ceramics, you can browse the workshops along Corso Vittorio Emanuele and Via Giuseppe Licata.

SciacCarnevale

SCIACCA'S CARNIVAL

In February Sciacca hosts a phantasmagorical carnival with huge grotesque figures mounted on floats that wind through the streets. The king of carnival Peppe Nappa opens the party with the traditional handover of the keys of the city. It ends on Shrove Tuesday with the burning of a puppet of the king.

Caltabellotta

A VILLAGE 1000M HIGH

Sitting high up on Mount Kratas, this hilltop village (949m) is definitely off the beaten track. Here you'll be treated to some spectacular panoramas, the best of which is from the ruined Norman castle. Wander its narrow streets and discover its 11th-century church of **Maria Santissima Assunta**. Over time Caltabellotta has been inhabited by the Greeks, Romans, Arabs and Normans, all of whom have left traces across town. The name derives from the Arabic 'Qal'at Ballutt' (Rock of Oaks) and you can go up to the **Monastero di San Pellegrino**, a former Arab fort. Below the church lies the **Dragon's Caves**, where legend has it a dragon lived, feeding on the children in the village.

 WHERE TO STAY IN SCIACCA

Domus Maris Relais
Overlooking the fishing port with airy rooms that feature names inspired by Greek mythology. €€

Casa dell'Aromatario B&B
On the main street in a blue building. Beautiful roof terrace and breakfast served in the cave. €€

Regina Bianca
Frescoed ceilings, historic floors and modern furnishings. On-site spa and a relaxing terrace. €€

A WALKING TOUR OF SCIACCA

Founded in the 5th century BCE as a thermal resort, the old spa town of Sciacca was originally named Xacca (water) by the Arabs. Start near the harbour at **1 Scalinata Artistica**, a staircase decorated with majolica. From here, head along Via Caricatore to see the **2 Santa Maria del Soccorso**, erected in 1108 and rebuilt in 1656. then continue to the panoramic **3 Piazza Scandaliato** from which there is a magnificent view of the sea. Take Via Incisa to admire the Renaissance portal of the former **4 Santa Margherita hospital**, **5 Porta San Salvatore**, the main gateway to the city dating back to the 14th century and rebuilt in 1581 in the Renaissance style, and **6 Chiesa del Carmine** with its bizarre mishmash facade. Continue along Via Gerardi to the 16th-century **7 Palazzo Steripinto** a fortified palace built in 1501 with a diamond-tipped facade. At the pastry shop **8 La Favola** taste the *cucchiteddi* made with almond paste and pumpkin jam. Explore the narrow alleys of the ancient Jewish quarter climbing the **9 Salita di San Michele** to the church of **10 San Michele Arcangelo**, founded by Count Guglielmo Peralta in 1371 and later reconstructed in the 17th century. Heading down Via Giglio, reach **11 Castello dei Luna**, built in 1382 and linked to the bloody dispute between two medieval families, Luna and Perollo.

BEST RESTAURANTS IN SCIACCA

Hostaria del Vicolo
Traditional Sicilian dishes with a contemporary twist. Don't miss the local dessert *ova murina:* an almond crepe filled with milk cream.

Pizzeria Steripinto
Always full of locals here for Sciacca's typical *pizza saccense,* or *tabisca:* tomato, sardines, pecorino cheese and onion.

Otto
Just in front of the cathedral, Otto has a stylish and minimalist setting and seasonal menu of excellent local dishes. Try the seared octopus.

La Lampara
A contemporary restaurant serving a creative fish menu by the sea. Tuna steak in sesame seeds is unmissable.

Trattoria Al Faro
A welcoming trattoria serving delicious fish at surprisingly low prices. Don't miss its *pasta con le sarde* (sardines, fennel, raisins and breadcrumbs).

FRANCESCA SCIARRA/SHUTTERSTOCK ©

Palma di Montechiaro

Sambuca di Sicilia

ANCIENT ZABUT

A destination that seems to have stopped in time, Sambuca di Sicilia is a place of churches and palaces. Its ancient name was Zabut, which derived from its founder, the emir Al Zabut, and this Arabic centre dates back to the 9th century. Today you'll find some 13 churches and several noble palaces including the **Palazzo Oddo**, now the town hall, **Palazzo Campisi** and **Palazzo Panitteri**. Also don't miss the Baroque balcony of the **Casino dei Marchesi Beccadelli**. During the Sagra delle Minni di Virgini in May you can taste a typical dessert evoking the shape of the Virgin's breast.

Palma di Montechiaro, Licata, Falconara, Butera & Gela

A ROAD TRIP ALONG THE COAST

Situated 30 minutes east of Agrigento, begin your road trip from **Palma di Montechiaro**, founded in 1637 by Carlo Caro

 WHERE TO EAT IN CALTABELLOTTA

M.A.T.E.S.
A family-run restaurant serving local and seasonal Sicilian food. Housed in a restored oil mill. €€

Osteria Gulèa
On a rooftop overlooking the village. Try the lamb and the *tuma* cheese with tangerine jam. €€

Trattoria La Ferla
No frills but good food at a reasonable price. Try the pasta with sausage. €

Tomasi, a forebear of the writer Giuseppe Tomasi di Lampedusa, author of the novel *Il Gattopardo* (The Leopard). The writer spent his childhood and set part of his masterpiece here. Along the coast is the Castello Chiaramontano, built in 1353 in a dominant position. In the 17th century it became the property of the Tomasi family. The town is 9km away, following the SS115. Discover the impressive Mother Church with a scenic staircase and the splendid Palazzo degli Scolopi.

Reaching **Licata** from Palma di Montechiaro takes 30 minutes. It was here in July 1943 that the Allies landed along this coast, but this sea also saw the famous naval Battle of Cape Ecnomus, fought in 256 BCE between Romans and Carthaginians. The relics of Punic and Roman ships can be seen in the Museo del Mare inside the Sant'Angelo cloister. Nearby, in a former Cistercian convent, is the Museo Archeologico della Badia, housing finds from the prehistoric age (5000 BCE) to the Hellenistic-Roman age (1st century BCE). On a hill above the city stands Castel Sant'Angelo, an Aragonese fire tower.

Continue towards **Falconara** to be amazed by its 14th-century castle overlooking the beach. From here head up to Butera, a further 24km away. Once a prosperous city under the rule of the Branciforte noble family, today it offers a lovely Mother Church, also known as Chiesa di Santa Maria Assunta, and a hilltop Arab-Norman castle with a stunning view. End the day driving towards **Gela** along the SS115 to see its remarkable archaeological museum for insights into the city's great past. It's undergoing renovations and due to reopen around March 2024. You can also see the well-preserved Greek fortifications at Capo Soprano built in 333 BCE by Timoleon, tyrant of Syracuse.

Sunset at Capo Ponente

THE SUN DROPPING INTO THE SEA

If you journey to Lampedusa – by plane, ferry or hydrofoil (Getting Around, p241) – the westernmost tip of the island is the best viewpoint to enjoy the sunset. Capo Ponente is 20 minutes drive from the town centre of Lampedusa. You can also get there by bus (Circolare Azzurra, blue line) but be aware the last return trip is at 9.15pm; just in time as the sun sets between 8pm and 8.30pm in summer. The sun drops into the sea while you sip an *aperitivo* supplied by a mobile bar (May to September). You can also witness a great sun-

BEST BEACHES EAST OF AGRIGENTO

Punta Bianca
This wild beach lapped by crystal-clear sea in a nature reserve is a paradise for divers. There's also a ruined stone house and a WWII bunker. No facilities.

Torre San Nicola
Right below a 16th-century tower is this sandy stretch of beach dotted with rocks. Across from here sits the islet of San Nicola. Parasols, a kiosk and changing rooms available.

Mollarella Bay
A popular sandy beach equipped with parasols, sunbeds and facilities.

Nicolizia
This wild beach is dotted with emerging flat rocks called *balatazze* and surrounded by Mediterranean shrubs. No facilities.

Torre di Gaffe
Between Palma and Licata, this windy beach is loved by surfers and kitesurfers. Parasols and sunbeds available.

 WHERE TO EAT IN LICATA

La Madia
Michelin-starred restaurant serving modern Sicilian food presented as a work of art. €€€

L'Oste e il Sacrestano
Freshly caught seafood and local meat. Order a la carte or a seven-course tasting menu. €€€

Oasi Beach Osteria del Mare
Right on the beach is this authentic place full of locals and great seafood. €€

Shot from
Fuocoammare

set from Albero Sole, the island's highest point (133m). It sits on the northern shore but it's not far from Capo Ponente (an eight-minute drive).

Otherworldly Photos at Tabaccara

FLYING BOATS

This natural pool on the southern shore of Lampedusa has water so transparent that anchored boats look as if they are flying! The best spot to take that perfect Instagram shot? Along the path towards the Spiaggia dei Conigli, which is just a 30-minute walk away. And the name? It's called Tabaccara due to the tobacco traders who conducted business here.

Hike & Dive in Cala Pulcino

EXPLORING A CANYON

A trail crossing a pine forest and a mini canyon leads to this little pebble cove between two rocky headlands on Lampedusa. Follow the signs for Casa Teresa and leave your car at the Cala Pulcino car park, then take the path to the left and walk for 30 to 40 minutes. The trail is easy and suitable for everyone but make sure you wear closed-toe shoes.

Cala Pulcino is paradise for snorkelers and divers. The crystal-clear water is deep enough to make you feel like you are flying while you swim among multicoloured fishes. **Marina Diving Center** (www.marinadivinglampedusa.it) can help you find the best spots to dive, such as a submerged cave. The beach has no facilities so bring water and food if you plan to stay for a while.

Lampedusa by Boat

BEACHES & CAVES

Ask down the main port in Lampedusa town to book a boat tour. It takes about four hours. After passing Punta Guitgia you'll see a sequence of lovely coves called Cala Croce, Cala Madonna, Cala Greca, Cala Galera and Cala Tabaccara, where the boat stops for you to take an unforgettable swim in the most crystalline waters you've ever seen. Likewise the nearby Spiaggia dei Conigli seems to have been borrowed from a Caribbean island and you'll be treated to spectacular views while out on the water. After a stop at Cala Pulcino, where you can swim, the tour continues towards the deep inlet Vallone dell'Acqua and Capo Ponente, Lampedusa's

WHERE TO STAY ON LAMPEDUSA

**Italianway
Ottoventi Apartments**
Fully equipped apartments
with lovely decor. Close to the
centre but in a quiet spot. €€€

B&B Giro Di Boa
Nice rooms, balcony with views
over the port and breakfast
served on the terrace. €€

B&B SoleLuna
Spacious rooms, a nice garden,
private parking and free
airport-shuttle service. €€

westernmost point. The boat takes you back to the port along the north shore of the island, a steeper coast made up of photogenic high cliffs.

A Day in Linosa

A VOLCANIC ISLAND

Linosa is part of the Pelagie islands and is located about 40km from Lampedusa, connected daily by ferry or hydrofoil. Despite its small size, this natural paradise can offer a lot and is far less touristy than Lampedusa. In ancient times, it was a refuge for those who crossed the Mediterranean and the Romans used it as a base during the Punic wars. Today there are about 430 inhabitants who live mainly from tourism, agriculture and fishing. Take a walk among the colourful houses of the small village around the harbour where you'll find bars and restaurants.

Linosa has a volcanic origin so its landscape is different from Lampedusa. It's a jewel for birders with migratory species passing through here from Africa, and its coasts are dotted with caves, inlets and stacks worth discovering during a boat ride. You may also spot dolphins. Rent a boat at the main port or book a tour to spend the day exploring the *faraglioni* (rock formations emerging from the sea) on the eastern shore, a natural pool connected to the sea through an underground cave, and the black-sand beach at Pozzolana Di Ponente on the western shore.

BEST RESTAURANTS ON LAMPEDUSA

Cavalluccio Marino
Taste amazing dishes such as swordfish *cannoli* or a great risotto with red prawns. In summer you can dine on a patio with sea views.

Trattoria Terranova
Much-loved local trattoria. Do not miss the antipasti: *caponata*, couscous, mackerel meatballs, marinated sardines.

Il Balenottero
A family-run 'home restaurant' serving excellent seafood. Their spaghetti with sea urchins is superb.

A Putia
A wine shop in the centre of Lampedusa town where you can try their rich platters with cheese, charcuterie, olives, bread and veggies, paired with Sicilian wines or craft beers.

GETTING AROUND

It's best to use a car while travelling along the Mediterranean coast. Favara is just 10km from Agrigento along the SS122 but note that it's almost impossible to park on the narrow streets around the Farm Cultural Park. Our tip? Find a spot along Via Umberto and walk from there.

To reach Scala dei Turchi, follow the coastal SS115 and exit at Porto Empedocle and follow the signs. You can reach Torre Salsa, Eraclea Minoa and Sciacca, as well as the coastal towns east of Agrigento, along the same highway. Sciacca is also connected by bus (Lumia, one hour).

Caltabellotta is best reached by car along the panoramic SP37. Be prepared to brave narrow

streets once you arrive in town and head up to Piazzale Ruggero di Lauria where you can park. And if you like scenic drives, then you will love the winding country road leading to Sambuca di Sicilia from Sciacca (SS624 and SS188).

Lampedusa is accessed by plane (DAT from Catania and Palermo; Volotea and ITA from other Italian cities), ferry (Siremar, nine hours) or hydrofoil (Liberty Lines, four hours, summer only). Once there, you can rent a car, bicycle, e-bike or scooter. Cycling is a great way to get around the relatively small island. Two circular bus routes cover the island: Linea Azzurra serving the west and Linea Rossa the northeast.

TOOLKIT

The chapters in this section cover the most important topics you'll need to know about in Sicily. They're full of nuts-and-bolts information and valuable insights to help you understand and navigate Sicily and get the most out of your trip.

Arriving
p244

Getting Around
p245

Money
p246

Accommodation
p247

Family Travel
p248

Health & Safe Travel
p249

Food, Drink & Nightlife
p250

Responsible Travel
p252

LGBTIQ+ Travellers
p253

Accessible Travel
p254

Nuts & Bolts
p255

Language
p256

Noto (p188)

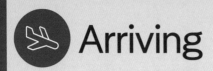

Arriving

TOOLKIT

Palermo and Catania are the primary airports for most travellers visiting Sicily. Smaller airports at Trapani and Comiso offer a handful of flights. Keep in mind that Comiso airport is not connected by public transport, so you will need to rent a car or call a taxi.

Visas

Not required for stays of up to 90 days, or at all for EU citizens. Some nationalities will need a Schengen visa. More info schengenvisainfo. com/who-needs-schengen-visa.

SIM cards

Local SIM cards offer affordable prepaid data plans, readily available for unlocked mobile phones. A photo ID is required to activate a local SIM card.

Wi-fi

Don't rely on finding free wi-fi everywhere, although it is available at airport terminals, hotels and many restaurants. Public wi-fi in cities is usually slow and unreliable. Better to get a local SIM card.

ATMs

ATMs are everywhere and major credit cards are widely accepted but some smaller shops and market stalls might not take them.

Public transport from airport to city centre

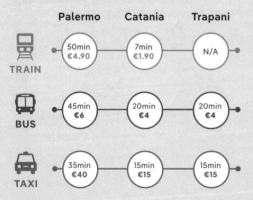

	Palermo	Catania	Trapani
TRAIN	50min €4.90	7min €1.90	N/A
BUS	45min €6	20min €4	20min €4
TAXI	35min €40	15min €15	15min €15

OVER THE SEA TO SICILY

If you are driving to Sicily, you need to catch a ferry at Villa San Giovanni in Calabria to cross the Strait of Messina, taking your car on board and disembarking in Messina. You can also take a ferry from Genoa, Livorno, Civitavecchia, Naples or Salerno to Palermo. If you do not have a car but would still rather travel via sea, catch the hydrofoil from Naples or Livorno (June to September). On overnight services travellers can choose between cabin accommodation or a *poltrona,* an airline-type armchair.

Getting Around

Nothing beats the freedom of having your own car in Sicily, especially if you are planning to explore the island's rural villages, its most secluded beaches and scenic back roads.

TRAVEL COSTS

Rental
From €45/day

Petrol
Approx
€1.90/litre

EV charging
€20 for full

Train ticket from
Palermo to Catania
from €15

Hiring a Car

Pre-book for lower costs. Renters must generally be over 21 and have a credit card. Most hire cars have manual transmission. Hiring a small car will make it easier to tackle narrow streets and tight parking spaces.

Road Conditions

Main motorways *(autostrada)* and high-traffic secondary roads (SS/SP) are generally in good condition. Smaller roads can be poorly maintained. Tolls are charged on the A18 (Messina–Catania) and A20 (Messina–Palermo).

GO WITH THE FLOW

Sicilians have a reputation for being among the worst drivers in Italy. They drive super fast and recklessly and will cut you off, so if you decide to rent a car in Sicily be careful. While Sicilians always seem to be in a hurry while driving, they are very relaxed with timetables and have a very nonchalant approach to getting anything done on time. Go with the flow, having a positive attitude is the best way to get the most out of your trip.

TIP

You can wheel your bike onto regional trains; simply purchase a separate bicycle ticket valid for 24 hours.

DRIVING ESSENTIALS

Drive on the right.

50

Speed limit is 130km/h on *autostrade*, 90km/h on smaller highways and 50km/h in built-up areas.

.05

Blood alcohol limit is 0.05%.

Parking

Free spaces are marked with white lines while blue lines denote pay-and-display parking. You can buy the ticket at the automated machines or from a tobacconist. Parking in the main cities can be difficult but you could get lucky looking for a free space in peripheral streets.

Train & Bus

Rail travel is cheap and reliable, though routes are limited and trains are often slow. Away from the main coastal routes, buses are the best way of getting around Sicily as they offer fast and direct service on many intercity routes. Sometimes they are the only form of public transport serving interior towns.

Plane & Boat

DAT (Danish Air Transport) operates flights from Catania and Palermo to Lampedusa and Pantelleria. You can also reach islands by boat. Hydrofoil and ferry connections to the smaller islands are guaranteed during high season, but decrease in winter and can be affected by sea conditions.

Money

CURRENCY: EURO (€)

Cash or card?

Always carry some cash. Most hotels and restaurants accept credit cards; smaller guesthouses and trattorias might not. Unattended petrol stations usually accept only Visa and MasterCard.

Digital payments

Major credit cards are widely accepted but some smaller shops, market stalls and toll booths on motorways might not take them, so have cash on hand.

Taxes and refunds

Prices in Sicily always include 22% VAT (4% on food and drinks). Non-EU passport holders can claim back the VAT on goods at the time of purchase if they buy from a store with a tax-free symbol. Ask for the tax-back form and get it stamped by customs.

Tipping

Restaurants If no *coperto* (a cover charge of around €2), consider rounding the bill up.

Cafes People often place a small coin (€0.10–0.20) on the bar when ordering coffee.

Hotels Not expected, but welcome.

Taxis Optional but polite to round up to the nearest Euro.

HOW MUCH FOR A...

Espresso
€1

Archaeological museum ticket
€8–10

Bus ticket from Palermo to Agrigento
€9

Train ticket from Catania to Syracuse
€8

HOW TO...

SAVE SOME EUROS

If you have a student card, or you are under 25, you can get reduced admission to almost all sights. Likewise, those aged over 65 with an ID proving their age will save money or enter for free. Many attractions offer combined tickets which allow you access to two or more sites. saving some euros on individually purchased tickets.

LOCAL TIP

ATMs are widely available but be aware of transaction fees. Some ATMs reject foreign cards so be prepared to try a few before assuming your card is the problem.

TO BARGAIN OR NOT TO BARGAIN?

Haggling is common in outdoor and flea markets (but not in food markets) as markets in Sicily are more similar to Arabic markets than in the rest of Italy. However, bargaining is generally unacceptable in stores. You can still try to get a better price, through good-humoured bargaining, in a craft shop or a small artisan store if you are making a huge purchase. In all other circumstances, you are expected to pay the stated price. It is up to the seller to decide to offer a discount.

Accommodation

Sleep like an aristocrat

Feel like part of the old Sicilian aristocracy by sleeping in a historic building. Many palaces, especially in recent years, are being restored and opened to the public. Sometimes they reserve a wing for hospitality. Despite the modern facilities they offer, each hotel respects its history and architectural traits. Rates start at around €150 per night but prices can vary a lot depending on the location.

Go rural

Many *agriturismi* (farm-stay accommodation), farmhouses and country houses offer rooms as well as delicious home-cooked meals using fresh ingredients, often grown on-site. Sometimes they are housed in ancient villas or old castles, offering you an immersion both in history and in nature. A breakfast based on local products is generally included and a restaurant usually provides other meals on request.

Into the wild

It's easy to find cheap accommodation in a *rifugio* (mountain hut) in national parks such as Nebrodi, Madonie and Etna. This is the best way for outdoor enthusiasts to connect with nature. Some are run like real hotels, but with more basic amenities. Others are open and always accessible or must be booked in advance (for free) by asking the forestry corps.

HOW MUCH FOR A NIGHT IN...

a palace
from €150

a wine estate
from €200

a B&B
€45

Camp out

Wild camping is generally prohibited but you can count on a wide range of paid camping options. Campgrounds are always equipped with hot showers and electrical hookups. Be aware that many seafront campgrounds can get crowded and noisy in summer. Feeling like some luxury? Choose glamping that combines the natural experience with the comforts of a hotel.

Fall in love with a B&B

Born as an economic and familiar alternative to the hotel, B&Bs are a delightful way to get in touch with locals. Breakfast is almost always included and is based on typical Sicilian products, served on an outdoor terrace or in a common area where you can interact with other guests or spend some time with your hosts.

SLEEP IN A WINE ESTATE

While food and wine tourism is constantly growing, many wineries offer accommodation as well as wine tasting. They are often located inside sumptuous villas or in more traditional *masserie* (farmhouses). You can book a room to stay overnight and take a relaxing walk through the vineyards, enjoy a picnic with stunning views over the countryside or visit *palmenti* (traditional wine cellars) and taste amazing Sicilian wines. It is an unusual but fascinating way to discover another facet of Sicily. The proceeds from the rooms are often invested in improving winemaking techniques or preserving historical buildings.

Family Travel

Sicily is a very family-friendly place and children of all ages are generally welcome in restaurants, hotels and cafes. A wide range of sights and activities is available for kids: a train adventure on a volcano, *gelaterie,* well-equipped beaches and amazing puppet theatres. As a family, you can also benefit from discounts on transport and accommodation.

Sights

Children are often given reduced entrance fees or free admission to tours and sights. EU kids aged under 18 do not pay to go to state-run museums and pay half price at private museums. Children under five enter for free. Even those attractions that do not offer discounted fees usually have a day free for everyone on the first Sunday of the month. A few museums offer specific tours and workshops for children.

Facilities

- Very few restaurants and museums have nappy-changing facilities.
- Cobbled streets make historic centres difficult with a pram; better to bring a baby carrier.
- Supplies for babies (food, nappies, milk) are available at pharmacies and supermarkets.
- Most hotels have cots available (sometimes costing extra) but reserve them in advance.
- Breastfeeding is quite common anywhere.

Getting around

Children under 15 accompanied by an adult do not pay on trains. A seat on a bus costs the same for everyone except for toddlers and babies sitting on a parent's lap. If you are hiring a car, book a child safety seat in advance.

Eating out

Children are warmly welcomed at restaurants but highchairs are rarely available. Some restaurants offer a kids' menu. If there is no kids' menu, it is perfectly acceptable to order a *mezza porzione* (half portion) or a simple pasta off the menu.

KID-FRIENDLY PICKS

Ferrovia Circumetnea, Mt Etna (p17)
Ascending the volcano by train, then strolling on the lunar landscape of Mount Etna.

Villa Romana del Casale (p216)
Spotting lions, tigers and other animals in the mosaics at this ancient Roman villa.

Teatro dei Pupi, Syracuse (p181) & Palermo (p75)
Children will love watching brave knights defeat evil monsters.

Farm Cultural Park, Favara (p233)
Creative labs for both children and teens.

Ruins of Selinunte (p97)
Ancient rubble to explore and open spaces in which to run.

A FARM STAY WITH CHILDREN

Sicily's brilliant *agriturismi* provide a perfect way to have an affordable holiday with children. Often they have a swimming pool and a playground on-site. Some are family-focused offering babysitting services and opportunities to learn how a farm works. Children can enjoy all kinds of animals, collect eggs and pick fruit from trees, living a bucolic adventure. Moreover, there is plenty of space for kids to run around and most of the food has travelled 0km to reach your plate so it is tasty, fresh and suitable for the little ones.

Health & Safe Travel

INSURANCE

Italy's public-health system provides urgent care to everyone, so it is not compulsory to have insurance in Sicily. Having said that, a travel insurance policy is a good idea as it covers theft, loss, flight cancellation and medical care. EU travellers can apply for the European Health Insurance Card covering medical treatment free of charge.

Solo travel

Sicily is a safe place for solo female travellers, just take the usual precautions you would in any other part of the world. Solo women may occasionally be subjected to unwanted attention by men. Ignore them and avoid eye contact. Note that intense staring is common in Sicily though this is not necessarily limited to women travellers.

Sunstroke

In Sicily, the summer heat can be exhausting. Make sure you have plenty of water, a hat and sunscreen, and avoid getting out and about in the hottest hours of the day. The risk of getting sunstroke is not limited to July and August. Even in May, June and September the sun is strong, especially for those with fair skin prone to being burnt.

PICK-POCKETING

Do not flash cash around in public. Pickpocketing is not common but it can happen in the most crowded tourist places.

SWIM SAFELY

Green flag
Safe to swim

Yellow flag
Moderate currents, swim with caution.

Red flag
Danger, no swimming allowed.

Double red flag
Water is closed to the public.

Purple flags
Dangerous marine life has been spotted.

Traffic

Sicilian traffic can be daunting, especially in Palermo and Catania. The general rule is to drive wherever your car can pass through. Always look twice before crossing the street or an intersection. Scooters are the biggest hazard to watch out for as they appear out of nowhere, often breaking the usual traffic rules. Take extra care on curving roads.

EARTHQUAKES & VOLCANIC ERUPTIONS

Sicily experiences regular earthquakes though they are very rarely destructive. The last major earthquake occurred in 1908, and casualties caused by the eruptions of Mount Etna are very low. The worst eruption occurred in 1669. During the eruption period, the highest part of the volcano is usually closed to tourists. Stromboli is a more restless volcano but both of them are constantly under control.

Food, Drink & Nightlife

When to eat

Colazione (breakfast) A standard Italian breakfast: coffee, *cornetto* (croissant), brioche or *granita*.

Pranzo (lunch) The biggest meal of the day, especially on Sundays. Most Sicilians eat after 1pm.

Aperitivo (pre-dinner drink) A post-work or a pre-dining-out drink between 7pm and 8pm. Your drink includes some snacks.

Cena (dinner) Restaurants usually open around 7pm but Sicilians dine after 9pm.

Where to eat

Trattoria Usually a family-run restaurant focusing on regional cuisine.

Osteria Typically a tavern focused on wine, today a more intimate trattoria with a relaxed atmosphere.

Enoteca A wine shop also serving platters with charcuterie or simple meals.

Ristorante A more formal restaurant with higher prices than a trattoria and a wider menu.

Pizzeria Where to enjoy a pizza and a cold beer in a convivial place.

Agriturismo A working farm serving meals based on produce grown on-site.

Friggitoria Informal street-food venue where you can taste fried snacks at very low prices.

MENU DECODER

Menu turistico A fixed-price, multicourse meal, often signals mediocre fare. Better to steer clear.

Menu alla carta You can choose whatever you like from the menu.

Menu degustazione A tasting menu consisting of four to eight 'tasting size' courses.

Piatto del giorno Dish of the day.

Nostra produzione/ fatto in casa Homemade/made in-house.

Antipasti Starters. Ask for an *antipasto misto* to taste a mix.

Primi First courses (pasta, rice, soup, couscous).

Secondi Second courses (meat or fish).

Contorni Side dishes (veggies, salads).

Dolci Sweets or desserts.

Frutta Fresh fruit. Traditional eateries serve it at the end of a meal.

Surgelato Frozen, is used for fish and seafood but also for veggies.

Coperto A fixed cover charge.

WHAT IS... **a coperto?**

The bill is higher than you expected and there is something about a *coperto* charge? It is not a tip nor a scam but a standard fixed cover charge and you must pay it. It is charged on a per-person basis in addition to the cost of your food and must be printed on the menu. The *coperto* is a charge for tableware, table linen and bread and you have to pay it even if you decline the bread. It is usually in the range of €1 to €2 a head and children also get charged. Fancy restaurants may charge more. To avoid surprises, check the menu before sitting down. At around €2, it usually won't break the bank, but if you have a quick €20 lunch for two, an unexpected increase of 20% will stick out on the bill. However, remember that tipping is not required in restaurants where there is a cover charge.

HOW MUCH FOR A...

Espresso
€1

Granita and brioche
€3–4

Gelato
€2.50

Arancino
€2

Cannolo
€2

Glass of wine
€5–7

Dinner at trattoria
€25

Dinner at a Michelin-star restaurant
€100–150

HOW TO... order a coffee the Sicilian way

In Sicily coffee is a serious matter, not just a simple tradition but a kind of ritual. Sicilians tend to drink coffee in the morning and in the afternoon. If you would like to blend in with the locals and not be labelled as a tourist, take a look at locals' habits and the typical coffee they order.

The morning always begins with an espresso to get a boost of energy, but it is always the right time to enjoy a good coffee. You can sit and have it chatting with friends or drink it at the bar, standing at the counter during a quick break. However you drink it, it is a pleasure to be savoured to the full.

Espresso A tiny cup of very strong black coffee. Just order a caffè.

Caffè lungo A weaker espresso, but stronger than an American coffee.

Caffè macchiato An espresso with a dash of milk.

Cappuccino A long espresso topped with hot foaming milk.

Sicilians typically drink it at breakfast, never after a meal. You will be instantly labelled as a tourist if you order it after 11am.

Caffe latte Hot milk with a dash of coffee. Only drunk in the morning.

Caffè freddo The local version of an iced coffee.

Caffè ammantecato

If you happen to be in the Trapani area, don't miss this local speciality prepared with coffee, almond milk and cinnamon. It is a very old recipe using almond milk instead of water in the coffee pot.

Caffè corretto An espresso with a splash of alcohol.

Caffè americano Usually made explicitly for American tourists.

HEADING OUT ON THE TOWN

A night out in Sicily usually starts with an after-work aperitivo. Order a drink, generally accompanied by snacks, while chatting with friends at a table outside. Even in winter, people often sit on a veranda or in an outdoor space. In summer, you can drink a beer while watching the sunset on the beach in a bar by the sea.

Sometimes the *aperitivo* is called *apericena* (aperi-dinner) as the snacks paired with the drink are reinforced with a huge platter of charcuterie taking the place of a proper dinner. Otherwise, it is off to a restaurant or a pizzeria to eat before heading to a lounge bar with a DJ or a pub to listen to live music.

If you prefer to have dinner at home, you can join in later. Places start getting crowded after 11pm. In summer, people flock to the streets, especially in the main cities.

If you want to dance, hit the clubs – not before 1am or you may find them completely empty. Most clubs are quite casual and do not have a strict dress code, others can refuse entry to those wearing shorts and sneakers or slippers. Sicilians love to dress up when they go out.

Many clubs offer free entry to women, others offer free admission to everyone with a minimum drink spend. For popular parties, you may need to get your name on the guestlist.

Responsible Travel

Climate change & travel

It's impossible to ignore the impact we have when travelling, and the importance of making changes where we can. Lonely Planet urges all travellers to engage with their travel carbon footprint. There are many carbon calculators online that allow travellers to estimate the carbon emissions generated by their journey; try resurgence.org/resources/carbon-calculator.html. Many airlines and booking sites offer travellers the option of offsetting the impact of greenhouse gas emissions by contributing to climate-friendly initiatives around the world. We continue to offset the carbon footprint of all Lonely Planet staff travel, while recognising this is a mitigation more than a solution.

Pizzo-free

Local businesses who refuse to pay the *pizzo* extortion money (Addiopizzo) challenge the Mafia and try to educate people. You can download a *pizzo*-free city map of Palermo from addiopizzotravel.it

Choose who to support

Often in Sicily residents cannot access well-paid jobs unless they know influential people and young folk leave the island to find work elsewhere. Tourism doesn't automatically benefit the local population, but as a traveller you can choose to support family-run accommodations and local shops.

Libera Terra

Libera Terra (Free Land, liberaterra.it) gives dignity to territories with a strong Mafia presence by creating self-sufficient cooperative farms producing high-quality produce (including wine), which respect both the environment and the dignity of workers.

Electric car

Hiring an electric car is a bit more expensive but you will save more on fuel and parking. Electric cars park for free and SicilyByCar (www.sicilybycar.it) has plenty of charging points throughout Sicily free of cost.

Recycled souvenirs

Litter is a huge problem in the larger cities and Sicily has a poor record on recycling. The project Fieri in Catania tackles the trash crisis and integrates migrants through recycling. It creates purses made of old door handles and African textiles, recycled copper ornaments and wooden souvenirs from discarded furniture.

Sustainable wineries

SOStain (fondazionesostainsicilia.it) promotes ethical and sustainable development in the Sicilian wine sector, helping wineries to reduce the impact that agricultural practices have on the territory and sharing best practices with a common goal: respecting the ecosystem.

Save the turtles

Volunteers from all parts of the world come to Lampedusa to assist in the conservation of the Caretta Caretta turtle (lampedusaturtlerescue.org). Do you have a passion for marine life? Work alongside scientists and marine biologists and meet new people from different cultures.

RESOURCES

SiciliaParchi
Information on Sicily's nature reserves.

Isole Sostenibili
Sustainable Islands Observatory's page.

Area Marina Protetta Isola di Ustica
Italy's first marine protected area.

LGBTIQ+ Travellers

Homosexuality is widely accepted in Sicily but discretion is advised in smaller towns as some negative attitudes still linger. Larger cities such as Palermo and Catania have well-established queer communities which can count on a safe network while rural areas remain largely conservative. Queer people will not face open discrimination but might receive some nasty comments.

Festivals and parades

The Sicilian LGBTIQ+ scene is centred on cities, mainly Palermo and Catania, but there is also a lively scene in Taormina and Syracuse. Palermo hosts the biggest Pride in Sicily, usually held in July (palermopride.it). In Catania, Pride is held around the end of June and the beginning of July. Another noteworthy event to mark on the calendar is the Sicilia Queer Film Fest held in the first week of June in Palermo. It was first held in 2013 and it hasn't stopped since, bringing in a series of screenings, talks and lectures.

FIRST GAY ORGANISATION IN ITALY

Arcigay (arcigay.it) is Italy's first gay organisation and was founded in Palermo in 1980 – then nationally established in Bologna only in 1985 – after a double murder took place in Giarre, near Catania, where the lifeless bodies of two boys were found holding hands.

CHANGING MINDSET

Sicily is generally welcoming and Taormina is considered the first openly gay tourist destination in Europe, frequented since the second half of the 19th century. However, cities are more progressive than smaller rural towns where older generations might make the occasional rude remark.

Queer tour

Claudia Fauzia is an economist with expertise in gender and women's studies and is the founder of La Mala Fimmina, an awareness-raising project on issues related to gender equity and southern transfeminism. Among the many initiatives, La Mala Fimmina arranges two-hour walking tours through Palermo to learn about Sicilian transfeminism – intertwined with the anti-Mafia movement – and discover many queer realities of the city.

Queer travel hints

Gay Friendly Italy (gayfriendlyitaly.com) is an ideal resource for travel tips in Sicily with up-to-date news about queer-friendly hotels, bars, clubs and beaches. You can even find a wedding planner!

A SAFE NETWORK

Protego (arcigay.it/en/palermo) has been operating in Palermo since May 2022. It is the first support centre against discrimination based on sexual orientation and gender identity. It offers 24-hour emergency help, a medical help desk, lawyers, psychologists and assistance to LGBTIQ+ migrants and refugees. It is set inside the Cantieri Culturali alla Zisa, a former industrial complex now housing art exhibitions, workshops and meeting spaces focused on intercultural dialogue.

Accessible Travel

Sicily has major accessibility issues, but great efforts are being made to promote more accessible tourism.

Accessible museums

Museums and galleries in the main cities and many archaeological sites are wheelchair accessible and offer apps or audio guides designed as alternative paths for those with sensory impairments.

Airports

Sicilian airports offer assistance for passengers with reduced mobility, visual or hearing impairments. You can request the service from your airline 48 hours before departure. Palermo and Catania have reserved parking spaces for free.

Accommodation

Only newer and larger hotels can cater to guests with special needs, offering adapted rooms and adequate bathrooms, while B&Bs and guesthouses often cannot. To make sure you find suitable accommodation, search on www.bookingbility.com.

Disability Pride

In July Palermo holds Disability Pride, an opportunity to focus attention on body integrity and the right to sexuality, which many people are denied due to their disability.

Cobbled streets

Even if trains and many buses are wheelchair-friendly, Sicily is not an easy place for travellers with special needs. Cobbled streets, high traffic and tiny lifts make life difficult for wheelchair users and the visually and hearing-impaired.

A FREE APP

TripStep is a free app designed for people with impaired sensory capacity who want to visit Sicily. All content is readable by screen readers and you can create a personalised itinerary.

RESOURCES

Sicily for All (*sicilyforall.com*) is part of Mobility Unesco Sustainable Tourism (MUST) and provides essential information about the accessibility of tourist services and facilities. You can independently plan your holiday or join an organised tour.

Sicilia Accessibile (*siciliaccessibile. it*) is an online guide that lists all the accessible historical, archaeological and naturalistic sites of Sicily as well as hotels, restaurants and beaches. There is also a list of restaurants for coeliacs.

SOUNDS OF CATANIA

Discover Catania through your sense of hearing. A map available on Google Maps includes over 500 sounds and about 60 interviews with people talking about Catania's most loved places, a kind of audio version of the famous Street View feature.

Catania hosts a 2000-sq-metre museum entirely dedicated to visually impaired people. It includes a tactile section with reproductions of works of art to explore by hand, a bar run by visually impaired people and a sensory garden.

📖 Nuts & Bolts

OPENING HOURS

May vary throughout the year, decreasing during low season.

Banks 8.30am to 2pm and 2.45pm to 3.45pm Monday to Friday.

Cafes 6am or 7am to 8pm (later if offering bar service at night).

Museums Hours vary, but many close on Monday.

Restaurants Noon to 3pm and 7.30pm to 11pm; many close one day per week.

Shops 9.30am or 10am to 1pm and 4pm to 8pm Monday to Friday, 10am to 1pm Saturday. In very touristy areas and during December open on Sundays.

Smoking

Smoking, including e-cigarettes, is prohibited in public spaces, except within designated areas. In restaurants and cafes you can only smoke outdoors.

Weights & measures

Sicily uses the metric system.

Toilets

With the exception of the main tourist sites and museums, public toilets are rare in Sicily. You can use facilities in bars and cafes.

GOOD TO KNOW

Time Zone
GMT/UTC+1 in winter

GMT/UTC+2 in summer

Country Code
+39

Emergency number
112

Population
5 million

Electricity 230V/50Hz

Type F
230V/50Hz

Type L
230V/50Hz

PUBLIC HOLIDAYS

On public holidays in Sicily many businesses and non-essential services may be closed. Note that individual towns have public holidays to celebrate their local patron saints.

New Year's Day
1 January

Epiphany 6 January

Easter March/April

Pasquetta (Easter Monday)

Liberation Day
25 April

Labour Day 1 May

Republic Day 2 June

Feast of the Assumption 15 August

All Saints' Day
1 November

Feast of the Immaculate Conception
8 December

Christmas Day
25 December

Santo Stefano (St Stephen's Day)
26 December

Language

TOOLKIT

Standard Italian (as presented in this section) is Sicily's official language and is spoken almost universally on the island, although most locals speak Sicilian among themselves. Sicilian is referred to as an Italian dialect, but is sufficiently different for some to consider it a language in its own right.

Basics

Good day/morning/afternoon.
Buongiorno. bwon·*jor*·no
Good evening. Buonasera.
bwo·na·*se*·ra
Hello. Salve (pol.)/Ciao (inf.).
sal·ve/*chow*
Goodbye. Arrivederci (pol.)/Ciao
(inf.). a·ree·ve·*der*·chee/*chow*
Yes. Sì. *see*
No. No. *no*
Please. Per favore. *per* fa·*vo*·re
Thank you. Grazie. *gra*·tsye
Excuse me. Mi scusi. mee *skoo*·zee
Sorry. Mi dispiace.
mee dees·*pya*·che
What's your name? Come si
chiama? (pol.) Come ti chiami? (inf.)
ko·me see *kya*·ma/
ko·me tee *kya*·mee
My name is ... Mi chiamo...
mee *kya*·mo...
Do you speak English? Parla/Parli
inglese? *par*·la/*par*·lee een·*gle*·ze
I don't understand. Non capisco.
non ka·*pee*·sko

Directions

Where's (the station)?
Dov'è (la stazione)?
do·*ve* (*la* sta·*tsyo*·ne)
What's the address?
Qual'è l'indirizzo?
kwa·*le* leen·dee·*ree*·tso
Could you please write it down?
Può/Puoi scriverlo, per favore?
pwo/*pwoy* *skree*·ver·lo *per* fa·*vo*·re
Can you show me (on the map)?
Può mostrarmi (sulla pianta)?
pwo mos·*trar*·mee (*soo*·la *pyan*·ta)

Time

What time is it? Che ora è?
ke o·ra e
It's one o'clock. È l'una. e *loo*·na
It's (10) o'clock. Sono le (dieci).
so·no le (*dye*·chee)
Half past (10). (Dieci) e mezza.
(*dye*·chee) e me·dza
in the morning di mattina
dee ma·*tee*·na
in the afternoon di pomeriggio
dee po·me·*ree*·jo
in the evening di sera *dee* se·ra
yesterday ieri *ye*·ree
today oggi *o*·jee
tomorrow domani do·*ma*·nee

Emergencies

Help! Aiuto! a·*yoo*·to
Go away! Vai via! *vai* vee·*a*
I don't feel well. Mi sento male.
mee *sen*·to ma·le
Call ...! Chiami... *kya*·mee
a doctor un medico *oon* me·dee·ko
the police la polizia
la po·lee·*tsee*·a

Eating & drinking

What would you recommend?
Cosa mi consiglia?
ko·sa mee con·*see*·lya
Cheers! Salute! sa·*loo*·te
That was delicious.
Era squisito. *e*·ra skwee·*zee*·to

NUMBERS

1
uno *oo*·no

2
due *doo*·e

3
tre *tre*

4
quattro *kwa*·tro

5
cinque *cheen*·kwe

6
sei *say*

7
sette *se*·te

8
otto *o*·to

9
nove *no*·ve

10
dieci *dye*·chee

256

DONATIONS TO ENGLISH

Numerous – most of us are familiar with **ciao, pasta, bella, maestro, mafia**...

DISTINCTIVE SOUNDS

The rolled *r*, stronger than in English; most other consonants can have a more emphatic pronunciation too (in which case they're written as double letters).

False friends

Warning: many Italian words look like English words but have a different meaning altogether, eg **camera** *ka·me·ra* is a room, not a camera (which is **macchina fotografica** *ma·kee·na fo·to·gra·fee·ka* in Italian).

Must-Know Grammar

Italian has a formal and informal word for 'you' (**Lei** *lay* and **tu** *too* respectively); the verbs have a different ending for each person, like the English 'I do' vs 'he/she does'.

5 phrases to learn before you go

Qual'è la specialità di questa regione? (What's the local speciality?) – A bit like the rivalry between medieval Italian city-states, these days the country's regions compete in speciality foods and wines.

Quali biglietti cumulativi avete? (Which combined tickets do you have?) – Make the most of your euro by getting combined tickets to various sights; they are available in all major Italian cities.

C'è un outlet in zona? (Where can I buy discount designer items?) – Discount fashion outlets are big business in major cities – get bargain-priced seconds, samples and cast-offs for *la bella figura*.

Sono qui con il mio marito/ragazzo. (I'm here with my husband/boyfriend.) – Solo women travellers may receive unwanted attention in some parts of Italy; if ignoring fails have a polite rejection ready.

Ci vediamo alle sei per un aperitivo. (Let's meet at 6pm for pre-dinner drinks.) – At dusk, watch the main *piazza* get crowded with people sipping colourful cocktails and snacking the evening away: join your new friends for this authentic Italian ritual!

TOOLKIT

WHO SPEAKS ITALIAN?

Thanks to widespread migration and the enormous popularity of Italian culture and cuisine – from 'spaghetti Western' to opera – Italian is often a language of choice in schools all over the world, despite the fact that Italy never established itself as a colonial power.

65 million speak Italian as their first language

20 million speak Italian as a second language

Switzerland

Italy*

Istria (Croatia & Slovenia)

Malta

Eritrea

*plus San Marino & Vatican City

257

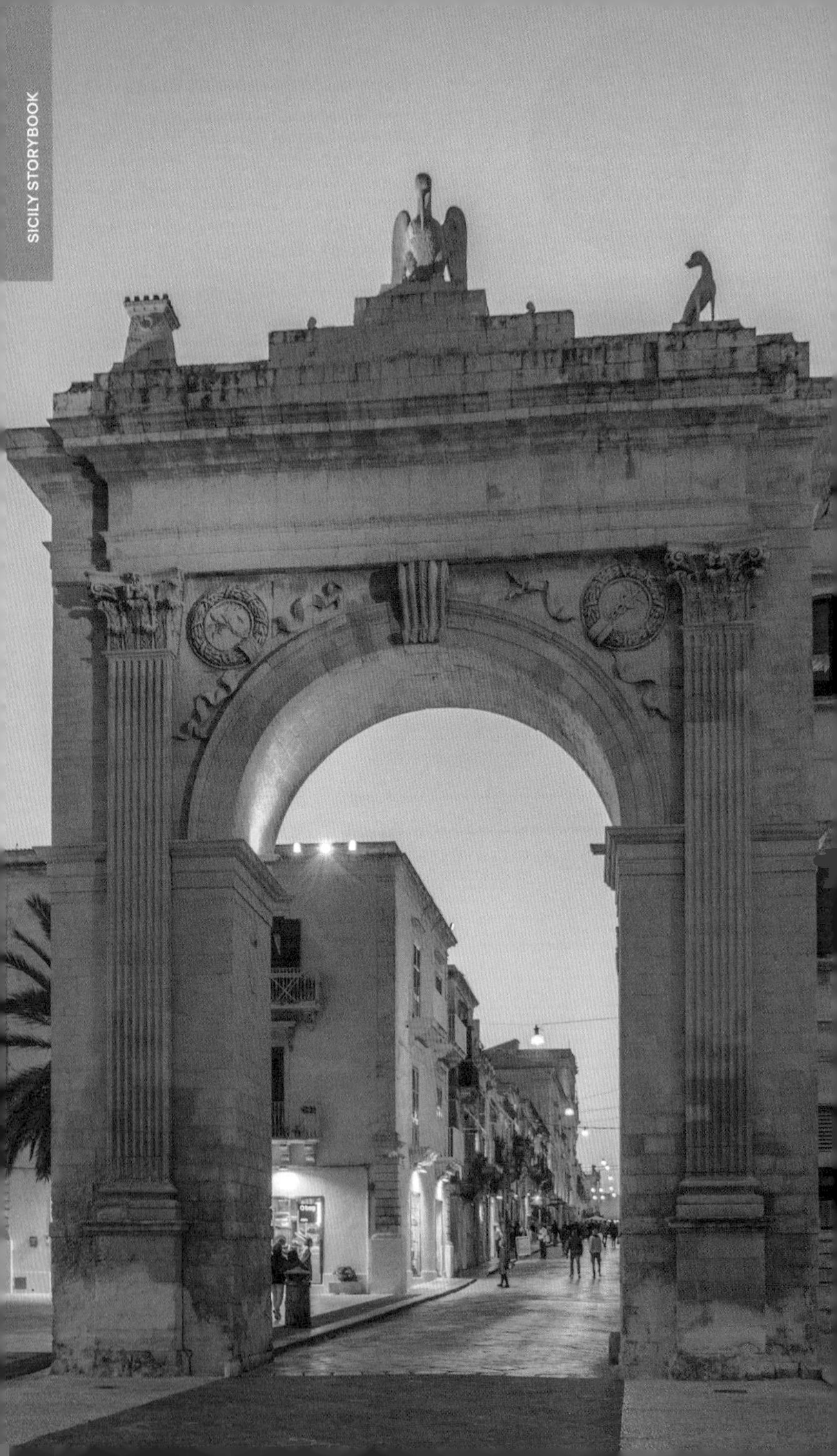

STORYBOOK

Our writers delve deep into different aspects of Sicilian life

Porta Ferdinandea (p262), Noto

A HISTORY OF SICILY IN
15 PLACES

Over the millennia, Sicily's strategic position in the middle of the Mediterranean has lured culture after culture to its shores, resulting in one of Europe's richest and most remarkable histories. This is not an itinerary: it's a journey through Sicily's pageant of diverse, powerful stories, from prehistory to modernity.

SICILY IS AN island that has historically been the subject of desire and dispute. For centuries it enticed a steady parade of ancient peoples, including the Greeks, Carthaginians and Romans, into its handsome lair. Subsequent rule by invading forces of Byzantines, Saracens, Normans, Germans, Angevins and the Spanish blessed Sicily with a lavish artistic and architectural legacy – and fair share of political angst – before finally claiming its pivotal role within a unified Italy in the early 1860s.

Sicily is an archaeologist's dream; a story of construction and transformation over a millennia of foreign domination. Mysterious grottoes hide ancient prehistoric civilisations. In the southeast, Syracuse was built to be one of the ancient world's most splendid, powerful cities. The Normans collaborated with Byzantine and Arab architects and artisans to transform Greek temples in the 12th century into dazzling basilicas with shimmering gold mosaics and intricate Arabesque wood carvings. Earthquakes in the 17th and 20th centuries led to dazzling new constructions. Sicily is an island of resilience and resistance, of hero farmers and creative artists and dogged innovators who – despite earthquakes and volcanoes and the modern Mafia menace – keep Sicily's wheels spinning.

1. Grotta del Genovese
A PALAEOLITHIC PLACE OF REFUGE

Imagine a time when the Egadi Islands were not islands, but part of a grassy limestone steppe attached to Sicily's far west. This was the case 12,000 years ago when prehistoric artists engraved animal and anthropomorphic figures inside Grotta del Genovese on the Aeolian island of Levanzo. More recent charcoal drawings of tuna and dolphins from the Neolithic period indicate that Sicily's culinary reliance on the ocean took root around 7000 BCE. A few hundred years later, between 7000 and 6500 BCE, sea levels rose and Levanzo became an island. *p104*

2. Castello di Venere
THE CULT OF VENUS

Virgil compared the spectacularly perched village of Eryx (modern-day Erice in western Sicily) to Mt Athos for its altitude and spiritual preeminence. Its history as a centre for the cult of Venus (Astarte to the Phoenicians and Aphrodite to the Greeks) is certainly head-turning. The mysterious Elymians settled in Sicily in the Bronze Age and claimed descent from Venus' famous Trojan son, Aeneas, who mentions their Eryx sanctuary as a holy landmark in the 'Aeneid'. *p93*

...aradiso

...DISE

...ing Athens' crushing de-
...forces during the Pelo-
...000 captured soldiers
...nland were thrown into
...e's Garden of Paradise' and left to
die. Citrus and magnolia trees now perfume the old limestone quarry-turned-pris-
on which, under merciless tyrant Dionysius
I (r. 432–367 BCE), was part of the largest
city in the ancient world. Dionysius eavesdropped on his prisoners from the slit entrance to Orecchio di Dionisio ('Ear of Dionysius'), a deep, precipitous cavern with
electrifying acoustics allowing the wick-
ed despot to hear every word muttered
23m below. *p182*

4. Ortygia

ARCHIMEDES' WAR MACHINES

Ingenious weapons developed by brilliant
Greek philosopher and engineer Archimedes (c 287–212/211 BCE) protected Syracuse
from Roman forces for two years. Giant cat-
apults hurled objects weighing more than
300kg, copper shields set vessels alight using only the sun's rays, and the Claw of Archimedes – a monstrous wooden crane –
grabbed galleys by the prow, lifted them
from the water and dropped them, making
them capsize or sink. Alas, Syracuse's independence ended abruptly in 211 BCE when
a small group of Roman soldiers scaled the
city walls to take control of the city. *p179*

5. Villa Romana del Casale

A ROMAN COUNTRY RETREAT

Sicily's wealth gap is nothing new. As Rome's
first colony (241 BCE–470 CE), Sicily suffered
the worst of Roman rule. Native inhabitants
were refused the right of citizenship and
forced into indentured slavery while Roman emperors and senators luxuriated in
palatial villas. This includes Villa Romana del Casale in central Sicily, with rooms
emblazoned with the world's finest Roman
floor mosaics; a powerful portrait of daily
life for the privileged in Roman Sicily. *p216*

6. Cattedrale di Monreale

ARAB-NORMAN SPLENDOUR

Sicily's rich melting pot of cultures harks
back to its golden era during the Norman
kingdom of Sicily (1130–94) when architects wed Arab, Byzantine and classical
art and craftsmanship to create one of the
most impressive architectural legacies of
the Italian Middle Ages. Norman king William II (1166–89) chose to construct the
golden Cattedrale di Monreale on his royal
hunting ground 8km southwest of Palermo after the Virgin appeared to him in a
vision there. She instructed him to dig for
treasure beneath the majestic carob tree
where he was napping and build a temple in her honour on that very spot. *p78*

7. Trapani

THE SPIRIT OF REBELLION

So inspirational was Sicily's spirit of rebellion during the Sicilian Vespers that Italian
composer Giuseppe Verdi wrote an entire
opera about it. The alleged rape of a local
girl by a gang of French troops incited peasants attending vespers in a Palermo church
in 1282 to lynch every French soldier they
could get their hands on. Some 2000 French
were massacred in one night, sparking off
a countrywide rebellion against tyrannical
Sicilian ruler Charles of Anjou (1266–82).
Sicilian barons formed an allegiance with
Peter of Aragon, who sailed into the harbour
at Trapani and was proclaimed king. *p88*

8. Alla Giudecca

JEWISH SICILY

Hidden in the basement of Residence Hotel
Alla Giudecca in Syracuse is Europe's oldest surviving *miqweh*. Some 18m deep, this
Jewish ritual bath was unearthed when the
15th-century *palazzo* became a hotel in the
1990s. It sits in the old Jewish quarter on
the island of Ortygia where Jews settled
from the 1st century CE until their expul-
sion from all Spanish territories in 1487.
This brutal end to religious tolerance ush-
ered in nearly three centuries of imprison-
ment, torture and killings in Sicily under
the Spanish Inquisition. *p181*

9. Porta Ferdinandea

THE TRIUMPHANT PHOENIX

Sicilians have always been ardent build-
ers. As urban planners in Catania aspire
to spruce up ramshackle buildings lost to
the ravages of time and non-existent budgets, the inscription on Catania's triumphal
stone arch – built in white Syracuse stone
and local black lava blocks in 1768 to com-

memorate the marriage of Bourbon king Ferdinand I – is no coincidence: *Melior de cinere surgo* (Better I arise from the ashes). Following a Mt Etna eruption in 1669 and earthquake in 1693, architects in Catania erected grandiose *palazzi* and churches out of the volcanic rock. *p164*

10. Mt Etna
ICON OF THE 18TH-CENTURY GRAND TOUR

No single natural feature has been the source of so much fascination and terror. The Greeks said Etna's fire-red cap hid the thunderbolt workshops of Hephaestus and the Cyclops, and in the 18th century its ascent became an essential stop on the Grand Tour for European aristocrats in Italy completing their education. 'We set off early this morning on mules, turning our heads every so often to look at the view behind us. After some time we reached the lava zone. Unsoftened by time, jagged clumps and slabs stared us in the face ...' wrote German writer Goethe in his *Italian Journey* (1816). *p169*

11. Castello di Nelson
THE ENGLISH IN SICILY

To thank Horatio Nelson for saving him from revolutionaries in Naples in 1796, Bourbon king Ferdinand IV gave the English admiral a castle in Sicily. Situated in the remote foothills northwest of Etna, Nelson's family recast this 12th-century abbey as an English country manor with Anglican chapel and English gardens dedicated to Admiral Nelson. A couple of years later, in Cambridge, England, a 25-year-old Irish student – who would later father the Brontë sisters – changed his name from Brunty to Brontë in a nod to his favourite English admiral's Sicilian escapades.

12. Piazza del Duomo, Syracuse
OPERATION MINCEMEAT

To prepare for their invasion to recapture mainland Italy during WWII, Allied forces implemented 'Operation Mincemeat' in 1943. Disguising the corpse of a recently deceased man in Royal Marine uniform, British intelligence officers planted a letter on him 'exposing' fake plans by the Allies to invade Sardinia and Greece. The dead body, a Londoner who'd died from consuming rat poison (later buried with full military honours), was then dropped in the Med and picked up by Germans who, upon reading the letter, redeployed their Sicily troops to Sardinia. Mission accomplished, Allied forces attacked Sicily in July 1943. In Syracuse locals took shelter from bombings in 4th-century catacombs beneath Chiesa di Santa Lucia and the Roman hypogeum beneath Piazza del Duomo. *p179*

13. Cretto di Burri
MODERN DESTRUCTION & DISPLACEMENT

Mother nature has dealt some cruel blows to Sicily over the centuries. In 1968 a series of consecutive earthquakes hit the Valle del Belice in western Sicily overnight, killing almost 400 people and leaving 100,000 homeless. Ten villages were severely damaged and two – Gibellina and Poggioreale – were completely destroyed. Both were rebuilt on new sites as sterile, post-modern towns without traditional *piazze* and historic backstreets. What was left of Gibellina was cemented over by Italian artist Alberto Burri (1915–95) to become a dramatic piece of land art entitled *Cretto di Burri. p99*

14. No Mafia Memorial
SHEDDING A TROUBLED PAST

The recent decision to make the superb 'No Mafia Memorial' exhibition – a museum, study centre and crucible for ideas – on Palermo's main pedestrian strip into a permanent fixture was a notable victory for Sicily's anti-Mafia movement. Since the Mafia supertrials of the 1990s, Palermo has slowly emerged from its past, with authorities embarking upon an ambitious program of revitalisation that continues to this day. On a grassroots level, an estimated 70% of businesses in Sicily still pay *pizzo* (protection money) to the Mafia in return for immunity from theft and vandalism. *p66*

15. La Mala Fimmina
A WOMAN'S PLACE

In Francis Ford Coppola's *The Godfather,* Fabrizio describes women as more dangerous than shotguns. A judge faced with a female Mafia suspect in the 1990s declared that women were too stupid to partake in the complexities of finance. Traditional gender roles and stereotypes are shaken on trans-feminist walking tours of Palermo led by feminist disruptor and organiser of the Malandrina Sicilian Feminist Fest, La Mala Fimmina (@la.malafimmina). *p253*

VOLCANO TOURISM

Living with volcanoes: a blessing, a curse and a timeless curiosity. By Nicola Williams.

RISING TEMPERATURES, INCREASED gas emissions and violent storms have impacted visitor access to Sicily's active volcanoes in recent years – check updated rules when planning your trip. But does global warming affect volcanoes and what does it mean for the future of volcano tourism in Sicily?

A Blessing

It is not difficult to understand why one-fifth of Sicily's population lives around fiery Mt Etna, a snip of a region that only accounts for 7% of the island's total and area: Europe's largest active volcano provides islanders with a wealth of natural resources.

Medieval *nivroli* (snow collectors) gathered snow from slopes soaring up to the clouds at 3357m and stored it in ice-cold *nivere* (stone caves) at high altitude to make *granita*. Arabs in the 9th century needed no persuasion to plant sweet white peaches, citrus fruits, almonds and pistachio nuts in Etna's fertile volcanic soils – a mineral-powered turbo mix of decomposed lava, ash and sand – and modern winemakers followed suit with vineyards producing respectable reds and whites under the Etna DOC appellation. (To this day, when Mt Etna threatens to erupt, islanders leave a bottle of local wine on their kitchen table before running to safety in

the superstitious belief that Etna will thus sparc their home). Blossoms from flowering citrus and eucalyptus groves, chestnut trees and wild thyme go into Italy's most sought-after honey; the traditional apiculture town of Zafferana Etnea on Etna's eastern slopes produces one-third of all Italy's honey. Little wonder really that Mt Etna and its primeval slopes form the protected national park Parco dell'Etna.

Historically, industrious Sicilians have profited from their volcanic heritage. Greeks and Romans exploited buxom seams of alum stone (alunite) as they pocketed rocks near active volcanoes on Lipari, Vulcano and Stromboli in the Aeolian Islands. Lipari's now-extinct Monte Pilato showered the island with glassy-black obsidian flow from its crater sometime between the Neolithic era and 5th century BCE, and with mountains of 'white gold' pumice stone in the Middle Ages. From the 17th century to early 1900s, mines on 'mainland' Sicily famously provided Europe with the bulk of its sulphur – at a price. American black activist and presidential advisor Booker Taliaferro Washington (1856–1915) famously wrote of the *carusi* or young Sicilian boys forced to work in mines: 'I am not prepared just now to say to what extent I believe in a physical hell in the next world, but a sulphur mine

in Sicily is about the nearest thing to hell that I expect to see in this life.'

A Curse

Living with an active volcano is not all sunset *aperitivi* with smouldering (literally) red sky and beach frolics on black volcanic sand. Sicily's Mt Etna was known as the home of Vulcan, arms supplier to the gods, in Greek and Roman mythology for good reason. Sicily's remaining three active volcanoes – Mt Etna near Catania, and Stromboli and Vulcano on the same-name Aeolian Islands – are in a constant state of activity. Eruptions do occur, most spectacularly in the case of Mt Etna from its four summit craters, and more dangerously, from new fissures and old craters on the mountain's flanks. Since 1500 BCE, it has exploded more than 200 times, most hideously in 1669 and 1928 when it destroyed entire towns and villages. In 2021 Mt Etna exploded 16 times; in February 2022 it shot a 12km-high plume of volcanic ash into the sky, closing airports and raining undesirable ash on surrounding villages, vineyards, beech woods and pistachio groves.

Italy's National Institute of Geophysics and Volcanology (INGV) in Catania monitors Etna's round-the-clock rumblings with 120 seismic-activity stations and satellites. Volcanologists can usually anticipate dangerous lava-rocketing eruptions or lava flows that threaten to bury villages, and evacuate high-risk zones when necessary to keep islanders safe. But no scientist or modern-day god can control the angry outbursts and fiery foibles of Europe's mightiest volcano.

It is a similar scenario on Stromboli where recorded volcanic eruptions date to 300 BCE. Thermal webcams managed by the INGV and University of Florence's Department of Earth Sciences on the slopes of the island's 924m-high volcano record regular but harmless mini-bombs of lava and ash shooting from Stromboli's summit craters. Nonetheless, in July 2019 the violent paroxysm (magma bubble explosion) that caused devastating fire damage in the village of Ginostra and killed one hiker on the trail below Punta Corvo unfortunately took everyone by surprise.

A Timeless Curiosity

Writers, intellectuals and romantics have been inspired by, and drawn to, Sicily's volcanoes ever since an exploding Mt Vesuvius on mainland Italy buried Pompeii in ash and rocks, preserving the ancient Roman city for eternity. Ironically, as contemporary travel trends dig deep into nature and encourage slower, more considered exploration of natural landscapes, a booming volcano tourism is becoming more challenging.

The volcano on Aeolian island Vulcano hasn't erupted since 1888–90, but it remains closely monitored. Tourists were briefly banned from the island in November 2019 after a significant leap in sulphurous gases emanating from the smoking crater (391m). The volcano – the island's star attraction as a popular walking spot – has been strictly off-limits ever since. A combination of rising air temperatures (about 1.5°C higher in Sicily in the last century) and increased volcanic activity also means Vulcano's famous mud baths, where tourists gleefully rolled and frolicked in warm coffee-coloured clay (29°C) prior to the Covid pandemic, are now too hot for comfort and unlikely to reopen anytime soon.

Since 2019 the crater summit on Stromboli has been inaccessible to tourists. In 2022 the toxic combo of a manmade fire destroying some 85% of volcanic vegetation – centurion olive trees, caper bushes and herbal scrub – and violent summer storms wreaked havoc with the island's traditional summer season. Torrential rain in August washed black mud and ash from the volcano's charred slopes into the village, wrecking houses and destroying designated footpaths up to Stromboli's viewing platforms at 290m and 400m. Hiking access to 400m with a professional guide was authorised again a month later, but until adequate vegetation regrows (count three years at least) the volcano remains perilously vulnerable – and the village, at its mercy.

Mt Etna

WHAT IS A PUTÌA?

With roots in Greek times, this is the history of the small Sicilian shops where you can buy a bit of everything. By Sara Mostaccio.

THE SICILIAN EXPRESSION *'casa e putìa'* means a person who not only embodies righteousness and good manners, but sticks to duties and is devoted to their *casa* (family house) and *putìa* (job). A similar expression exists in Italian: *'casa e chiesa'* (home and church), which refers to a person who has no leisure and sticks to familiar places and travelling the same route. By extension, it also comes to mean a narrow-minded or bigoted person. But what does putìa exactly mean, and what are its origins?

Putìa is an institution of Sicilian popular culture, and one that persists in small towns and in some neighbourhoods in larger cities. While today it is mostly mistaken for a modern inn – one where you can indulge in wine while eating something genuinely Sicilian – traditionally the word putìa defined not only a place dedicated to food and wine but every small craft activity. In past centuries it actually indicated tiny shops including seamstresses, barbers, bakeries, butchers and shoemakers; just so long as they were small and family-run.

A *putìa ro vinu* (wine shop), on the other hand, was considered a place to avoid if you didn't want to lose your reputation and ruin your liver as well! Widespread until about 40 years ago, it was a place where bulk wine was sold to a predominantly male, working-class clientele. Some patrons of this

A Putìa Do Calabrisi, Catania

putìa were disreputable characters (not to mention drunkards), so the term, depending on the context, was often derogatory. Despite this, it's still possible to find these small shops in Sicily – usually food-related businesses such as grocers or butchers where the owner welcomes you as a friend and perhaps has known you your entire life. In the past you could buy on credit thanks to this deep bond based on trust. The owner kept a *libretta* (notebook) in which they wrote down customers' names and the sums to be paid at the end of the month.

Dating back to Greek times, *putìa* is a word with a long history. Every *putìa* shares a common etymology which goes back to the Greek (then Latin) word *apotheke* (literally, a warehouse). In Italian, and in other dialects of the peninsula, it has become 'workshop'. Its existence, therefore, concerns a much broader and much older Mediterranean context than one might suspect.

The noun *apotheke* derives from the verb *apotithemi,* which literally means to put aside, therefore it was a place used for the conservation and custody of goods. Over the centuries the term became part of the so-called lingua franca used in various ports of the Mediterranean Sea and began to diversify, giving life to the German *Apotheke* (pharmacy), the French boutique (shop) and the Spanish bodega (wine cellar). In Sicily it has kept the original meaning to the present day, indicating a place where goods are stored and sold.

In Greek times, merchants' shops were located in the *agora* (the main square where public life took place), while artisans' workshops were housed inside their homes. They displayed their goods on the street to attract customers and often worked outside the door to take advantage of the daylight. In the Roman period, the artisan workshop remained almost the same, though the entrance was surmounted by a pergola or a balcony belonging to the upper floor, where the house was. The shop was located on the ground floor, overlooking the street.

> **...AN INSTITUTION OF SICILIAN POPULAR CULTURE, AND ONE THAT PERSISTS IN SMALL TOWNS**

In the Middle Ages, the artisan shops flourished and the medieval urban structure spread not only in Italy and the Mediterranean but also in Western Europe, remaining unaltered until the industrial revolution in the 19th century. In Sicily, however, artisan shops were still widespread in the 20th century. In the northeast, Messina has a modern example of 19th-century houses with shops below. These are called Case Cicala and clearly show the division between the residential top floor and the shop below.

Today a *putìa* is usually intended as a tiny food shop or a traditional wine bar with a small kitchen providing a few dishes, giving priority to quality and traditional cuisine. It could also be an artisan workshop where local handmade products such as pottery or delicatessen produce are bought. And yet, in the most secluded and authentic villages, a *putìa* is a little shop where you can find all sorts of goods – bread, groceries, detergents, glue, socks or whatever you need – and, just as importantly, stop for a friendly chat with the owner.

Bar and delicatessen, Cefalù

LEFT: FOTOKON/SHUTTERSTOCK © RIGHT: NOEL. BENNETT/SHUTTERSTOCK ©

SICILY'S LOVE AFFAIR WITH THE BIG SCREEN

Take a cinematic journey through Sicily as you pass through great international productions set among stunning natural beauty. By Sara Mostaccio

BEYOND ALL THE *Godfather* cliches, Sicily has become a setting for a multitude of Italian and foreign movies. Thanks to its beauty and variety of captivating scenery – beachfront, desert, vibrant cities, sleepy villages, volcanoes and forests – Sicily never ceases to enchant movie makers. Films shot here also often incorporate a clever perspective on local traditions, without failing to capture the island's fascinating cultural history and the vivaciousness of its people.

Sicily is one big movie set. Since the beginning of the 20th century, two film industries were set up in Palermo and Catania, while Taormina hosts one of the most prestigious film festivals in Italy. 'Cinema is interested in Sicily because Sicily is Cinema', said the writer Leonardo Sciascia, whose works have been the basis for various films, including *A Ciascuno Il Suo* (We Still Kill the Old Way), shot by Elio Petri in 1967 in the beautiful town of Cefalù. Here directors and screenwriters have been inspired by literature and many films were adapted from novels and short stories. Sicilian writers such as Verga, Martoglio and Pirandello all took an interest in the nascent movie industry.

Many notable neorealist movies were filmed in Sicily in the 1940s and '50s. Depicting the hard life of Sicilian fishermen, *La Terra Trema* (The Earth Trembles; 1948) by Luchino Visconti was an adaptation of Verga's novel *I Malavoglia* and was filmed in Aci Trezza. *Stromboli Terra di Dio* (Stromboli, Land of God) and *Vulcano* (Volcano) were shot simultaneously in 1950 on two different Aeolian islands. In both films, the wild beauty of the islands enchants even more than the stories themselves.

The 1960s were a golden era for cinema in Sicily. Michelangelo Antonioni opened the decade with his mysterious *L'Avventura* (The Adventure) set in Lipari. The same year *Il bell'Antonio* (Handsome Antonio) was released by Mauro Bolognini, set in Catania and inspired by Vitaliano Brancati's novel. Pietro Germi filmed his acclaimed *Divorzio all'Italiana* (Divorce Italian Style; 1961) in Catania, Ragusa and the surrounding area; a very funny movie starring Marcello Mastroianni that's a satire of Sicilian traditions and the stranglehold of the Roman Catholic Church. Francesco Rosi told the story

HOS FILMS *présente*

N FILM DE
**ICHELANGELO
NTONIONI**

GABRIELE FERZETTI
MONICA VITTI
LEA MASSARI
RENZO RICCI
et DOMINIQUE BLANCHAR
LELIO LUTTAZZI

CINO DEL DUCA

L'AVVENTURA

MES ADDAMS · DOROTHY DE POLIOLO · GIOVANNI PETRUCCI · ESMERALDA RUSPOLI

ES GAILLARD PARIS

Imprimé en France

3 FOIS PRIMÉ AU FESTIVAL DE CANNES

SUNSET BOULEVARD/GETTY IMAGES ©

The set of *Il Gattopardo*

of Salvatore Giuliano (1962), a contentious figure in Sicily, equally considered a criminal and a local Robin Hood fighting for independence. All these movies shed light on Sicily's historical, social and economic situation.

But the undisputed masterpiece of the 1960s was *Il Gattopardo* (The Leopard; 1963) directed by Luchino Visconti and starring Burt Lancaster, Alain Delon and Claudia Cardinale. An unforgettable scene was filmed in the ballroom at Palazzo Valguarnera-Gangi in Palermo. The movie is an adaptation of Giuseppe Tomasi di Lampedusa's novel set in revolutionary Sicily in the mid 1800s.

In 1974, Vittorio De Sica chose Syracuse to shoot *Il Viaggio* (The Voyage), an adaptation from a novella by Luigi Pirandello starring Sophia Loren. The Taviani brothers also took inspiration from Pirandello for *Kaos* (Chaos, 1984), which takes its name from the district where the Sicilian author was born near Agrigento.

The masterpiece of the 1980s is definitely *Nuovo Cinema Paradiso* (Cinema Paradiso; 1988) by Giuseppe Tornatore. It's a semi-autobiographical movie set in Palazzo Adriano, a location virtually unchanged to this day. In the town square here you'll find the Cinema Paradiso Museum with exhibits of film stills, movie posters and memorabilia.

The Oscar-winning director Tornatore also set other films in Sicily, including *L'uomo delle stelle* (The Star Maker; 1995), *Malèna* (2000) and *Baarìa* (2009). The first renders the betrayed hopes of Sicilians in its portrayal of an itinerant filmmaker who travels through rural Sicily. The filming locations include Ragusa Ibla, Gangi, Marzamemi, Iblei, Madonie, Gurfa caves and the Morgantina archaeological area. It's like taking a trip through deepest Sicily without getting up from your armchair. *Malèna* is set in Messina but was shot in Syracuse and tells the story of a woman facing the wrath of judgemental townspeople and her husband's absence during WWII. *Baarìa* (also known as Bagheria) is named after Tornatore's hometown and follows the story of a Sicilian family through three generations.

The turquoise water surrounding the Aeolian island of Salina and its volcano peaks provide an enchanting setting to many scenes of *Il Postino* (The Postman; 1994) by Michael Radford. Costanza Quatriglio also let herself be inspired by life on an island. Her *L'Isola* (The Island; 2003), a revelation at Cannes, was shot on Favignana and recounts the difficulties of growing up on a small, secluded islet.

Emanuele Crialese has chosen the Sicilian islands for most of his films. *Respiro* (2002) is set on Lampedusa, while *Nuovomondo* (Golden Door; 2006) takes place in early-20th-century Sicily and tells the story of a family's courage and loss as they are forced to emigrate to America in search of a better life. *Terraferma* (Dry Land; 2011) comes back to the Pelagic islands, and more precisely to Linosa, as it seeks to understand the relationship between inhabitants and migrants who reach the island.

There has been no lack of films about the Mafia in Sicily. In 2005, Marco Turco directed *In un altro paese* (Excellent Cadavers), a docudrama telling the story of Giovanni Falcone and Paolo Borsellino, anti-Mafia judges who were killed in 1992. Letizia Battaglia, photojournalist and anti-Mafia activist, plays a role in the film shot around Palermo; Rai (the Italian public broadcasting service) has dedicated a miniseries to her, and her work entitled *Solo per Passione* (Just for Passion; 2022).

Directed by Giuseppe Ferrara, *100 Giorni a Palermo* (One Hundred Days in Palermo; 1984) recounts the true story of General Carlo Alberto dalla Chiesa, who was killed in 1982 after being appointed prefect of Palermo and tasked with fighting the Mafia. In 1991 Roberto Benigni directed *Johnny Stecchino,* a comedy about a bus driver named Dante who looks like a Sicilian mafioso. Known for its humorous plot, the movie highlights a big Sicilian issue and at the same time shows gorgeous corners of the island. On the small screen, *La Piovra,* starring Michele Placido and directed by Damiano Damiani, was a series that brought the Mafia to television between 1984 and 2001.

Also taking an ironic look at the Mafia is *Tano da Morire* (To Die for Tano; 1997), a grotesque musical by Roberta Torre set in the noisy Vucciria market in Palermo. In 2014, the satirist Franco Maresco shot *Belluscone,* a wry documentary about former prime minister Silvio Berlusconi and his alleged link to the Mafia. Others to more recently tell the contemporary Mafia story through the filter of comedy include director Pif with his 2013 *La mafia uccide solo d'estate* (The Mafia Kills Only in Summer, 2013), later adapted for TV, and the acting duo Ficarra and Picone with their series *Incastrati* (Framed! A Sicilian Murder Mystery, 2022–) More recently, the director Pif and the actors Ficarra and Picone have tried to tell the contemporary Mafia story through the filter of comedy. But the most touching film on the Sicilian mafia is *I cento passi* (One Hundred Steps; 2000) by Marco Tullio Giordana. It's set in Cinisi, near Palermo, and reconstructs the story of Peppino Impastato, born a hundred steps from the house of Tano Badalamenti, a powerful Mafia boss.

In *Shooting Palermo* (2008), Wim Wenders chose Palermo to tell the story of a young photographer wandering the city's streets in search of a break from his past, while John Turturro came back to his ancestral city to shoot *Rehearsal For A Sicilian Tragedy* (2009), a documentary about the art of Sicilian puppetry. But it was Emma Dante who depicted a faithful image of Palermo's hectic life in her *Via Castellana Bandiera* (A Street in Palermo; 2013).

And then there's the popular TV series *Inspector Montalbano,* which was adapted from the detective books by Andrea Camilleri and introduces the beauties of southeastern Sicily to the world. Baroque cities such as Ragusa Ibla, Scicli and Modica were used to create the fictional city of Vigàta. The series ended in 2021 after 15 seasons but there is already another Sicilian detective to follow on screen; *Màkari,* loosely based on the novels by Gaetano Savatteri, follows journalist and investigator Saverio Lamanna and is set mainly in the Trapani area.

Resisting Sicily's timeless charm is not easy, as the international film industry recently proved once again by choosing the island for productions such as Joe Wright's *Cyrano* set in Noto and on Mt Etna, and the newest instalment of the *Indiana Jones* series, filmed in Syracuse, Cefalù, Marsala, San Vito Lo Capo, Castellammare del Golfo and Segesta. Sicily was also used as a backdrop for the fortchoming adaptation of Dino Buzzati's masterpiece *The Desert of the Tartars* by director Jessica Woodworth.

Meanwhile, local director Beppe Fiorello shot *Stranizza d'Amuri,* a 2021 film loosely based on a true story of homophobia involving a brutal double murder in 1980 in Giarre, near Catania, where the lifeless bodies were found holding hands. This episode influenced public opinion to such an extent that it gave impetus to the foundation in Palermo of Italy's first gay rights organisation.

'CINEMA IS INTERESTED IN SICILY BECAUSE SICILY IS CINEMA,' SAID THE SICILIAN WRITER LEONARDO SCIASCIA, WHOSE WORKS HAVE BEEN THE BASIS FOR VARIOUS FILMS.

SICILY'S FUTURE:
SOUTH WORKING & €1 HOUSES

Sicily is seizing some unique opportunities to overcome the economic gap separating it from regions of northern Italy. By Sara Mostaccio

THE OPPORTUNITY TO work remotely arose as an unexpected silver lining during the first weeks of the pandemic in 2020. Unlike other European states, almost no companies in Italy had previously provided opportunities to work remotely – then suddenly it was enough to have a computer and internet connection to be able work from home. With this came the desire for many to move back to the south to stay with their families while continuing to work remotely, saving money at the same time. And so Sicily discovered the phenomena known as 'smart working' and 'south working'.

Since the pandemic, south working has become a widespread and rapidly growing phenomenon. It allows northern-based companies to recruit geographically distant employees so workers can continue living in their home region. Likewise, non-local workers can now choose to live in warmer places, all while bringing talent and resources to Sicily.

Hence over the past few years, Sicily – along with destinations such as Puglia and Sardinia – has become very popular. Living in the South not only costs less and saves time in commuting to the workplace, but

Clockwise from top left: Cummari, Catania; co-working space, Castelbuono; Pollina; Castiglione di Sicilia

for many it also means an improved quality of life and increased productivity. Add in the more scenic surroundings in the countryside or the coast and a milder climate year-round, and the south beckons as an attractive option for those seeking a healthier work-life balance.

'Smart working' has changed working life throughout Italy and 'south working' is increasingly becoming an opportunity to relaunch the Sicilian economy and tackle population decline. According to estimates, by 2030 the number of inhabitants aged between 20 and 64 will shrink by 11%, so many hope south working can be decisive in addressing demographic and economic issues in southern Italy by supporting local suppliers and reversing the brain drain. But whether this can really represent a long-term reversal that's sustainable in the future is something that remains to be seen.

Fast and reliable internet connection has long been an issue outside big cities. However, the process of providing adequate digital infrastructure has now started and a greater demand for co-working spaces and fast connections by companies could create a virtuous circle. Many hope this will give Sicily an extraordinary opportunity to foster the growth of a skilled local workforce without uprooting people from their birthplace, all while reducing the economic and social gaps between the different areas of the country.

In Sicily, the towns that offer co-working spaces have been multiplying. For instance Castelbuono, near Palermo, is pursuing a south-working experiment in the Madonie mountains, inside a magnificent natural park with a sea view from above. It's been proven that productivity standards do not decrease if meetings are held online, meaning you can look out the window at amazing views and breathe clean air while avoiding hours spent commuting.

One of the most interesting projects in Sicily is Cummari. Taking its name from

an old Sicilian word denoting female solidarity, Cummari was set up by New Yorker Michelle Titus, who after living in 18 different countries in 15 years decided to settle in Catania with her husband to transform an abandoned home into a co-working space. Combining classic Sicilian architecture and modern design, she created a space which offers luxurious accommodation in the heart of the old city, as well as a place for women to work, relax and share ideas in what has become Europe's first co-working house for solo female travellers. Here digital nomads, entrepreneurs and artists from around the world live and work side by side in a welcoming, safe and inclusive environment. Located at the base of Mt Etna – which in Sicily is also considered feminine – here the daily frenzy is put aside as workers revel in the advantages offered by south working. Though men are not excluded altogether, precedence is given to people who identify as female.

BUYING A HOME IN A SECLUDED TOWN DOESN'T JUST MEAN RESTORING IT AS YOUR PERSONAL REFUGE BUT ALSO HELPING A VILLAGE TO RESTORE ITS COMMUNITY AND ATTRACT NEW TOURISTS AND INVESTORS.

ALONGSIDE SOUTH WORKING, there's another strategy being developed to improve island's fortunes: the €1 housing project. First proposed back in 2008 by art critic Vittorio Sgarbi (then mayor of Salemi) to save the town's crumbling old quarter, the idea of selling properties at the symbolic price of €1 is to not only counter depopulation but to both reverse the progressive wear and tear of social infrastructures and the urban decay generated by abandoned houses.

Recovering dilapidated properties, left unused by owners who consider them a burden, ensures decorum in the city centre. The municipality acts as a bridge between sellers and potential buyers and preference is given to buyers who also submit a project to encourage the development of the village. Many of this projects focus on social programmes, accommodation facilities or even south-working hubs. The long-term goal here is to bring abandoned villages back to life. They are almost always places off the tourist routes which over the years have suffered from drastic depopulation, but remain immersed in the beauty of the Sicilian countryside and rich in history and charm.

Though it is easy to fall in love with forgotten villages where time stands still, the logistics can be tricky: alleys are narrow, the oldest districts are usually accessible only on foot and sometimes the houses need extensive renewals. Yet nonetheless, costs remain very low and grabbing a slice of Italian dolce vita (in a very affordable way!) and immersing in the slow rural life is an opportunity that attracts many.

And while Sicily has been offering €1 houses for more than a decade, since the pandemic other municipalities throughout Italy are likewise luring new residents with the same offer to revive their dying communities and bring some buzz into the town. Castiglione di Sicilia, not far from Taormina, was among the first municipalities to adhere to the project, offering plenty of opportunities to buy a cheap house in a historic centre full of monuments, noble palaces and intertwining narrow streets. Many buyers are using their €1 dilapidated houses to give back to the community by turning them into social projects. Danny McCubbin is among them, and he and a dozen foreigners bought a €1 house in Mussomeli, a few kilometres from the historic temples of Agrigento. Here he converted the house into a community kitchen providing meals to elderly and vulnerable people, as he partnered with local farms and supermarkets to rescue leftover food.

For a region more accustomed to watching people leave instead of staying, all this brings new life, energy and, ideas. In addition to the €1 houses there are often other vacant properties in the range of €5000 to €20,000 that usually require minor restoration work but are still very cheap compared to market prices. The idea is to encourage people to live in Sicily permanently rather than build a holiday home. Furthermore, an old house transformed into an accommodation facility can also generate tourist flows and boost local businesses as owners establish partnerships with local restaurants, cafes etc. The €1 housing project gives the chance not only to live in Sicily, but also to experience real local culture off the beaten track. Leading a slower life is an aspiration that seems to have become a priority after the pandemic, and for many, the idea of snapping up an Italian home is a dream come true. At the same time, buying a home in a secluded town doesn't just mean restoring it as your personal refuge or and enchanted place from which to work remotely, but also helping a village to restore its community and attract new tourists and investors.

INDEX

Map Pages **000**

281

Map Pages **000**

Taormina's remarkable, horseshoe-shaped Teatro Greco (p159), built in the 3rd century BCE, is equipped with a dramatic volcanic backdrop thanks to Mt Etna.

Cinematic Cefalù (p112) boasts a stunning combo of architectural marvel and sweeping golden sands, seducing tourists and filmmakers alike.

THIS BOOK

Design development
Marc Backwell

Content development
Mark Jones, Sandie Kestell, Anne Mason, Joana Taborda

Cartography development
Katerina Pavkova

Production development
Sandie Kestell, Fergal Condon

Series development leadership
Darren O'Connell, Piers Pickard, Chris Zeiher

Commissioning Editor
Sandie Kestell

Product Editor
James Appleton

Book Designer
Catalina Aragón

Cartographer
Chris Lee-Ack

Assisting Editors
Katie Connolly, Melanie Dankel, Clare Healy, Trent Holden,

Alison Killilea, Michael MacKenzie, Claire Naylor

Cover Researcher
Ania Lenihan

Thanks Gwen Cotter, Esteban Fernandez, Karen Henderson, Darren O'Connell, Katerina Pavkova

Paper in this book is certified against the Forest Stewardship Council™ standards. FSC™ promotes environmentally responsible, socially beneficial and economically viable management of the world's forests.

Published by Lonely Planet Global Limited
CRN 554153
10th edition - May 2023
ISBN 978 1 83869 941 3
© Lonely Planet 2023 Photographs © as indicated 2023
10 9 8 7 6 5 4 3 2 1
Printed in China